Cisco Networking Academy Program
CCNP 3: Multilayer Switching Lab Companion
Second Edition

Cisco Systems, Inc.

Cisco Networking Academy Program

Wayne Lewis, Ph.D.

Cisco Press

800 East 96th Street

Indianapolis, IN 46240 USA

Cisco Networking Academy Program

CCNP 3: Multilayer Switching Lab Companion

Second Edition

Cisco Systems, Inc.

Cisco Networking Academy Program

Wayne Lewis, Ph.D.

Copyright © 2005 Cisco Systems, Inc.

Published by:

Cisco Press

800 East 96th Street

Indianapolis, IN 46240 USA

Printed in the United States of America   1 2 3 4 5 6 7 8 9 0

First Printing   October 2004

ISBN: 1-58713-144-7

Warning and Disclaimer

This book is designed to provide information on Multilayer Switching. Every effort has been made to make this book as complete and as accurate as possible, but no warranty or fitness is implied.

The information is provided on an "as is" basis. The author, Cisco Press, and Cisco Systems, Inc. shall have neither liability nor responsibility to any person or entity with respect to any loss or damages arising from the information contained in this book or from the use of the programs that may accompany it.

The opinions expressed in this book belong to the author and are not necessarily those of Cisco Systems, Inc.

This book is part of the Cisco Networking Academy® Program series from Cisco Press. The products in this series support and complement the Cisco Networking Academy Program curriculum. If you are using this book outside the Networking Academy program, then you are not preparing with a Cisco trained and authorized Networking Academy provider.

For information on the Cisco Networking Academy Program or to locate a Networking Academy, please visit www.cisco.com/edu.

CISCO SYSTEMS

Trademark Acknowledgments

All terms mentioned in this book that are known to be trademarks or service marks have been appropriately capitalized. Cisco Press or Cisco Systems, Inc., cannot attest to the accuracy of this information. Use of a term in this book should not be regarded as affecting the validity of any trademark or service mark.

Corporate and Government Sales

Cisco Press offers excellent discounts on this book when ordered in quantity for bulk purchases or special sales.

For more information please contact: U.S. Corporate and Government Sales 1-800-382-3419 corpsales@pearsontechgroup.com

For sales outside the U.S. please contact: International Sales international@pearsoned.com

Feedback Information

At Cisco Press, our goal is to create in-depth technical books of the highest quality and value. Each book is crafted with care and precision, undergoing rigorous development that involves the unique expertise of members of the professional technical community.

Readers' feedback is a natural continuation of this process. If you have any comments regarding how we could improve the quality of this book, or otherwise alter it to better suit your needs, you can contact us at networkingacademy@ciscopress.com. Please be sure to include the book title and ISBN in your message.

We greatly appreciate your assistance.

Publisher	John Wait
Editor-in-Chief	John Kane
Executive Editor	Mary Beth Ray
Cisco Systems Representative	Anthony Wolfenden
Cisco Press Program Manager	Nannette M. Noble
Production Manager	Patrick Kanouse
Development Editor	Sheri Cain
Technical Editors	Jim Lorenz, Arthur Tucker
Copy Editor	Gill Editorial Services
Cover and Interior Design	Louisa Adair
Composition	Mark Shirar

Corporate Headquarters
Cisco Systems, Inc.
170 West Tasman Drive
San Jose, CA 95134-1706
USA
www.cisco.com
Tel: 408 526-4000
     800 553-NETS (6387)
Fax: 408 526-4100

European Headquarters
Cisco Systems International BV
Haarlerbergpark
Haarlerbergweg 13-19
1101 CH Amsterdam
The Netherlands
www-europe.cisco.com
Tel: 31 0 20 357 1000
Fax: 31 0 20 357 1100

Americas Headquarters
Cisco Systems, Inc.
170 West Tasman Drive
San Jose, CA 95134-1706
USA
www.cisco.com
Tel: 408 526-7660
Fax: 408 527-0883

Asia Pacific Headquarters
Cisco Systems, Inc.
Capital Tower
168 Robinson Road
#22-01 to #29-01
Singapore 068912
www.cisco.com
Tel: +65 6317 7777
Fax: +65 6317 7799

Cisco Systems has more than 200 offices in the following countries and regions. Addresses, phone numbers, and fax numbers are listed on the **Cisco.com Web site at www.cisco.com/go/offices.**

Argentina • Australia • Austria • Belgium • Brazil • Bulgaria • Canada • Chile • China PRC • Colombia • Costa Rica • Croatia • Czech Republic
Denmark • Dubai, UAE • Finland • France • Germany • Greece • Hong Kong SAR • Hungary • India • Indonesia • Ireland • Israel • Italy
Japan • Korea • Luxembourg • Malaysia • Mexico • The Netherlands • New Zealand • Norway • Peru • Philippines • Poland • Portugal
Puerto Rico • Romania • Russia • Saudi Arabia • Scotland • Singapore • Slovakia • Slovenia • South Africa • Spain • Sweden
Switzerland • Taiwan • Thailand • Turkey • Ukraine • United Kingdom • United States • Venezuela • Vietnam • Zimbabwe

About the Author

Wayne Lewis is the Cisco Academy manager for the Pacific Center for Advanced Technology Training, based at Honolulu Community College (HCC). Since 1998, Wayne has taught routing and switching, remote access, troubleshooting, network security, and wireless networking to instructors from universities, colleges, and high schools in Australia, Canada, Central America, China, Hong Kong, Indonesia, Japan, Mexico, Singapore, South America, Taiwan, and the U.S., both onsite and at HCC. Prior to teaching computer networking, Wayne began teaching math at age 20 at Wichita State University, followed by the University of Hawaii and HCC. Wayne received a Ph.D. in math from the University of Hawaii in 1992. Wayne works as a contractor for Cisco Systems, developing curriculum for the Cisco Networking Academy Program. Wayne enjoys surfing the North Shore of Oahu when he's not distracted by work.

About the Technical Reviewers

Jim Lorenz is an instructor and curriculum developer for the Cisco Networking Academy Program. He has over 20 years of experience in information systems and has held various IT positions in Fortune 500 companies, including Honeywell and Motorola. Jim has developed and taught computer and networking courses for both public and private institutions for more than 15 years. He is coauthor of the Cisco Networking Academy Program Fundamentals of UNIX course, contributing author for the CCNA Lab Companion manuals and technical editor for the Companion Guides. Jim is a Cisco Certified Academy Instructor (CCAI) for CCNA and CCNP courses. He has a bachelor's degree in Computer Information Systems and is currently working on his masters in Information Networking and Telecommunications. Jim and his wife Mary have two daughters, Jessica and Natasha.

Arthur Tucker is a Cisco certified network security consultant in the Dallas/Ft Worth area specializing in intrusion detection. Arthur has more than nine years of experience in networking and troubleshooting, and he teaches the CCNA track at Richland College in Dallas.

Table of Contents

Chapter 8 Quality of Service 181

Chapter 9 Monitoring and Security 217

Chapter 10 Transparent LAN Services 253

Foreword

Throughout the world, the Internet has brought tremendous new opportunities for individuals and their employers. Companies and other organizations are seeing dramatic increases in productivity by investing in robust networking capabilities. Some studies have shown measurable productivity improvements in entire economies. The promise of enhanced efficiency, profitability, and standard of living is real and growing.

Such productivity gains aren't achieved by simply purchasing networking equipment. Skilled professionals are needed to plan, design, install, deploy, configure, operate, maintain, and troubleshoot today's networks. Network managers must ensure that they have planned for network security and for continued operation. They need to design for the required performance level in their organization. They must implement new capabilities as the demands of their organization, and its reliance on the network, expands.

To meet the many educational needs of the internetworking community, Cisco Systems established the Cisco Networking Academy Program. The Networking Academy is a comprehensive learning program that provides students with the Internet technology skills essential in a global economy. The Networking Academy integrates face-to-face teaching, web-based content, online assessment, student performance tracking, hands-on labs, instructor training and support, and preparation for industry-standard certifications.

The Networking Academy continually raises the bar on blended learning and educational processes. All instructors are Cisco Certified Academy Instructors (CCAIs). The Internet-based assessment and instructor support systems are some of the most extensive and validated ever developed, including a 24/7 customer service system for Networking Academy instructors and students. Through community feedback and electronic assessment, the Networking Academy adapts the curriculum to improve outcomes and student achievement. The Cisco Global Learning Network infrastructure designed for the Networking Academy delivers a rich, interactive, and personalized curriculum to students worldwide. The Internet has the power to change the way people work, live, play, and learn, and the Cisco Networking Academy Program is in the forefront of this transformation.

This Cisco Press title is one of a series of best-selling companion titles for the Cisco Networking Academy Program. Designed by Cisco Worldwide Education and Cisco Press, these books provide integrated support for the online learning content that is made available to Academies all over the world. These Cisco Press books are the only authorized books for the Networking Academy by Cisco Systems and provide print and CD-ROM materials that ensure the greatest possible learning experience for Networking Academy students.

I hope you are successful as you embark on your learning path with Cisco Systems and the Internet. I also hope that you will choose to continue your learning after you complete the Cisco Networking Academy Program curriculum. In addition to its Cisco Networking Academy Program titles, Cisco Press also publishes an extensive list of networking technology and certification publications that provide a wide range of resources. Cisco Systems has also established a network of professional training companies—the Cisco Learning Partners—who provide a full range of Cisco training courses. They offer training in many formats, including e-learning, self-paced, and instructor-led classes. Their instructors are Cisco certified, and Cisco creates their materials. When you are ready, please visit the Learning & Events area on Cisco.com to learn about all the educational support that Cisco and its partners have to offer.

Thank you for choosing this book and the Cisco Networking Academy Program.

The Cisco Networking Academy Program Team
Cisco Systems, Inc.

Introduction

CCNP 3: Multilayer Switching Lab Companion, Second Edition, supplements your classroom and laboratory experience with the Cisco Networking Academy Program.

This book contains all the labs in the current CCNP course in the Cisco Networking Academy Program. The labs are hands-on and require access to Cisco routers and switches or a lab simulator. Successful completion and understanding of the topics covered in the labs help you to prepare for the Building Cisco Multilayer Switched Networks exam (642-811), which is a qualifying exam for the Cisco Certified Network Professional (CCNP) certification.

Audience for This Book

This book is written for anyone who wants to learn about multilayer switching, especially students enrolled in the CCNP 3 Networking Academy course. Students in any educational environment could use this book as both a textbook companion and as a lab manual.

How This Book Is Organized

Table I-1 outlines all the labs in this book, the corresponding Target Indicator (TI) in the online curriculum, and the time it should take to complete the lab.

Table I-1 Master Lab Overview

Lab TI	Title	Estimated Time (Minutes)
1.6.1	Catalyst 2950T and 3550 Series Basic Setup	30
1.6.2	Catalyst 2950T and 3550 Configuration and IOS Files	60
1.6.3	Catalyst 2950T and 3550 Series Password Recovery	30
1.6.4	Introduction to Fluke Network Inspector	90
1.6.5	Introduction to Fluke Protocol Expert	90
2.9.1	Catalyst 2950T and 3550 Series Static VLANS	60
2.9.2	Catalyst 2950T and 3550 Series VTP Domain and VLAN Trunking	120
2.9.3	Catalyst 2950T and 3550 Series VTP Pruning	60
2.9.4	Catalyst 2950 and 3550 Series Intra-VLAN Security	90
3.10.1	Spanning Tree Protocol (STP) Default Behavior	60
3.10.2	Use Network Inspector to Observe STP Behavior	120
3.10.3	Advanced PVST+ Configuration	60
3.10.4	Implementing MST	120
3.10.5	Configuring Fast EtherChannel	90
3.10.6	Per-VLAN Spanning-Tree Load Balancing	90
3.10.7	Port Level Tuning to Control STP Behavior	120
4.3.1	Inter-VLAN Routing with an External Router	90

continues

Table I-1 Master Lab Overview (Continued)

Lab TI	Title	Estimated Time (Minutes)
4.3.2	Inter-VLAN Routing with the Internal Route Processor	90
4.3.3	Routing Between an External Router and an Internal Route Processor	90
5.4.1	Monitoring Cisco Express Forwarding	120
6.5.1	Hot Standby Router Protocol	120
6.5.2	Multigroup Hot Standby Router Protocol	120
8.9.1	Classifying Traffic Using Class of Service at the Access Layer	90
8.9.2	Introduction to the Modular QoS Command-Line Interface	60
8.9.3	QoS Classification and Policing Using CAR	60
8.9.4	Weighted Fair Queuing	60
8.9.5	Configuring WRED on an Interface	60
8.9.6	Configuring WRED with CBWFQ	60
8.9.7	Configuring Low Latency Queuing (LLQ)	90
8.9.8	Configuring Generic Traffic Shaping (GTS)	60
8.9.9	QoS Manually Configured Frame Relay Traffic Shaping	90
8.9.10	Quality of Service Dynamic Frame Relay Traffic Shaping	60
8.9.11	Configuring Link Fragmentation and Interleaving	120
8.9.12	QoS Compressed Real Time Protocol	60
9.9.1	Creating a Switched Port Analyzer (SPAN) Session	90
9.9.2	Creating a VSPAN Session	90
9.9.3	Creating a RSPAN Session	120
9.9.4	Setting Encrypted Passwords	60
9.9.5	Using Local Usernames and Passwords	60
9.9.6	Using Advanced Username Options	60
9.9.7	Configuring the Management VLAN on a Single Switch	60
9.9.8	Restricting Virtual Terminal Sessions with Access Lists	60
9.9.9	Restricting Web Interface Sessions with Access Lists	60
9.9.10	Configuring Protected Ports	60
9.9.11	Configuring VLAN Maps	90

This Book's Features

Many of the book's features will help facilitate your full understanding of the networking and routing topics covered in the labs:

- **Objective**—Identifies the goal or goals that are to be accomplished in the lab.

- **Scenario**—Allows you to relate the lab exercise to real-world environments.

- **Questions**—As appropriate, the labs include questions that elicit particular points of understanding. These questions help to verify your comprehension of the technology being implemented.

The conventions used to present command syntax in this book are the same conventions used in the *Cisco IOS Command Reference*:

- **Bold** indicates commands and keywords that are entered literally as shown. In examples (not syntax), bold indicates user input (for example, a **show** command).

- *Italic* indicates arguments for which you supply values.

- Braces ({ }) indicate a required element.

- Square brackets ([ ]) indicate an optional element.

- Vertical bars (|) separate alternative, mutually exclusive elements.

- Braces and vertical bars within square brackets (such as [x {y | z}]) indicate a required choice within an optional element. You do not need to enter what is in the brackets, but if you do, you have some required choices in the braces.

Chapter 1

Campus Networks and Design Models

Lab 1.6.1: Catalyst 2950T and 3550 Series Basic Setup

Estimated Time: 30 Minutes

Note: This lab has no questions for students to answer.

Objective

In this lab, you configure a Cisco Catalyst 2950T or 3550 series Ethernet switch for the first time using the command-line interface (CLI) mode. You complete basic first-time tasks such as configuring a switch name, assigning passwords, and assigning an IP address to the Management VLAN for remote management purposes. Figure 1-1 shows the topology for this lab.

Figure 1-1 Topology for Lab 1.6.1

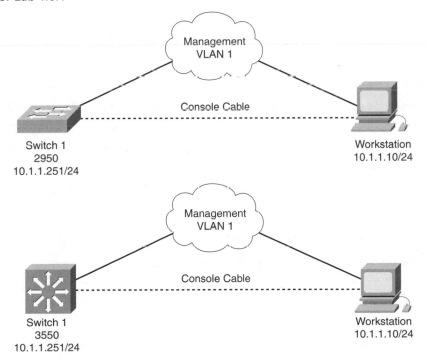

Scenario

The standard switch pod that is used for this course contains Cisco Catalyst WS-C3550-24-EMI and WS-C2950T-24-EI switches. The Catalyst 3550 has 24 10/100 ports and two Gigabit Interface Converter (GBIC) ports. The Catalyst 2950T has 24 10/100 ports and two fixed GBIC-based 1000BASE-X uplink ports. Both switches are standardized on IOS 12.1(11)EA1 with the Enhanced Multilayer Image (EMI) on the 3550 and the Enhanced Image (EI) on the 2950T. The respective system image filenames are c3550-i5q312-mz.121-11.EA1.bin and c2950-i6q412-mz.121-11.EA1.bin.

The basic first-time setup for the 2950T and 3550 series switches is similar with the exception of the fixed 1000BASE-T uplink ports on the 2950T versus the GBIC ports on the 3550.

Step 1

Select a 2950T or 3550 switch, but do not plug the power cord into the power socket or outlet. Neither switch has an on/off power button or switch. Use the standard process for establishing a HyperTerminal console connection from a workstation with either switch using a rollover cable and a serial adapter. The communication settings are as follows:

- 9600 bits per second
- 8 data bits
- No parity
- 1 stop bit
- No flow control

Clear the switch configuration by issuing the **delete vlan.dat** and **erase startup-config** commands from privileged EXEC mode. Then restart the switch using the **reload** command.

Watch the boot process on the HyperTerminal display screen. After the boot process is complete, a prompt for the System Configuration dialog box is displayed. If no previously saved configuration exists, the following prompt is shown:

```
--output omitted--

--- System Configuration Dialog ---

Would you like to enter the initial configuration dialog? [yes/no]:
```

Notice that the prompt is the same as a router upon bootup without a previously saved configuration. Similarly, the switch has a Basic and an Extended Management Setup option.

Respond **no** to the configuration dialog prompt because you will complete initial configuration using the CLI mode. You might want to redo the lab later using the System Configuration dialog box.

After you respond **no** to the configuration prompt, you might need to press the **Enter** key to display the **Switch >** prompt.

```
Press RETURN to get started!

01:06:37: %LINK-5-CHANGED: Interface Vlan1, changed state to
administratively down
01:06:38: %LINEPROTO-5-UPDOWN: Line protocol on Interface Vlan1, changed
state to down
Switch>
```

Step 2

Look at the default configuration from the privileged EXEC mode before you configure the switch. Sample outputs from a 2950T-24 and a 3550-24 switch are shown here. The configurations are similar to an IOS-based router:

```
Switch>enable
Switch#show running-config
```

Use the default configuration for the Catalyst 2950T-24:

```
Building configuration...

Current configuration : 1449 bytes
!
version 12.1
no service pad
service timestamps debug uptime
service timestamps log uptime
no service password-encryption
!
hostname Switch
!
!
ip subnet-zero
!
spanning-tree extend system-id
!
!
interface FastEthernet0/1
no ip address
!
interface FastEthernet0/2
no ip address
!
interface FastEthernet0/0
no ip address
!
interface FastEthernet0/4
no ip address
!
interface FastEthernet0/5
no ip address
!
interface FastEthernet0/6
no ip address
!
interface FastEthernet0/7
no ip address
!
interface FastEthernet0/8
no ip address
!
interface FastEthernet0/9
no ip address
!
interface FastEthernet0/10
no ip address
!
interface FastEthernet0/11
no ip address
!
interface FastEthernet0/12
no ip address
!
interface FastEthernet0/13
no ip address
!
interface FastEthernet0/14
no ip address
!
interface FastEthernet0/15
no ip address
!
interface FastEthernet0/16
no ip address
```

```
!
interface FastEthernet0/17
no ip address
!
interface FastEthernet0/18
no ip address
!
interface FastEthernet0/19
no ip address
!
interface FastEthernet0/20
no ip address
!
interface FastEthernet0/21
no ip address
!
interface FastEthernet0/22
no ip address
!
interface FastEthernet0/23
no ip address
!
interface FastEthernet0/24
no ip address
!
interface GigabitEthernet0/1
no ip address
!
interface GigabitEthernet0/2
no ip address
!
interface Vlan1
no ip address
no ip route-cache
shutdown
!
ip http server
!
!
line con 0
line vty 5 15
!
end
```

Use the default configuration for the Catalyst 3550-24:

```
Building configuration...

Current configuration : 1451 bytes
!
version 12.1
no service pad
service timestamps debug uptime
service timestamps log uptime
no service password-encryption
!
hostname Switch
!
!
ip subnet-zero
!
!
spanning-tree extend system-id
!
!
!
interface FastEthernet0/1
no ip address
```

```
!
interface FastEthernet0/2
no ip address
!
interface FastEthernet0/3
no ip address
!
interface FastEthernet0/4
no ip address
!
interface FastEthernet0/5
no ip address
!
interface FastEthernet0/6
no ip address
!
interface FastEthernet0/7
no ip address
!
interface FastEthernet0/8
no ip address
!
interface FastEthernet0/9
no ip address
!
interface FastEthernet0/10
no ip address
!
interface FastEthernet0/11
no ip address
!
interface FastEthernet0/12
no ip address
!
interface FastEthernet0/13
no ip address
!
interface FastEthernet0/14
no ip address
!
interface FastEthernet0/15
no ip address
!
interface FastEthernet0/16
no ip address
!
interface FastEthernet0/17
no ip address
!
interface FastEthernet0/18
no ip address
!
interface FastEthernet0/19
no ip address
!
interface FastEthernet0/20
no ip address
!
interface FastEthernet0/21
no ip address
!
interface FastEthernet0/22
no ip address
!
interface FastEthernet0/23
no ip address
!
```

```
!
no ip address
!
interface GigabitEthernet0/1
no ip address
!
interface GigabitEthernet0/2
no ip address
!
interface Vlan1
no ip address
shutdown
!
ip classless
ip http server
!
!
!
line con 0
line vty 5 15
!
end
```

Step 3

Configure a switch name, enable password, privileged password, console password, and virtual terminal password. The commands are the same that you have used to configure routers in previous courses and labs:

```
Switch#configure terminal
Enter configuration commands, one per line. End with CNTL/Z.
Switch(config)#hostname Switch1
Switch1(config)#enable password cisco
Switch1(config)#enable secret class
Switch1(config)#line con 0
Switch1(config-line)#password cisco
Switch1(config-line)#login
Switch1(config-line)#line vty 0 15
Switch1(config-line)#password cisco
Switch1(config-line)#login
Switch1(config-line)#^z
```

Issue a **show running-config** command to check the operating configurations.

Issue a **copy running-config startup-config** command to save the configurations.

Issue the **show startup-config** command to view the configuration in NVRAM, which is also known as the startup configuration.

Step 4

By default, the 2950T and 3550 series switches use VLAN 1 as the Management VLAN for network connection. The VLAN 1 interface is displayed in the following switch configuration:

```
--output omitted--

interface GigabitEthernet0/2
no ip address
!
interface Vlan1
no ip address
shutdown
!
ip classless
ip http server

--output omitted--
```

To enable a network connection, you must assign an IP address to VLAN 1. You also must configure a default gateway to the router to enable inter-VLAN communication. Although you do not need to configure a default gateway in this lab because you are not using a router and no inter-VLAN communication will occur, configure one for practice.

Configure an IP address, subnet mask, and default gateway on the switch for access to the network for management purposes:

```
Switch1#configure terminal
Switch1(config)#interface vlan 1
Switch1(config-if)#ip address 10.1.1.251 255.255.255.0
Switch1(config-if)#no shutdown
Switch1(config-if)#exit
Switch1(config)#ip default-gateway 10.1.1.1
Switch1(config)#exit
```

You can create additional VLAN interfaces by issuing the **interface vlan** command. The IP address that you assign to the VLAN must be a valid one from the subnet to which the VLAN belongs. Remember that a VLAN is equated with a subnet.

Step 5

By default, all ports are members of VLAN 1. Therefore, all devices that are plugged into any port must belong to the same subnet as the IP address that previously was assigned to VLAN 1. Configure the workstation with the IP address and subnet mask, which is 10.1.1.10 255.255.255.0.

Plug a straight-through cable from the workstation into any switch port. This should enable communications between the workstation and the switch. Verify connectivity with a ping from the workstation to the switch, which is 10.1.1.251, and from the switch to the workstation.

You can now access the switch from the workstation by using Telnet or through a web browser. Notice in the following sample output that the HTTP capability has been enabled by default:

```
--output omitted--

interface GigabitEthernet0/2
no ip address
!
interface Vlan1
no ip address
shutdown
!
ip classless
ip http server

--output omitted--
```

Telnet from the workstation to the switch with the Management VLAN 1 IP address that was assigned previously, which is 10.1.1.251. Respond to the password prompt with the vty cisco login password that was configured previously.

Open a web browser on the workstation and enter the Management VLAN 1 IP address, which is 10.1.1.251, in the Address field. No username is required. Respond to the password prompt with the privileged password "class." An output that is similar to the sample 3550 output appears to indicate a successful connection:

```
Cisco Systems
Accessing Cisco WS-C3550-24 "Switch1"
Web Console - Manage the Switch through the web interface.
Telnet - to the router.
Show interfaces - display the status of the interfaces.
Show diagnostic log - display the diagnostic log.
Monitor the router - HTML access to the command line interface at level 0,1,2,3,4,5,6,7,8,9,10,11,12,13,14,15
Connectivity test - unavailable, no valid nameserverdefined.
Extended Ping - Send extended ping commands.
Show tech-support - display information commonly needed by tech support.

Help resources
CCO at www.cisco.com - Cisco Connection Online, including the Technical Assistance Center (TAC).
```

```
tac@cisco.com - e-mail the TAC.
1-800-553-2447 or +1-408-526-7209 - phone the TAC.
cs-html@cisco.com - e-mail the HTML interface development group.
```

Using the CLI mode, you have successfully completed a basic first-time configuration of a Catalyst 2950T or Catalyst 3550 switch with network access capability for management purposes.

Save the configuration for use in the next lab.

Lab 1.6.2: Catalyst 2950T and 3550 Configuration and IOS Files

Estimated Time: 60 Minutes

Objective

In this lab, you upload and download configuration files and the IOS system image files. Figure 1-2 shows the topology for this lab.

Figure 1-2 Topology for Lab 1.6.2

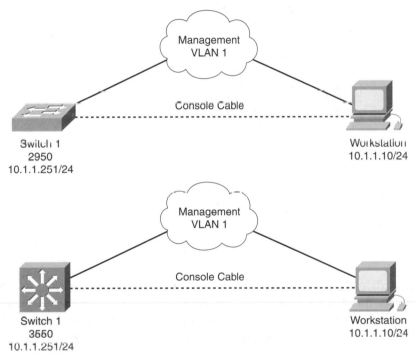

Scenario

You need to be familiar with the fundamental aspects of working with configuration files and the IOS file system for general housekeeping, maintenance, and backup purposes.

As was covered in the previous lab, both the 2950T and 3550 switches are standardized on IOS 12.1(11)EA1 with the EMI for the 3550 and the EI for the 2950T. The respective system image filenames are c3550-i5q312-mz.121-11.EA1.bin and c2950-i6q412-mz.121-11.EA1.bin.

Specifics differ among certain aspects of the 2950T and 3550 series of switches. However, the basic procedure for uploading and downloading configuration files and software images is essentially the same. This is true regardless of the model.

Step 1

Select a 2950T or 3550 switch that you used in the previous lab. If necessary, power up the switch and use the standard process to establish a HyperTerminal console connection from a workstation.

The configuration from the previous lab should be in the switch already. Issue the **show running-config** command to ensure that VLAN 1 has the appropriate IP address, which is 10.1.1.251, and that the interface is not shut down.

Make sure the workstation has been assigned the appropriate IP address, which is 10.1.1.10, and is connected to a switch port in VLAN 1. Validate connectivity with a ping from the workstation to the switch, which is 10.1.1.251, or from the switch to the workstation.

Step 2

Issue the **show file systems** command from the privileged mode to display the available file systems in the switch. The following output is a sample:

```
Switch1#show file systems
File Systems:

        Size(b)     Free(b)        Type   Flags   Prefixes
*     15998976     7104512       flash      rw    flash:
            -           -        opaque      ro    bs:
            -           -        opaque      rw    vb:
      15998976     7104512     unknown      rw    zflash:
        393216      391712       nvram      rw    nvram:
            -           -        opaque      rw    null:
            -           -        opaque      rw    system:
            -           -       network      rw    tftp:
            -           -        opaque      ro    xmodem:
            -           -        opaque      ro    ymodem:
            -           -       network      rw    rcp:
            -           -       network      rw    ftp:
```

Note: You can obtain additional information about file systems from http://www.cisco.com/univercd/cc/td/doc/product/lan/c3550/1214ea1/3550scg/swiosfs.pdf.

Save the various switch files externally to the switch to protect against the internal files becoming corrupted or other factors that would require the files to be restored. The switch files that should be saved are the system image file, which is the IOS that resides in Flash memory, and the startup configuration file, which resides in the NVRAM section of Flash memory. The running or operating configuration resides in DRAM and does not need to be the same as the startup configuration. You can make temporary changes to the running configuration, and you should retain an external copy.

Step 3

You can retain an external copy of the running and startup configurations in several ways. You can generate a text file through the HyperTerminal capture process, or you can copy the output from a **show running-config** or **show startup-config** command and paste it into a text-editing program (such as Notepad) or a word processing program. Other ways to retain a binary version of a configuration file include TFTP, FTP, and Remote Copy Protocol (RCP).

The method you use to copy configuration files from the switch depends on the type of server you are using. The FTP and RCP mechanisms provide more reliable delivery because they are built on and use TCP, which is connection oriented. This lab uses the TFTP process, which is a simple FTP that is implemented in User Datagram Protocol (UDP).

If necessary, download, install, and start TFTP server software and designate the directory to which the switch configuration file will be saved on the workstation or TFTP file server.

Note: You can download the Solarwinds TFTP Server Software from http://solarwinds.net. The workstation that is being used to console into the switch does not need to be the TFTP server to which files will be saved. Another workstation that is acting as the TFTP file server or running the TFTP server software can be used to store and retrieve files. For the purposes of this lab, one workstation is being used as a console connection for working with both the switch and the TFTP file server.

Step 4

Copying a switch file to an external file server is called *uploading*, and copying a file from an external file server to the switch is called *downloading*. The basic command format for both of these is the same: copy from source to destination. The source and destination determine whether the copy is an upload, a download, or between internal files.

Issue a **copy ?** command from the privileged mode. The following output is a sample:

```
Switch1#copy ?
  bs:              Copy from bs: file system
  flash:           Copy from flash: file system
  ftp:             Copy from ftp: file system
  null:            Copy from null: file system
  nvram:           Copy from nvram: file system
  rcp:             Copy from rcp: file system
  running-config   Copy from current system configuration
  startup-config   Copy from startup configuration
  system:          Copy from system: file system
  tftp:            Copy from tftp: file system
  vb:              Copy from vb: file system
  xmodem:          Copy from xmodem: file system
  ymodem:          Copy from ymodem: file system
  zflash:          Copy from zflash: file system
```

Although all the descriptions say "Copy from," it is not clear whether the copy direction is an upload or a download. The source and destination ultimately determine the direction; the basic format is to copy from the source to the destination.

Issue a **copy startup-config ?** command from the privileged mode. A sample output follows:

```
Switch1#copy startup-config ?
  bs:              Copy to bs: file system
  flash:           Copy to flash: file system
  ftp:             Copy to ftp: file system
  null:            Copy to null: file system
  nvram:           Copy to nvram: file system
  rcp:             Copy to rcp: file system
  running-config   Update (merge with) current system configuration
  startup-config   Copy to startup configuration
  system:          Copy to system: file system
  tftp:            Copy to tftp: file system
  xmodem:          Copy to xmodem: file system
  ymodem:          Copy to ymodem: file system
  zflash:          Copy to zflash: file system
```

The second part of the command is represented by a question mark (?), which designates the destination.

The command **copy startup-config tftp** copies the startup configuration from the switch to the TFTP file server, which is an upload. The command **copy tftp startup-config** copies a startup configuration from the TFTP file server to the switch, which is a download.

Step 5

You can use different command formats to copy the running and startup configurations. One command format includes all parameters, whereas the other prompts for additional information. The full command syntaxes for copying the running and startup configurations to a TFTP file server are as follows:

```
copy system:running-config tftp:[[[//location]/directory]/filename]
copy nvram:startup-config tftp:[[[//location]/directory]/filename]
```

If you enter all the optional parameters in the commands, a prompt confirms the copy operation:

```
Switch1#copy nvram:startup-config tftp://10.1.1.10/Switch1-switch-confg
Write file Switch1-switch-confg on host    10.1.1.10? [confirm]
!!!!!
664 bytes copied in 3.264 secs (221 bytes/sec)
```

The exclamation points (!) indicate that the file is being copied.

If you use an abbreviated version of the **copy** command, prompts for the location and filename also appear:

```
Switch1#copy startup-config tftp
Address or name of remote host []? 10.1.1.10
Destination filename [Switch1-switch-confg]?
!!!!!
664 bytes copied in 3.264 secs (221 bytes/sec)
```

You might need to do some coordination between the settings of the TFTP server software and the location to save the uploaded configuration file. Regardless of the command you use to copy a configuration file to a TFTP file server, designate the default directory in the TFTP file server with the TFTP server software, which is described in Step 3.

Copy or upload the startup configuration of the switch to the TFTP file server using either of the following commands:

```
Switch1#copy nvram:startup-config tftp:[[[//location]/directory]/filename]
Switch1#copy startup-config tftp
```

Step 6

Download the configuration file from the TFTP file server to the startup configuration of the switch and change the filename in the commands as needed. Use either of the following commands:

```
Switch1#copy tftp:Switch1-switch-confg nvram:startup-config
Address or name of remote host []? 10.1.1.10
Source filename [Switch1-switch-confg]?
Destination filename [startup-config]?
Accessing tftp://10.1.1.10/Switch1-switch-confg...
Loading Switch1-switch-confg from 10.1.1.10 (via Vlan1): !
[OK - 664/1024 bytes]
[OK]
1682 bytes copied in 20.632 secs (84 bytes/sec)
Switch1#
01:42:30: %SYS-5-CONFIG_I: Configured from tftp://10.1.1.10/switch1-switch-
confg by console
Switch1#copy tftp startup-config
Address or name of remote host []? 10.1.1.10
Source filename []? Switch1-switch-confg
Destination filename [startup-config]?
Accessing tftp://10.1.1.10/Switch1-switch-confg...
Loading Switch1-switch-confg from 10.1.1.10 (via Vlan1): !
[OK - 664/1024 bytes]
[OK]
1682 bytes copied in 20.632 secs (84 bytes/sec)
Switch1#
01:42:30: %SYS-5-CONFIG_I: Configured from tftp://10.1.1.10/switch1-switch-
confg by console
```

You can copy the startup configuration to the running configuration internally or from an external source. You replace certain commands in the running configuration, whereas you add others. The result is a mixture of configurations. Think of copying to the running configuration as a merge of files rather than a replacement of the configuration. Copying to a running configuration generally is not recommended. Copying to a startup configuration always results in the replacement or overwriting of any existing configuration.

Step 7

You can upload the IOS image file for backup purposes, download it to replace the current image, or add it with the current image kept in Flash if memory is sufficient. If Flash has more than one image file, you can designate which one to use in the boot process with the following configuration command:

```
boot system [directory/filename]
```

Just as with the configuration files, you can upload and download the IOS image file with TFTP, FTP, or RCP; the process is similar.

To see the version and filename of the IOS image that is running currently, use the privileged mode commands **show version** or **dir**. Sample outputs for the 2950T-24-EI and 3550-24-EMI switches are shown.

Note: The **dir** command is an abbreviated version of **dir flash:** or **dir flash:/** and displays the names of files in the root Flash directory and the names of any subdirectories. The IOS image file in a new 3550 switch might be located in a Flash subdirectory with the same name as the image file. If so, the output of the **show version** and **dir** commands differs slightly from the 3550-24 EMI switch outputs that were generated with the IOS image file in the root Flash directory. If the IOS image file is in a subdirectory, the output of the **show version** command shows the Flash subdirectory name followed by the name of the IOS image file, which is flash:directory name/IOS image filename. The output of the **dir** command shows the name of the Flash subdirectory where the IOS image file is located instead of the IOS image filename.

The following sample output is for a 2950T-24-EI switch:

```
Switch1#show version
Cisco Internetwork Operating System Software
IOS (tm) C2950 Software (C2950-I6Q4L2-M), Version 12.1(11)EA1, RELEASE
SOFTWARE(fc1)
Copyright  1986-2002 by cisco Systems, Inc.
Compiled Wed 28-Aug-02 10:25 by antonino
Image text-base: 0x80010000, data-base: 0x80528000

ROM: Bootstrap program is CALHOUN boot loader

Switch1 uptime is 33 minutes
System returned to ROM by power-on
System image file is "flash:/c2950-i6q4l2-mz.121-11.EA1.bin"

cisco WS-C2950T-24 (RC32300) processor (revision G0) with 20402K bytes of
memory.
Processor board ID FHK0652W0J6
Last reset from system-reset
Running Enhanced Image
24 FastEthernet/IEEE 802.3 interface(s)
2 Gigabit Ethernet/IEEE 802.3 interface(s)

32K bytes of flash-simulated non-volatile configuration memory.
Base ethernet MAC Address: 00:0B:BE:C6:B7:80
Motherboard assembly number: 73-6114-08
Power supply part number: 34-0965-01
Motherboard serial number: FOC065201SN
Power supply serial number: PHI064709UP
Model revision number: G0
Motherboard revision number: A0
Model number: WS-C2950T-24
System serial number: FHK0652W0J6
Configuration register is 0xF

Switch#dir
Directory of flash:/

    2  -rwx    2664051    Mar 01 1993 00:03:18  c2950-i6q4l2-mz.121-11.EA1.bin
    3  -rwx        270    Jan 01 1970 00:01:46  env_vars
    4  -rwx       1641    Mar 01 1993 00:12:24  config.text
    5  -rwx          5    Mar 01 1993 00:12:24  private-config.text
    7  drwx        704    Mar 01 1993 00:03:54  html
   19  -rwx        109    Mar 01 1993 00:03:55  info
   20  -rwx        109    Mar 01 1993 00:03:55  info.ver

7741440 bytes total (3777024 bytes free)
```

The following sample output is for a 3550-24-EMI switch:

```
Switch1#show version
Cisco Internetwork Operating System Software
IOS (tm) C3550 Software (C3550-I5Q3L2-M), Version 12.1(11)EA1, RELEASE
SOFTWARE(fc1)
Copyright  1986-2002 by cisco Systems, Inc.
Compiled Wed 28-Aug-02 10:03 by antonino
Image text-base: 0x00003000, data-base: 0x0071D658

ROM: Bootstrap program is C3550 boot loader

Switch1 uptime is 36 minutes
System returned to ROM by power-on
System image file is "flash:c3550-i5q3l2-mz.121-11.EA1.bin"

cisco WS-C3550-24 (PowerPC) processor (revision G0) with 65526K/8192K bytes
of memory.
Processor board ID CHK0650V0SY
Last reset from warm-reset
Bridging software.
Running Layer2/3 Switching Image

Ethernet-controller 1 has 12 Fast Ethernet/IEEE 802.3 interfaces

Ethernet-controller 2 has 12 Fast Ethernet/IEEE 802.3 interfaces

Ethernet-controller 3 has 1 Gigabit Ethernet/IEEE 802.3 interface

Ethernet-controller 4 has 1 Gigabit Ethernet/IEEE 802.3 interface

24 FastEthernet/IEEE 802.3 interface(s)
2 Gigabit Ethernet/IEEE 802.3 interface(s)

The password-recovery mechanism is enabled.
384K bytes of flash-simulated non-volatile configuration memory.
Base ethernet MAC Address: 00:0B:BE:4F:BC:00
Motherboard assembly number: 73-5700-09
Power supply part number: 34-0966-02
Motherboard serial number: CAT06490ERT
Power supply serial number: DCA06471TBA
Model revision number: G0
Motherboard revision number: A0
Model number: WS-C3550-24-EMI
System serial number: CHK0650V0SY
Configuration register is 0x10F

Switch#dir
Directory of flash:/

2  -rwx       273   Jan 01 1970 00:01:21  system_env_vars
3  -rwx         5   Mar 12 1993 21:42:57  private-config.text
4  -rwx         0   Jan 01 1970 00:01:21  env_vars
5  -rwx   3703698   Mar 01 1993 22:53:42  c3550-i5q3l2-mz.121-11.EA1.bin
8  -rwx      1504   Mar 12 1993 21:42:57  config.text

15998976 bytes total (7104512 bytes free)
```

Step 8

To view the system image filename and other Flash files that you can copy from the root directory, issue the **copy flash:?** command:

```
Switch1#copy flash:?
flash:c2950-i6q4l2-mz.121-11.EA1.bin         flash:config.text
flash:env_vars           flash:html       flash:info
flash:info.ver           flash:private-config.text
```

```
Switch1#copy flash:?
flash:c3550-i5q3l2-mz.121-11.EA1.bin          flash:config.text
flash:env_vars                    flash:private-config.text      flash:system_env_vars
```

Note that several files are in Flash memory. Refer to http://www.cisco.com/univercd/cc/td/doc/product/lan/c3550/1214ea1/ 3550scg/swiosfs.pdf or other sources for more information about the various files.

Copy or upload the IOS image from Flash to the TFTP file server and use the appropriate filename for the 2950T or the 3550 switch. Just as with copying configuration files, you can include the filename parameter with the initial **copy** command or in response to prompts. Remember to include the subdirectory name if the IOS image is not in the root directory:

```
Switch1#copy flash:c2950-i6q4l2-mz.121-11.EA1.bin tftp
Address or name of remote host []?10.1.1.10
Destination filename [c2950-i6q4l2-mz.121-6.EA2c.bin]?
!!!!!!!!!!!!!!!!!!!!!!!!!!!!!!!!!!!!!!!!!!!!!!!!!!!!!!!!!!!!!!!!!!!!!!!!!!!!!!!!!
!!!!!!!!!!!!!!!!!!!!!!!!!!!!!!!!!!!!!!!!!!!!!!!!!!!!!!!!!!!!!!!!!!!!!!!!!!!!!!!!!
!!!!!!!!!!!!!!!!!!!!!!!!!!!!!!!!!!!!!!!!!!!!!!!!!!!!!!!!!!!!!!!!!!!!!!!!!!!!!!!!!
!!!!!!!!!!!!!!!!!!!!!!!!!!!!!!!!!!!!!!!!!!!!!!!!!!!!!!!!!!!!!!!!!!!!!!!!!!!!!!!!!
!!!!!!!!!!!!!!!!!!!!!!!!!!!!!!!!!!!!!!!!!!!!!!!!!!!!!!!!!!!!!!!!!!!!!!!!!!!!!!!!!
!!!!!!!!!!!!!!!!!!!!!!!!!!!!!!!!!!!!!!!!!!!!
2253443 bytes copied in 25.616 secs (90137 bytes/sec)

Switch1#copy flash tftp
Source filename []? c2950-i6q4l2-mz.121-11.EA1.bin
Address or name of remote host []? 10.1.1.10
Destination filename [c2950-i6q4l2-mz.121-11.EA1.bin]?
!!!!!!!!!!!!!!!!!!!!!!!!!!!!!!!!!!!!!!!!!!!!!!!!!!!!!!!!!!!!!!!!!!!!!!!!!!!!!!!!!
!!!!!!!!!!!!!!!!!!!!!!!!!!!!!!!!!!!!!!!!!!!!!!!!!!!!!!!!!!!!!!!!!!!!!!!!!!!!!!!!!
!!!!!!!!!!!!!!!!!!!!!!!!!!!!!!!!!!!!!!!!!!!!!!!!!!!!!!!!!!!!!!!!!!!!!!!!!!!!!!!!!
!!!!!!!!!!!!!!!!!!!!!!!!!!!!!!!!!!!!!!!!!!!!!!!!!!!!!!!!!!!!!!!!!!!!!!!!!!!!!!!!!
!!!!!!!!!!!!!!!!!!!!!!!!!!!!!!!!!!!!!!!!!!!!!!!!!!!!!!!!!!!!!!!!!!!!!!!!!!!!!!!!!
!!!!!!!!!!!!!!!!!!!!!!!!!!!!!!!!!!!!!!!!!!!!
2253443 bytes copied in 28.444 secs (80480 bytes/sec)
```

The exclamation points (!) indicate that the file is being copied.

Step 9

Copy or download the IOS image file from the TFTP file server to Flash and use the appropriate filename for the 2950T or 3550 switch. Doing so downloads the file that you just uploaded. A message indicates that the file already exists. Confirm to overwrite because this restores the same file for practice:

```
Switch1#copy tftp flash:c2950-i6q4l2-mz.121-11.EA1.bin
Address or name of remote host []? 10.1.1.10
Source filename []? c2950-i6q4l2-mz.121-11.EA1.bin
Destination filename [c2950-i6q4l2-mz.121-11.EA1.bin]?
%Warning: There is a file already existing with this name
Do you want to over write? [confirm]
Accessing tftp://10.1.1.10/ c2950-i6q4l2-mz.121-11.EA1.bin...
Loading c2950-i6q4l2-mz.121-11.EA1.bin from 10.1.1.10 (via Vlan1): !!!!!!!!!!!!!
!!!!!!!!!!!!!!!!!!!!!!!!!!!!!!!!!!!!!!!!!!!!!!!!!!!!!!!!!!!!!!!!!!!!!!!!!!!!!!!!!
!!!!!!!!!!!!!!!!!!!!!!!!!!!!!!!!!!!!!!!!!!!!!!!!!!!!!!!!!!!!!!!!!!!!!!!!!!!!!!!!!
!!!!!!!!!!!!!!!!!!!!!!!!!!!!!!!!!!!!!!!!!!!!!!!!!!!!!!!!!!!!!!!!!!!!!!!!!!!!!!!!!
!!!!!!!!!!!!!!!!!!!!!!!!!!!!!!!!!!!!!!!!!!!!!!!!!!!!!!!!!!!!!!!!!!!!!!!!!!!!!!!!!
!!!!!!!!!!!!!!!!!!!!!!!!!!!!!!!!!!!!!!!!!!!!!!!!!!!!!!!!!!!!!!!!!!!!!!!!!!!!!!!!!
!!!!!!!!!!!!!!!!!!!!!!!!!!!!!!!!!!!!!
[OK - 2253443/4506624 bytes]

2253443 bytes copied in 61.504 secs (36941 bytes/sec)

Switch1#copy tftp flash
Address or name of remote host []? 10.1.1.10
Source filename [c2950-i6q4l2-mz.121-11.EA1.bin]?
Destination filename [c2950-i6q4l2-mz.121-11.EA1.bin]?
%Warning: There is a file already existing with this name
Do you want to over write? [confirm]
```

```
Accessing tftp://10.1.1.10/c2950-i6q4l2-mz.121-11.EA1.bin...
Loading c2950-i6q4l2-mz.121-11.EA1.bin from 10.1.1.10 (via Vlan1):
!!!!!!!!!!!!!!!!!!!!!!!!!!!!!!!!!!!!!!!!!!!!!!!!!!!!!!!!!!!!!!!!!!!!!!!!!!!!!!!!
!!!!!!!!!!!!!
!!!!!!!!!!!!!!!!!!!!!!!!!!!!!!!!!!!!!!!!!!!!!!!!!!!!!!!!!!!!!!!!!!!!!!!!!!!!!!!!
!!!!!!!!!!!!!!!!!!!!!!!!!!!!!!!!!!!!!!!!!!!!!!!!!!!!!!!!!!!!!!!!!!!!!!!!!!!!!!!!
!!!!!!!!!!!!!!!!!!!!!!!!!!!!!!!!!!!!!!!!!!!!!!!!!!!!!!!!!!!!!!!!!!!!!!!!!!!!!!!!
!!!!!!!!!!!!!!!!!!!!!!!!!!!!!!!!!!!!!!!!!!!!!!!!!!!!!!!!!!!!!!!!!!!!!!!!!!!!!!!!
!!!!!!!!!!!!!!!!!!!!!!!!!!!!!!!!!!!!!!
[OK - 2253443/4506624 bytes]

2253443 bytes copied in 72.48 secs (31297 bytes/sec)
```

This successfully completes the procedure for uploading and downloading the switch startup configuration and IOS system image files.

Reflection

Why should you save a copy of the switch startup configuration and IOS system image files?

_____

_____

_____

_____

_____

_____

Lab 1.6.3: Catalyst 2950T and 3550 Series Password Recovery

Estimated Time: 30 Minutes

Note: This lab has no questions for students to answer.

Objective

In this lab, you recover passwords while retaining configurations for the Cisco Catalyst 2950T and 3550 series of Ethernet switches. Figure 1-3 shows the topology for this lab.

Figure 1-3 Topology for Lab 1.6.3

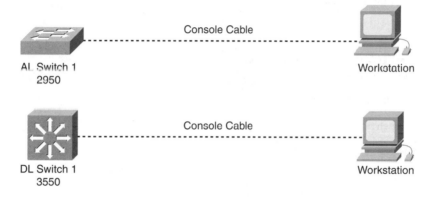

Scenario

Access to a network device might be denied because of an incorrect password. Sometimes password documentation is unavailable for reference. In that case, the device usually contains configurations that should not be changed. Therefore, it is important that you learn the password recovery procedure for devices in the network. This lab covers the password recovery procedure for the Cisco Catalyst 2950T and 3550 series of Ethernet switches. The password recovery procedure for the 2950T and the 3550 switch is identical.

Step 1

Establish a HyperTerminal console connection with a 2950T or a 3550 switch. Enter **enable secret** *password*.

```
Switch>enable
Switch#configure terminal
Switch(config)#enable secret password
Switch(config)#exit
Switch#copy running-config startup-config
Switch#exit
```

Access to the user mode should be successful. However, you cannot access the privileged mode without knowing the password.

Step 2

Begin the password recovery procedure by unplugging the switch power cord.

Step 3

Hold down the **Mode** button located on the left side of the front panel while reconnecting the power cord to the switch.

On the 2950T switch, release the Mode button after instructions that are similar to the sample output appear. On the 3550 switch, release the Mode button after the Fast Ethernet 0/1 light goes out:

```
--output omitted--
The system has been interrupted prior to initializing the flash file system.
```

The following commands initiate the flash file system and finish loading the operating system software:

```
        flash_init
        load_helper
        boot
switch:
```

Step 4

Finish initializing flash by issuing the **flash_init** command:

```
switch: flash_init
Initializing Flash...
flashfs[0]: 14 files, 2 directories
flashfs[0]: 0 orphaned files, 0 orphaned directories
flashfs[0]: Total bytes: 7741440
flashfs[0]: Bytes used: 3972096
flashfs[0]: Bytes available: 3769344
flashfs[0]: flashfs fsck took 6 seconds.
...done initializing flash.
Boot Sector Filesystem (bs:) installed, fsid: 3
Parameter Block Filesystem (pb:) installed, fsid: 4
switch:
```

Step 5

Load the default configuration by issuing the **load_helper** command. This is similar to changing the configuration register on a router to boot into the ROM Monitor mode. Then issue the **dir flash:** command to identify the configuration file that contains the password definition. A sample output is as follows:

```
switch: load_helper
switch: dir flash:
Directory of flash:/
2     -rwx   2253443    <date>           c2950-i6q412-mz.121-6.EA2c.bin
3     -rwx   269        <date>           env_vars
4     -rwx   109        <date>           info
6     -rwx   698        <date>           config.text
7     drwx   640        <date>           html
18    -rwx   109        <date>           info.ver

3767808 bytes available (3973632 bytes used)
switch:
```

The config.text file contains the password definitions and other switch configuration parameters.

Enter a **?** at the **switch:** prompt to list all available commands. In addition to the **dir** command used previously, note the **cat**, **rename**, and **boot** commands. You will use these commands subsequently. Display the contents of the config.text file using the **cat flash:config.text** command.

Step 6

Rename the original configuration file that contains the password definitions; then reboot the switch. The switch does not find the config.text file and continues with the default boot process. You might need to press the **Enter** key a few times during the boot process. The switch goes into the setup mode and presents the System Configuration Dialog prompt. Respond with **no** at the prompt.

```
switch: rename flash:config.text flash:config.old
switch: boot

--output omitted--

--- System Configuration Dialog ---

Would you like to enter the initial configuration dialog? [yes/no]:no

Press RETURN to get started!

Switch>
```

This enables access into the switch and bypasses passwords.

Step 7

Enter the privileged mode and restore the name of the configuration file to its original. Then copy the configuration file to running-config to retain any previously entered switch configurations:

```
Switch>enable
Switch#rename flash:config.old flash:config.text
Destination filename [config.text]? <press ENTER>
Switch#copy flash:config.text system:running-config
Destination filename [running-config]? <press ENTER>
698 bytes copied in 0.576 secs
Switch#
```

Step 8

You now can reassign and document all passwords without losing a switch configuration from the original configuration file. Be sure to save the configuration after changing the passwords:

```
Switch#configure terminal
Enter configuration commands, one per line.  End with CNTL/Z.
Switch(config)#enable password cisco
Switch(config)#enable secret class
Switch(config)#line con 0
Switch(config-line)#password cisco
Switch(config-line)#login
Switch(config)#line vty 0 15
Switch(config-line)#password cisco
Switch(config-line)#login
Switch(config-line)#exit
Switch(config)#exit
Switch#copy running-config startup-config
Destination filename [startup-config]? <press ENTER>
Building configuration...
[OK]
Switch#
```

The process of bypassing passwords to access a 2950T or 3550 series switch is now complete. Passwords have been changed, but all other switch configurations that might have been entered previously have been retained. Document the new passwords and place them in a secure location for future reference.

Lab 1.6.4: Introduction to Fluke Network Inspector

Estimated Time: 90 Minutes

Note: This lab references several toolbar buttons from the Fluke Network Inspector interface. Refer to the section "Appendix: Toolbars and Function Keys" at the end of this chapter for a detailed description of each button.

Objective

This tutorial lab demonstrates how to use the Network Inspector (NI) from Fluke Networks to discover and analyze network devices in a broadcast domain. Figure 1-4 shows the topology for this lab.

Figure 1-4 Topology for Lab 1.6.4

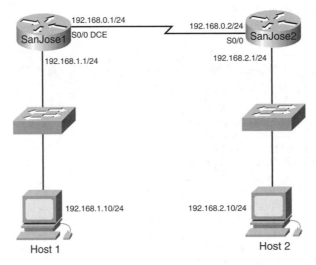

This lab demonstrates the key product features of NI. However, NI has a limited number of devices. The software can distinguish the following components if they have been assigned network addresses:

- Workstations
- Servers
- Network printers
- Switches
- Routers
- Managed hubs

After you complete the lab, consider repeating the steps in a larger environment, such as a classroom, so that you can see more variety. Before you attempt to run NI on a school LAN, make sure it is okay with the instructor. Consider the following points:

- NI detects the devices within a network subnet or VLAN. It does not search beyond a router. It also does not inventory the entire network of the school unless it is all on one subnet.
- NI is not a Cisco product and it is not limited to detecting only Cisco devices.
- NI is a detection tool, but it is not a configuration tool. You cannot use NI to reconfigure devices.

The output in this lab is representative only. The output varies depending on factors such as the number of devices, device MAC addresses, device host names, the LAN that is joined, and protocols used.

Scenario

This lab introduces the Fluke NI software, which might be useful in troubleshooting labs and in the field. The NI software is a valuable part of the Networking Academy program. It also is representative of the features that are available with other products on the market.

At least one host must have the NI software installed. If the lab is done in pairs, the software should be installed on both machines so that each person can perform the lab steps.

Step 1

Cable and configure the devices as shown in Figure 1-4. The switches pictured can be any Catalyst switches. Be sure to use the default switch configurations on these switches. If necessary, erase the configuration files on the switches.

Because the software discovers devices on the network, the demonstration improves as you add more devices to the network.

If available, add additional hosts to both LANs.

Step 2

From the Start menu, launch the Network Inspector Console (see Figure 1-5).

Click the **Agent** button at the left end of the toolbar to start the Agent.

Figure 1-5 Network Inspector Console

If necessary, select the **Agent** tab in the window, click on the **Start** button, and watch the Status box until it says that the Agent is running (see Figure 1-6). This process might take several minutes to start.

Figure 1-6 Network Inspector Agent

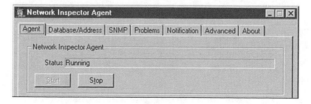

You can see the Agent status on the bottom of the Console window. Figure 1-7, which is shown in Step 3, indicates that the Agent has been running since 9:57 p.m.

Use the **Close** button in the lower-right corner of the Agent window to send the Agent away. Some versions might have a Hide button. If you use the **Stop** button, the discovery process ceases.

Step 3

The NI software is designed to collect network data quietly. NI can perform this data collection either passively or actively. It takes time for the devices to appear. This small network should be discovered in a minute or two. Active collection of statistical data is delayed for the first 10 minutes. An actual production network might take 30 minutes or more to discover most data.

After a few minutes, the Console window should display information about the network. In Figure 1-7, two additional workstations were added.

Figure 1-7 Network Inspector Console

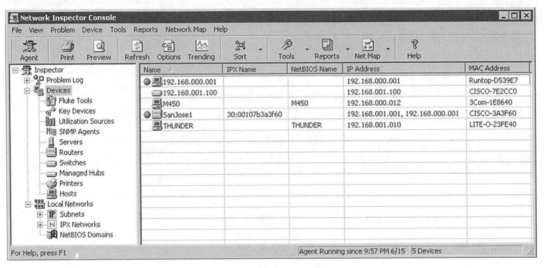

Note: You can see entries from previous sessions. It takes a few minutes for the entries to match the network. In the Agent window, under the Database/Address tab (see Figure 1-8), there is a checkbox for Overwrite. If that box is checked, the current database content is discarded, and a fresh data set is discovered and loaded when the Agent starts. If the box is not checked, any new data is integrated with the existing database as it is discovered.

Referring to the Figure 1-7 output, the MAC address has been configured to interpret the first half of the 48-bit MAC address to show the vendor name. You can use the Options button in the toolbar to change this display.

Figure 1-8 Database/Address Tab

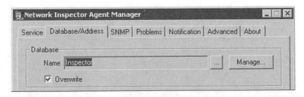

The Network Inspector console in Step 3 lists M450, SanJose1, and Thunder as the host names. Host names on PCs are different. This window also lists the IP address and MAC address for each discovered device. SanJose1 and SanJose2 each have two IP addresses assigned to the LAN interface.

NI does not investigate beyond the router interface. It collects information only on the devices that share the same broadcast domain as the computer network interface card (NIC).

Step 4

Double-click a device name. If a router is present, choose it and look over the available device properties (see Figure 1-9). Remember that the results depend on the devices that are included in the LAN subnet.

Figure 1-9 Device Properties of a Router

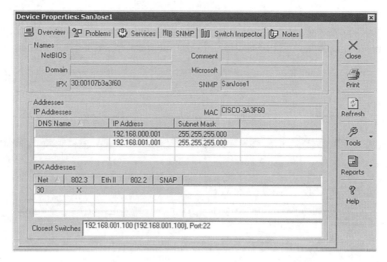

The Overview tab in Figure 1-9 shows IP addresses, the Internet Packet Exchange (IPX) address, the IPX networks that are attached, the IPX data frame used for 802.3, and the MAC address. Notice that the Organizational Unique Identifier (OUI) has been converted to identify the manufacturer in this example.

Closest switches appear only if you have provided NI with a valid SNMP community string for the switch.

The Problems tab reveals that one of the IP addresses is duplicated within the network (see Figure 1-10). This occurs if you configured an optional host when you defined Step 1. The red ball to the left of the Description indicates a problem.

Figure 1-10 Problems Tab

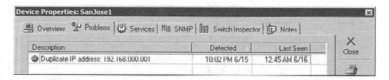

The Services tab reveals that IP and IPX services are running on the routers (see Figure 1-11).

Figure 1-11 Services Tab

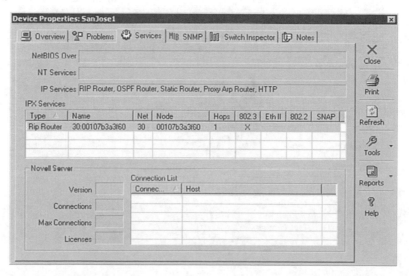

The preceding IP Services example reveals that the IP HTTP Server service has been turned on. This means that you can access the router with a web browser.

Scrolling to the right reveals MTU and Description, which is Fast Ethernet 0/0 or Token Ring 0/1, details.

The IPX Services shows that the IPX Network ID is 30 and the node address is MAC. It also indicates the frame type and the fact that IPX RIP is running.

The bottom third of the window shows the information that would have been revealed if the device had been a Novell server. A multihomed server that has more than one NIC connection in separate networks is working as a router or bridge.

The MIB SNMP tab reveals Simple Network Management Protocol (SNMP) information and the router IOS information (see Figure 1-12).

Figure 1-12 MIB SNMP Tab

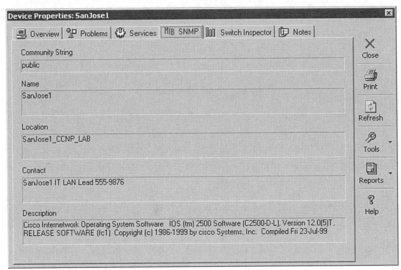

The Switch Inspector tab creates a variety of charts of the switch interface data for the selected device. This data is not collected during the initial 10-minute period. The Switch Inspector test provides basic utilization graphs for any SNMP-enabled device. The level of information that this test offers depends on which MIBs the selected devices support. For example, SanJose1 is a router that cannot display the address of directly connected devices for a highlighted port. The buttons on the left side of the window change the chart format. The Graph Legend button at the bottom-left corner displays the floating legend shown in Figure 1-13.

Figure 1-13 Floating Legend

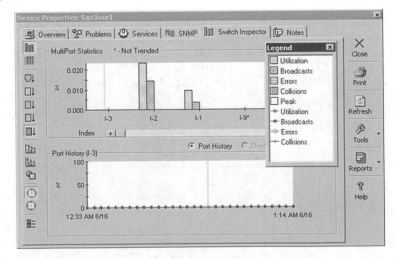

The second button on the left is the Tabular View button. This option details each interface on the selected device, whether the interface is up or down. The check box at the left of each line determines whether statistics are gathered for trending on that interface. Scrolling to the right reveals maximum transmission unit (MTU) and description details such as Ethernet 0 or Token-Ring 0/1 (see Figure 1-14).

Figure 1-14 Tabular View

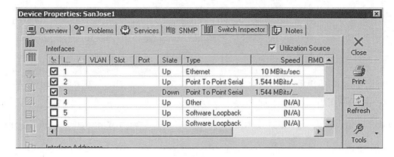

The two clock-like buttons switch between a 1-hour or 24-hour history, which can create an interesting comparison if the NI runs for an extended time (see Figure 1-15). The results are the same in this short exercise.

Figure 1-15 1-Hour and 24-Hour History Buttons

In the Switch Inspector, the Reports button on the right side of the screen expands to show two options: Switch Performance and Switch Detail (see Figure 1-16). Select the **Switch Performance** choice to reveal a multipage report with various charts. Look over the results.

Figure 1-16 Reports Button

The Switch Detail option works only with a switch.

After you examine the Device Properties window, click the **Close** button in the upper-right corner to return to the Network Inspector Console.

Step 5

At the Network Inspector Console, experiment with expanding and contracting the choices in the left-side pane. As with the Explorer, if an item on the left side is selected, the right side illustrates the details. As shown in Figure 1-17, expanding the Problems Log and selecting **Errors** reveals the devices with errors on the right side. This makes it easy to spot the duplicate IP address device.

Figure 1-17 Problem Log

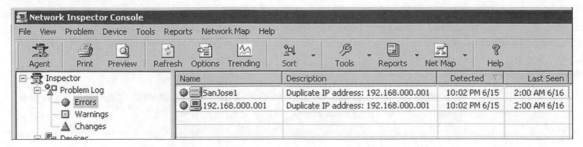

Try different options on the left pane and note the result in the right pane. Because of the limited number of devices, some will be empty. Try it later with a larger sample.

In the left pane, select **Devices** to show all devices in the right pane. Note the format of the MAC address.

Click the **Options** button or choose **View**, **Options** in the toolbar. Note that you have a choice between Manufacturer Prefix and Hex (see Figure 1-18). Select the one that is not chosen, look over the other options, and then click **OK**. Note the result.

Figure 1-18 Options Dialog Box

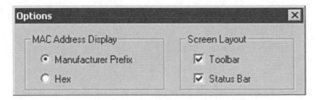

To get help in the Console main screen, check that the Problem Log is selected. Highlight a device shown in the detail window. Press the **F1** or the **Help** function key to show a list of problems by category.

If one of the problems created by the current lab configuration is a duplicate IP address, you can view this by providing a duplicate IP address for one of the devices. To learn about duplicate IP addresses, identify the symptoms, and determine what can be done about them, select the **Duplicate IP Address** hyperlink from the Network Inspector Console Help list (see Figure 1-19). The Help window for this software contains considerable information.

Figure 1-19 Hyperlinks in Network Inspector Console Help

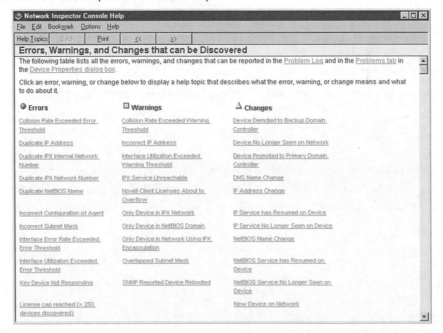

Experiment with the Preview, Sort, and Reports buttons in the toolbar. Focus on the troubleshooting and documentation possibilities of the reports.

Select a host. Then click the **Tools** button in the toolbar and choose **Ping**.

The Select Parameter dialog box includes the LAN IP addresses that you can ping (see Figure 1-20). Select an address and click **OK**.

Figure 1-20 Select Parameter Dialog Box

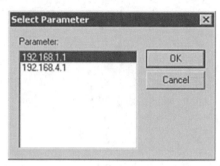

A command or MSDOS window appears to show the results.

Use the **exit** command to close the new window when you are finished.

Select a router or switch in the Console display and then choose **Tools>Telnet**. A window appears with an open Telnet session. Traceroute works the same way.

The Web option on the Tools button opens a web session with a device if the IP HTTP Server feature is turned on.

In the sample lab, the switch is a Catalyst 1924 with an assigned IP address. The window shown in Figure 1-21 appears if the Web choice is selected while the switch is highlighted.

Figure 1-21 Catalyst 1900 Web GUI

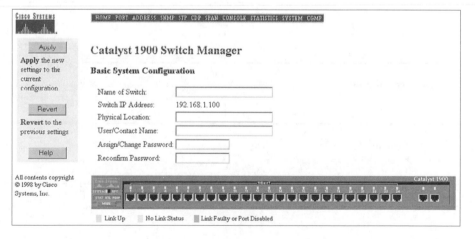

Experiment with the toolbar options so that you can become familiar with the features.

Step 6

If Visio is installed on the workstation, the Net Map button on the toolbar activates the application and create a network map of the broadcast domain. The following example uses the Router Connections in a Switched Network on the Net Map button. It draws the network whether or not a switch is included (see Figure 1-22).

Figure 1-22 Router Connections in a Switched Network

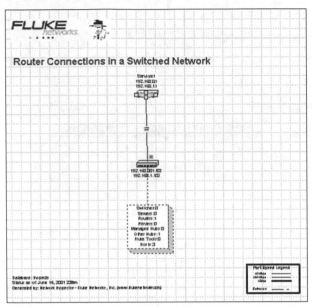

Visio is fully integrated into NI. Double-clicking one of the devices in the drawing displays the Device Properties window that you saw in Step 4.

Step 7

Use the skills acquired in this lab to select the router and document the following information:

1. What is the name of the device?

_____

2. What IP services is the device running?

_____

3. What IPX services is the device running?

_____

4. What is the SNMP community string?

_____

5. What is the location?

_____

6. Who is the contact?

_____

7. Which interfaces are available?

_____

8. Which interfaces are up?

_____

9. List any problem that the software has discovered.

_____

_____

_____

_____

Step 8

Connect the two switches with a crossover cable and watch the NI output as new devices are discovered. If a crossover cable is not available, remove one of the switches and plug the host and router into the second switch. Although this is not usually done in a production environment, you should see how the NI responds.

New devices should show up initially with blue triangles, which indicate that they are newly discovered. Many devices should eventually get a yellow warning rectangle, which indicates a potential problem. This process could take 10 or more minutes.

Eventually, you will see the other subnets and the second router.

Step 9

Click the **Agent** button in the toolbar. The Agent has been collecting data all this time. Click the **Stop** button and then confirm the intentions when prompted.

Examine the tabs to discover the database options that you can set. Note the Problems tab and the choices for focusing the investigation (see Figure 1-23).

Figure 1-23 Problems Tab

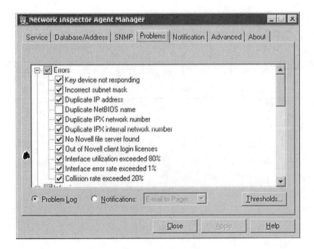

On the Notification tab (shown in Figure 1-24), observe that you can send e-mail notifications. To use this feature, you need to have the same information that is required to set up an Internet or Outlook e-mail account.

Figure 1-24 Notification Tab

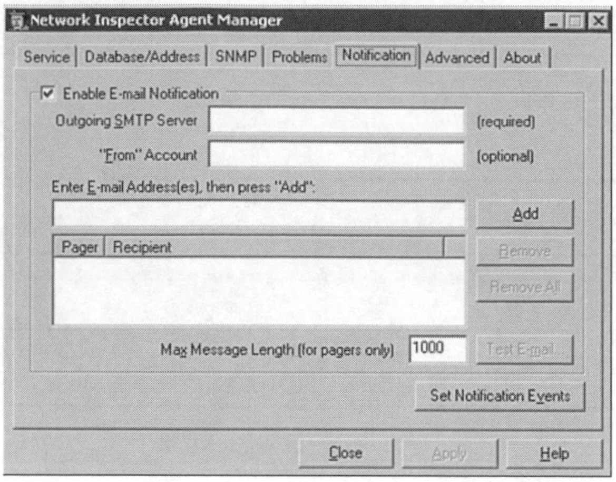

If the Agent is started again, it might take a few minutes to detect any changes that occurred while the Agent was off.

Step 10

Experiment with the NI tool by looking at the different devices.

If NI is installed on the classroom computers, investigate the devices on the larger network.

Reflection

How might you use this information in troubleshooting?

What advantages might NI have over HyperTerminal for troubleshooting documentation?

Lab 1.6.5: Introduction to Fluke Protocol Expert

Estimated Time: 90 Minutes

Note: This lab references several toolbar buttons from the Fluke NI interface. Refer to the section "Appendix: Toolbars and Function Keys" at the end of this chapter for a detailed description of each button.

Objective

This tutorial lab demonstrates how to use the Fluke Networks OptiView Protocol Expert (PE) to analyze network traffic. In this lab, you see the key features of the tool so that you can incorporate it into various troubleshooting efforts. Figure 1-25 shows the topology for this lab.

Figure 1-25 Topology for Lab 1.6.5

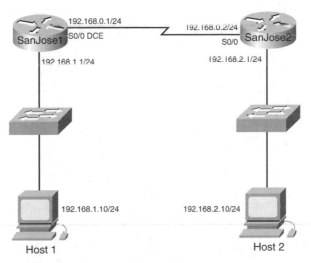

Note: The output in this lab is representative only. The output varies depending on the number of devices in the network, such as device MAC addresses and host names.

Scenario

This lab introduces PE, which can be useful in later troubleshooting labs and in the field. The PE software is a valuable part of the Networking Academy. It provides many of the same features as other products on the market.

If PE is installed on all classroom machines, each person can run the lab steps. However, each host might display slightly different results.

Step 1

Note: This lab configuration is the same as the previous lab's configuration.

Cable and configure the devices, as pictured in Figure 1-25. The switches pictured can be any Catalyst switches that are preferred. Be sure to use the default switch configurations on these switches. If necessary, erase the configuration files on the switches.

Step 2

From the Start menu, launch the OptiView Protocol Expert EDV program.

Note: The first time you run the program, a message appears that asks if you have any Fluke analyzer cards or Fluke taps in the local system.

If you are using the educational version, click **No**. If the answer is yes or if the following screen appears (see Figure 1-26), click **OK** without selecting any ports.

Figure 1-26 Scanning Ports

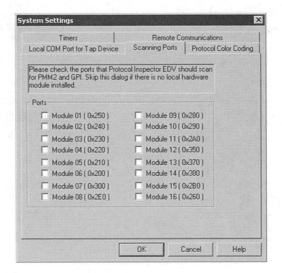

Four main PE views exist:

- Summary View

- Detail View

- Capture View of Capture Buffers

- Capture View of Capture Files

The program opens in the Summary View. This view shows several windows that the tool uses. The Resource Browser window in the upper-left corner shows the only monitoring device that is available in this lab, which is the NDIS 802.3 Module NIC of the host. Any Protocol Media Monitors are displayed with the associated host devices. The Alarm Browser on the left side and Message Area at the bottom are covered later in this chapter.

The Monitor View, which is the main window in the upper-right corner, monitors one resource per window in a variety of viewing options. The example shown in Figure 1-27 shows no information in the Monitor View window. The Stop in the upper-left corner of the Monitor View window confirms that no monitoring is occurring.

Figure 1-27 Monitor View

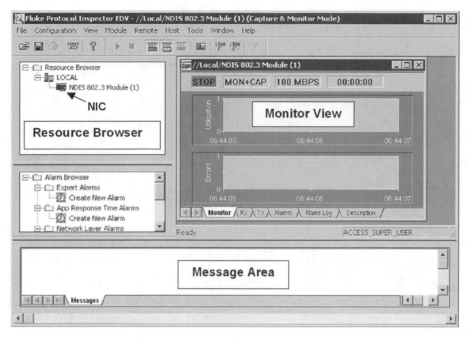

Step 3

Use the Start button or choose **Module > Start** from the menu system to begin the monitoring and capturing process. The Utilization chart should start showing activity, as demonstrated in Figure 1-28.

Figure 1-28 Utilization Chart Showing Activity

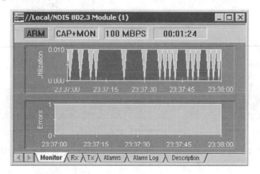

The word "ARM" should appear where Stop had been before. The Module menu shows that Stop is now an option and Start has been muted. Do not stop the process yet; restart it if necessary.

The tabs at the bottom of the window show the resulting data in a variety of forms. Click each tab and note the results. The Tx tab, which represents transmit, is blank. The Alarms and Alarm Log are also blank. Figure 1-29 shows the Rx, or received frames, which indicates that Broadcast and Multicast frames are being received. However, it might not show Unicasts.

Figure 1-29 Rx Tab

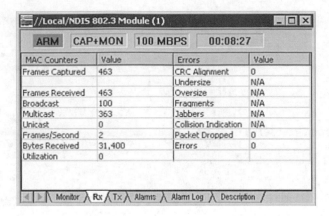

Use the console connection to the router to ping the monitoring host, which is 192.168.1.10 or 192.168.2.10. Unicast frames appear. Dedicated hardware protocol analyzers such as Fluke Network OptiView can show a more complete picture of traffic on the network.

The Description tab reveals the MAC address, manufacturer, and model of the NIC. It also shows which error counters are on (see Figure 1-30).

Figure 1-30 Description Tab

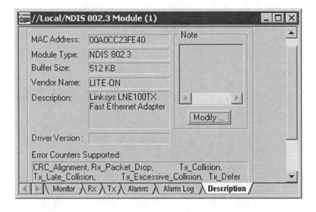

Take a few minutes to become familiar with the tabs and the scroll features of the window.

Step 4

Click the **Detail View** button in the toolbar or double-click anywhere on the **Monitor View** chart to access the Detail View window. This opens a second window that should resemble what is shown in Figure 1-31 after the Utilization/Errors Strip Chart or RX window has been maximized to fill the screen.

Figure 1-31 Detail View

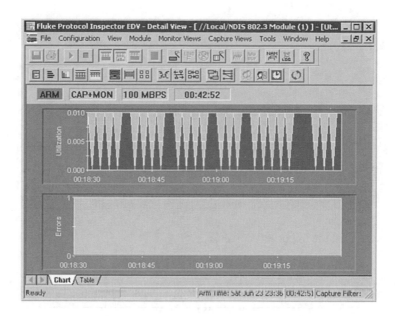

Note: If necessary, activate all toolbars on the View menu.

Initially, the chart output will be the same as before, but many more toolbar and menu options are available than in the Summary View. Confirm that the Chart and Table tabs still contain the same information.

The Detail View window is covering the Summary View window from earlier. Use the taskbar to move between the windows.

Like all Windows-compliant programs, when you place the mouse over a button, a screen tip appears to identify the purpose of the button. Move the mouse over the buttons and notice that some of them are muted. This muting indicates that the feature is not appropriate under the current circumstances or it might not be supported on the educational version.

Note: A complete display of the toolbars and what they do is included in the Appendix at the end of this lab.

Click the **Mac Statistics** button to view the Rx frame table data in a different format. The result should be obvious. Maximize the resulting window. The one piece of new information is the Speed, which shows the NIC transmission rate.

Click the **Frame Size Distribution** button to see a distribution of the size of the frames that the NIC is receiving. When you place the mouse over any bar, a small summary like the one shown in Figure 1-32 appears. Maximize the resulting window.

Figure 1-32 Summary of Frame Size Distribution

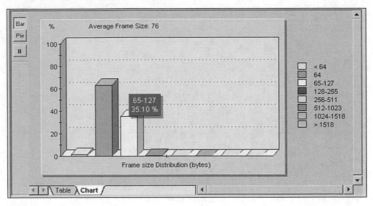

Try the Pie, Bar, and Pause buttons in the upper-left corner.

Note: Pause stops the capture, so click it again to resume the capture. Look at both the Table and Chart tab displays, too.

The sample configurations mainly produce small frames because routing updates are occurring. Try using the extended ping feature from the router console connection and specifying 100 pings with a larger packet size.

After you maximize each new display, use the Window menu to return to any previous view. You can also tile the windows. Experiment with the Window menu features and then close any unwanted views.

Click the **Protocol Distribution** button to see a distribution of the protocols that the NIC is receiving (see Figure 1-33). Place the mouse over any bar to view a small summary panel. Maximize the resulting window.

Figure 1-33 Distribution of Protocols That the NIC Is Receiving

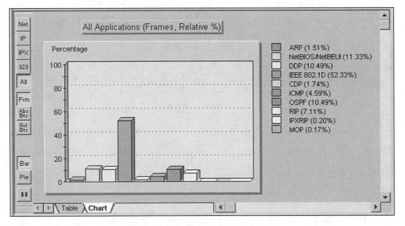

Try each of the buttons and tabs to see the results. The Net button shows only network protocols. Depending on the version of Protocol Expert you are using, you will see a button labeled either 323 or MoIP. The 323 button refers to the H323 protocol, and MoIP is Multimedia over IP. Both refer to Voice and Video over IP protocols. Look at the frame (Frm), the absolute bytes (Abs Bts), and the relative bytes (Rel Bts) to see the results. Remember that the Pause button stops the capture.

Click the **Host Table** button to see the MAC stations and related traffic (see Figure 1-34).

Figure 1-34 MAC Stations and Related Traffic

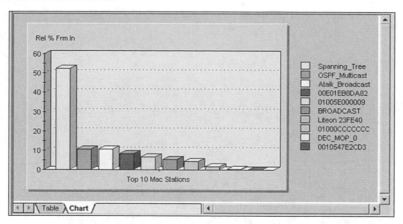

Notice in Figure 1-34 that Spanning Tree, AppleTalk, and Open Shortest Path First (OSPF) traffic are present. The results include only the protocols that are present on the network. Be sure to look at the Table tab to see the actual values.

Click the **Network Layer Host Table** button to see the network IP or IPX stations and related traffic (see Figure 1-35).

Figure 1-35 Network IP and IPX Stations and Related Traffic

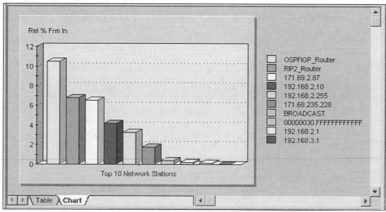

Any pings and any additional hosts that you have added to the configuration impact the actual addresses that appear on the right.

Click the **Application Layer Host Table** button to see the network station traffic for each application (see Figure 1-36).

Figure 1-36 Network Station Traffic

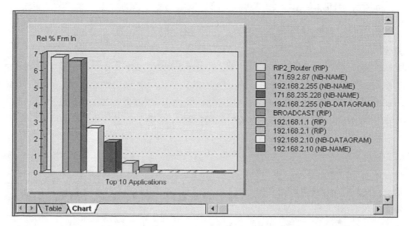

Experiment with the Host Matrix, Network Layer Matrix, and the Application Layer buttons. They create host-to-host matrices for MAC, network layer, and application layer conversations. Figure 1-37 gives an example of the network layer IP or IPX conversations.

Figure 1-37 Example of Network IP or IPX Conversations

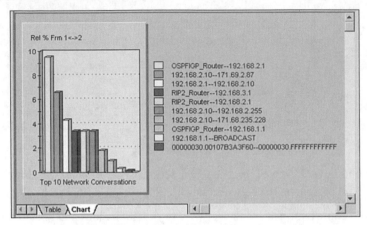

The VLAN button shows network traffic on VLANs. If this lab does not use VLANs, remember to try it in future VLAN labs.

The Address Map button creates a matrix that compares MAC and network station addresses to names. In Figure 1-38, the second row is a Novell station.

Figure 1-38 Comparison of MAC and Network Station Addresses to Their Names

MAC Station Name	MAC Station Address	Network Station Name	Network Station Address
00107B3A3F60	00107B3A3F60	192.168.1.1	192.168.1.1
00107B3A3F60	00107B3A3F60	00000030.00107B3A3F60	00000030.00107B3A3F60
Liteon 23FE40	00A0CC23FE40	192.168.2.10	192.168.2.10
00E01EB8DA82	00E01EB8DA82	192.168.2.1	192.168.2.1
00E01EB8DA82	00E01EB8DA82	192.168.3.1	192.168.3.1

The Name Table button opens the current name table for viewing or editing (see Figure 1-39).

Figure 1-39 Name Table Entries

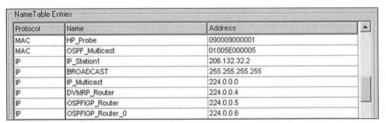

Protocol	Name	Address
MAC	HP_Probe	090009000001
MAC	OSPF_Multicast	01005E000005
IP	IP_Station1	206.132.32.2
IP	BROADCAST	255.255.255.255
IP	IP_Multicast	224.0.0.0
IP	DVMRP_Router	224.0.0.4
IP	OSPFIGP_Router	224.0.0.5
IP	OSPFIGP_Router_0	224.0.0.6

The Expert View button shows the expert symptoms that were discovered (see Figure 1-40). These statistics identify potential problems. The underlined options bring up additional detail windows if any values are recorded. The sample for this lab does not show much. However, you should review the options for debugging Inter-Switch Link (ISL), Hot Standby Router Protocol (HSRP), and other types of problems that you might see in later labs.

Figure 1-40 Expert Category of Symptoms

Expert Category	Value	Expert Category	Value
ICMP All Errors	368	Duplicate Network Address	0
ICMP Destination Unreachable	368	Unstable MST	0
ICMP Redirects	0	SAP Broadcast	0
Excessive Bootp	0	OSPF Broadcast	923
Excessive ARP	0	RIP Broadcast	25
NFS Retransmissions	0	ISL Illegal VLAN ID	0
TCP/IP SYN Attack	0	ISL BPDU/CDP Packets	0
TCP/IP RST Packets	0	IP Time to Live Expiring	0
TCP/IP Retransmissions	0	IP Checksum Errors	0
TCP/IP Zero Window	0	Illegal Network Source Address	0
TCP/IP Long Acks	0	Illegal MAC Source Address	0
TCP/IP Frozen Window	0	Total MAC Stations	11
Network Overload	0	Broadcast/Multicast Storm	0
Non Responsive Stations	0	Physical Errors	0
		HSRP Errors	0
		TCP Checksum Errors	0

Step 5

Click the **Stop** button or choose **Module > Stop** from the menu to stop the frame capture so that you can look at individual frames.

After you have stopped the capture, click the **Capture View** button. The education version displays a message box that says the capture is limited to 250 packets. Click **OK**.

The resulting window looks complicated at first (see Figure 1-41). Maximize it.

Figure 1-41 Captured Frames

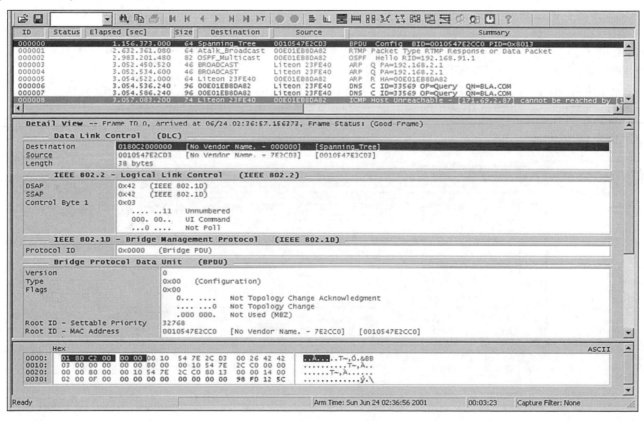

Looking over the results, note that three horizontal windows are open. The top window lists the captured packets. The middle window shows the details of the selected packet in the top window, and the bottom window shows the HEX values for the packet.

When you position the mouse over the borders between the three windows, a line mover or two-headed arrow should appear, which you can use to change the distribution of space to each window. You should make the middle window as large as possible and leave five to six rows in each of the other two, as shown in Figure 1-41.

Look over the packets that are listed in the top window. Domain Name System (DNS), Address Resolution Protocol (ARP), and Routing Table Maintenance Protocol (RTMP) packets should be included. When a switch is used, Cisco Discovery Protocol (CDP) and Spanning Tree Protocol (STP) packets should be displayed. Notice that when rows in the top window are selected, the contents of the other two windows change.

When you select information in the middle window, the HEX display in the bottom window changes to show where the specific information is stored. As shown in Figure 1-42, when you select the source address or IP, the HEX values from the packet are displayed.

Figure 1-42 HEX Values of the Packet

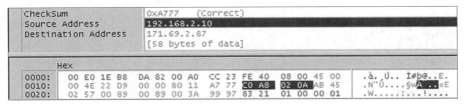

The color coding makes it easier to locate information from the middle window in the HEX window. With a DNS packet, for example, the data in the Data Link Control (DLC) section of the middle window is purple, whereas the IP section is green. The corresponding HEX values are the same colors.

Notice that, in Figure 1-43, the EtherType is 0x0800, which indicates that it is an IP packet. You can see the MAC addresses for both the destination and source hosts and the storage location of that data in the HEX display.

Figure 1-43 HEX Window

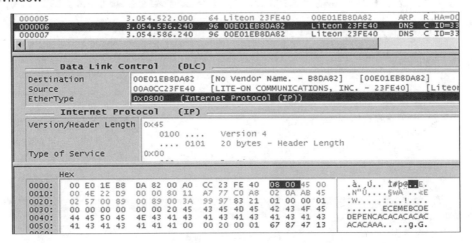

In the same example, the section in the middle window is the UDP, which contains information such as the UDP port numbers (see Figure 1-44).

Figure 1-44 UDP Information

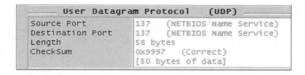

Note: The structure of the middle window is different for each type of packet.

Select different packet types in the top window and look over the resulting display in the other two windows. Pay attention to the EtherType, port numbers, and source and destination addresses. These can be both MAC and network layer addresses. You also might see Routing Information Protocol (RIP), OSPF, and AppleTalk RTMP packets in the capture. You should be able to find and interpret the important data. Figure 1-45 shows that this is a RIP version 2 packet. This version has a multicast destination address of 224.0.0.9, and you can see the actual route table entries. You should find the multicast destination address in version 1.

Figure 1-45 RIPv2 Packet

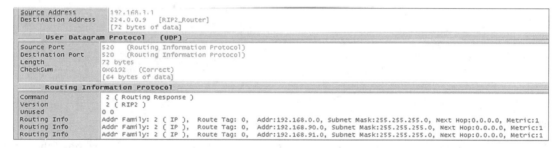

If CDP packets exist, determine the platform. Figure 1-46 is from a Catalyst 1900 switch.

Figure 1-46 Catalyst 1900 Switch Platform

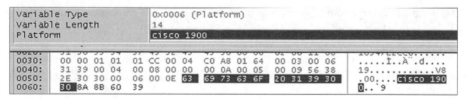

Experiment until the tools are familiar.

Step 6

Click the **Save Capture** button or choose **File > Save Capture** from the menu system to save the captured data. Click the **Continue** button to accept the All option. You can save a range of captured frames with this window (see Figure 1-47).

Figure 1-47 Save Options Window

Use a first name or anything that could be recognized as a name and store the file on the data floppy disk. If the CAP extension is showing when the window shown in Figure 1-48 opens, make sure it is there after you type the name.

Figure 1-48 Save As Window

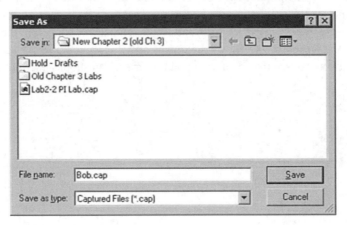

Click the **Open Capture File** button to open the file that you just saved.

The Capture View of Capture Files is being used now. The tools are the same, but the title bar at the top of the screen indicates that a file is being viewed instead of a capture in memory.

Step 7

Select a frame in the top window and try the navigation buttons. The basic arrows move up or down one frame. The arrow with the single line moves to the top or bottom of the current window. The arrow with two lines moves to the top or bottom of the entire list. The arrow with the T also moves to the top of the list.

Use the Search buttons to perform searches. Type text such as "OSPF" in the list box. Then click on the binoculars to move from one OSPF entry to the next.

Experiment until the tools are familiar.

Reflection

How might you use this tool in troubleshooting?

_____

Is all of the data on the network being analyzed?

_____

What is the impact of being connected to a switch?

_____

You have only been receiving broadcast traffic and unicasts for the monitor host. In Lab 9.9.1, you will learn how to mirror ports to direct a copy of any data to the protocol analyzer.

Appendix: Toolbars and Function Keys

This appendix describes the various toolbar buttons that are used in this chapter's labs. It also describes many function keys for your reference.

Toolbars

Figure 1-49 shows the PE toolbar.

Figure 1-49 PE Toolbar

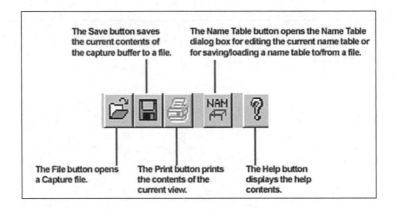

Figure 1-50 shows the Module toolbar.

Figure 1-50 Module Toolbar (Summary View)

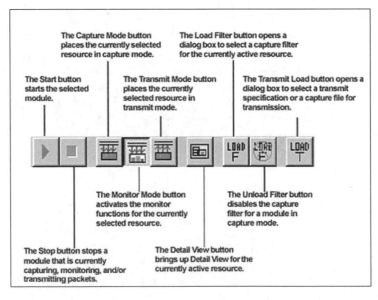

Figure 1-51 shows the Detail View toolbar.

Figure 1-51 Detail View Toolbar

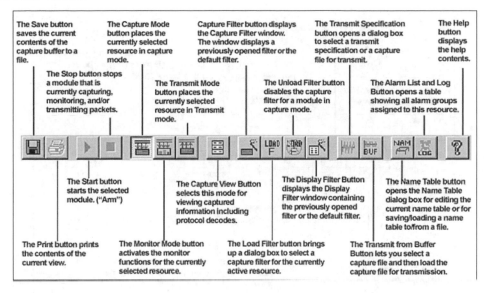

Figure 1-52 shows the Data Views toolbar. Note that only some of the views are available with GMM cards.

Figure 1-52 Data Views Toolbar

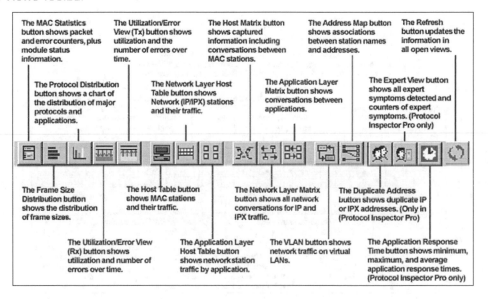

Figure 1-53 shows the Create/Modify Filter toolbar.

Figure 1-53 Create/Modify Filter Toolbar

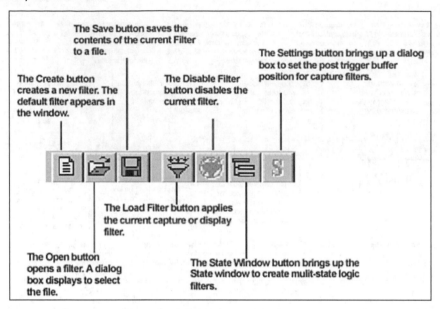

Figure 1-54 shows the State toolbar.

Figure 1-54 State Toolbar

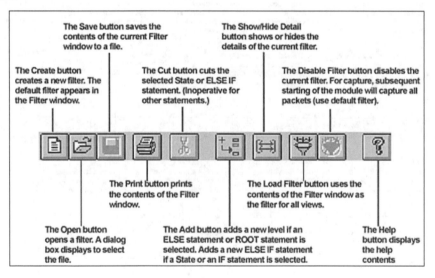

Figure 1-55 shows the Capture View toolbar.

Figure 1-55 Capture View Toolbar

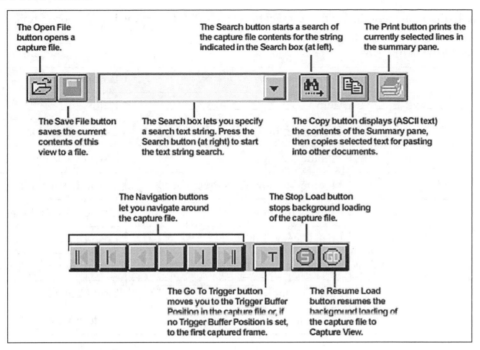

Figure 1-56 shows the easy-access PE toolbar.

Figure 1-56 Easy-Access PE Toolbar

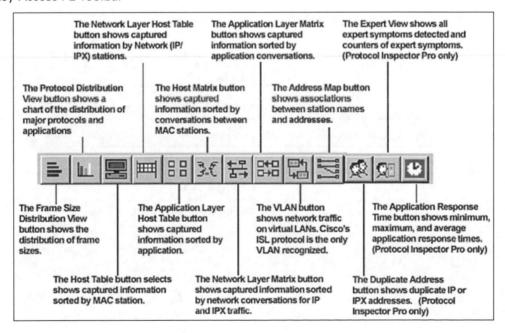

Function Keys

Function keys perform different operations within different PE views. Table 1-1 explains these operations.

Table 1-1 PE Function Keys and Views

Function Key	Summary View	Detail View
F1	Help	Help
F2	System Settings	Capture View Display Options
F3	Module Settings	Module Settings
F4	Module Monitor View Preferences	Create Display Filter
F5	Connect to Remote	Create Capture Filter
F6	Load Capture Filter	Load Capture Filter
F7	Open Caption File	Expert Summary View
F8	Save Capture	Save Capture
F9	Go to Detail View	Capture View
F10	Start/Stop	Start/Stop
F11	N/A	N/A
F12	N/A	N/A

Table 1-2 lists some keyboard shortcuts that you might find helpful.

Table 1-2 Keyboard Shortcuts

Key Combination	Action
Alt-F4	Closes window
Ctrl-O	Opens
Ctrl-S	Saves
Ctrl-T	Starts module
Ctrl-P	Stops module

Chapter 2

VLANs and VTP

Lab 2.9.1: Catalyst 2950T and 3550 Series Static VLANs

Estimated Time: 60 Minutes

Objective

In this lab, you create and maintain VLANs on a Cisco Catalyst 2950T or 3550 series Ethernet switch using the command-line interface (CLI) mode. Figure 2-1 shows the topology for this lab.

Figure 2-1 Topology for Lab 2.9.1

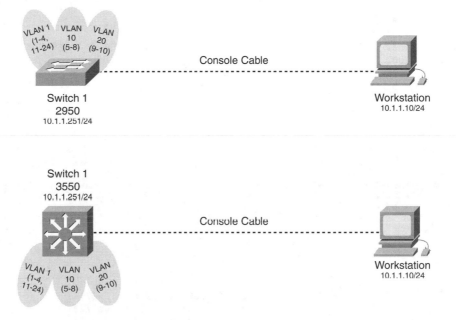

Scenario

VLANs must segment a network logically by function, team, or application regardless of the physical location of the users. End stations in a particular IP subnet often are associated with a specific VLAN. VLAN membership on a switch that is assigned manually for each interface is known as *interface-based* or *static VLAN membership*.

The basic procedures for creating and maintaining VLANs on the 2950T and 3550 series of Ethernet switches are essentially the same.

Step 1

Select a 2950T or 3550 switch. Both of these switches have 24 Fast Ethernet ports and 2 Gigabit Ethernet ports. If necessary, power up the switch and use the standard process for establishing a HyperTerminal console connection from a workstation. It does not matter if the switch configuration from the previous lab is running or if you start with no configuration.

Issue a **show vlan** command from the privileged mode.

The following sample output is for a 2950T switch:

```
Switch#show vlan

VLAN Name                             Status    Ports
---- -------------------------------- --------- -------------------------------
1    default                          active    Fa0/1, Fa0/2, Fa0/3, Fa0/4
                                                Fa0/5, Fa0/6, Fa0/7, Fa0/8
                                                Fa0/9, Fa0/10, Fa0/11, Fa0/12
                                                Fa0/13, Fa0/14, Fa0/15, Fa0/16
                                                Fa0/17, Fa0/18, Fa0/19, Fa0/20
                                                Fa0/21, Fa0/22, Fa0/23, Fa0/24
                                                Gi0/1, Gi0/2
1002 fddi-default                     active
1003 token-ring-default               active
1004 fddinet-default                  active
1005 trnet-default                    active


VLAN Type  SAID       MTU   Parent RingNo BridgeNo Stp  BrdgMode Trans1 Trans2
---- ----- ---------- ----- ------ ------ -------- ---- -------- ------ ------
1    enet  100001     1500  -      -      -        -    -        0      0
1002 fddi  101002     1500  -      -      -        -    -        0      0
1003 tr    101003     1500  -      -      -        -    -        0      0
1004 fdnet 101004     1500  -      -      -        ieee -        0      0
1005 trnet 101005     1500  -      -      -        ibm  -        0      0

Remote SPAN VLANs
-------------------------------------------------------------------------------


Primary Secondary Type             Ports
------- --------- ---------------- -----------------------------------------------
```

The following sample output is for a 3550 switch:

```
Switch#show vlan

VLAN Name                             Status    Ports
---- -------------------------------- --------- -------------------------------
1    default                          active    Fa0/1, Fa0/2, Fa0/3, Fa0/4
                                                Fa0/5, Fa0/6, Fa0/7, Fa0/8
                                                Fa0/9, Fa0/10, Fa0/11, Fa0/12
                                                Fa0/13, Fa0/14, Fa0/15, Fa0/16
                                                Fa0/17, Fa0/18, Fa0/19, Fa0/20
                                                Fa0/21, Fa0/22, Fa0/23, Fa0/24
                                                Gi0/1, Gi0/2
1002 fddi-default                     active
1003 token-ring-default               active
1004 fddinet-default                  active
1005 trnet-default                    active


VLAN Type  SAID       MTU   Parent RingNo BridgeNo Stp  BrdgMode Trans1 Trans2
---- ----- ---------- ----- ------ ------ -------- ---- -------- ------ ------
1    enet  100001     1500  -      -      -        -    -        0      0
1002 fddi  101002     1500  -      -      -        -    -        0      0
1003 tr    101003     1500  -      -      -        -    -        0      0
1004 fdnet 101004     1500  -      -      -        ieee -        0      0
```

```
1005 trnet 101005    1500  -    -    -      ibm  -    0    0

Remote SPAN VLANs
-------------------------------------------------------------------------


Primary Secondary Type              Ports
------- --------- ---------------- -------------------------------------------
```

Note the default VLAN numbers, names, associated types, and that all switch ports are automatically assigned to VLAN 1.

Step 2

Issue the **switchport mode ?** command for interface Fast Ethernet 0/1.

The switch port mode of all ports is set to access by default. This means that the port is intended to be a single port to which a standard device such as a workstation will be attached, or the port will be a single VLAN to which standard devices will be attached.

The following command is for a 2950T switch:

```
Switch#config terminal
Switch(config)#interface FastEthernet 0/1
Switch#(config-if)#switchport mode ?
  access   Set trunking mode to ACCESS unconditionally
  dynamic  Set trunking mode to dynamically negotiate access or trunk mode
  trunk    Set trunking mode to TRUNK unconditionally
```

The following command is for a 3550 switch:

```
Switch#config terminal
Switch(config)#interface FastEthernet 0/1
Switch(config-if)#switchport mode ?
  access       Set trunking mode to ACCESS unconditionally
  dot1q-tunnel Set trunking mode to DOT1Q TUNNEL unconditionally
  dynamic      Set trunking mode to dynamically negotiate access or trunk
  mode
  trunk        Set trunking mode to TRUNK unconditionally
```

A port on the 2950T switch can operate in one of three modes, whereas a port on the 3550 switch can operate in one of four modes.

The command for setting a single port to the access mode is shown in the following example, which uses the Fast Ethernet 0/1 port:

```
Switch#config terminal
Switch(config)#interface FastEthernet 0/1
Switch(config-if)#switchport mode access
```

Use the **show vlan** command to determine the mode of a port. Ports that are configured for a particular VLAN are shown in that VLAN. Ports that are configured to a mode other than access do not appear in any of the VLANs. For example, a port that is configured to trunk ports does not appear in any of the VLANs. The **show interfaces switchport** command lists the configured mode of each port in detail.

The following partial sample output is for a 2950T switch:

```
Switch#show interfaces switchport
--output omitted--
Name: Fa0/24
Switchport: Enabled
Administrative Mode: dynamic desirable
Operational Mode: static access
Administrative Trunking Encapsulation: dot1q
Operational Trunking Encapsulation: native
Negotiation of Trunking: On
Access Mode VLAN: 1 (default)
```

```
Trunking Native Mode VLAN: 1 (default)
Administrative private-vlan host-association: none
Administrative private-vlan mapping: none
Operational private-vlan: none
Trunking VLANs Enabled: ALL
Pruning VLANs Enabled: 2-1001

Protected: false

Voice VLAN: none (Inactive)
Appliance trust: none
Name: Gi0/1
Switchport: Enabled
Administrative Mode: dynamic desirable
Operational Mode: down
Administrative Trunking Encapsulation: dot1q
Negotiation of Trunking: On
Access Mode VLAN: 1 (default)
Trunking Native Mode VLAN: 1 (default)
Administrative private-vlan host-association: none
Administrative private-vlan mapping: none
Operational private-vlan: none
Trunking VLANs Enabled: ALL
Pruning VLANs Enabled: 2-1001

Protected: false

Voice VLAN: none (Inactive)
Appliance trust: none
--output omitted--
```

The following partial sample output is for a 3550 switch:

```
Switch#show interfaces switchport
--output omitted--
Name: Fa0/24
Switchport: Enabled
Administrative Mode: dynamic desirable
Operational Mode: down
Administrative Trunking Encapsulation: negotiate
Negotiation of Trunking: On
Access Mode VLAN: 1 (default)
Trunking Native Mode VLAN: 1 (default)
Administrative private-vlan host-association: none
Administrative private-vlan mapping: none
Operational private-vlan: none
Trunking VLANs Enabled: ALL
Pruning VLANs Enabled: 2-1001

Protected: false
Unknown unicast blocked: disabled
Unknown multicast blocked: disabled

Voice VLAN: none (Inactive)
Appliance trust: none
Name: Gi0/1
Switchport: Enabled
Administrative Mode: dynamic desirable
Operational Mode: down
Administrative Trunking Encapsulation: negotiate
Negotiation of Trunking: On
Access Mode VLAN: 1 (default)
Trunking Native Mode VLAN: 1 (default)
Administrative private-vlan host-association: none
Administrative private-vlan mapping: none
Operational private-vlan: none
Trunking VLANs Enabled: ALL
Pruning VLANs Enabled: 2-1001
```

```
Protected: false
Unknown unicast blocked: disabled
Unknown multicast blocked: disabled

Voice VLAN: none (Inactive)
Appliance trust: none

--output omitted--
```

Ports that are configured as access ports are not identified as such in the output of a **show running-config** command. Ports that are configured otherwise are noted specifically.

The following partial sample output is for a 2950T switch:

```
--output omitted--
!
interface FastEthernet0/1
 switchport mode trunk
 no ip address
!
interface FastEthernet0/2
 switchport mode trunk
 no ip address
!
interface FastEthernet0/3
 no ip address
!
interface FastEthernet0/4
 no ip address
!
--output omitted--
```

The following partial sample output is for a 3550 switch:

```
--output omitted--
!
interface FastEthernet0/11
 switchport trunk encapsulation dot1q
 switchport mode trunk
 no ip address
!
interface FastEthernet0/12
 switchport trunk encapsulation dot1q
 switchport mode trunk
 no ip address
!
interface FastEthernet0/13
 no ip address
!
interface FastEthernet0/14
 no ip address
!
--output omitted--
```

Step 3

Create a VLAN in one of two ways. One way is to assign a port to a VLAN that does not exist. The switch automatically creates the VLAN to which the port has been assigned. Another way is to create VLANs without assigning port membership.

The 2950T and 3550 switches have a **range** command that you can use to designate multiple individual ports or a contiguous range of ports for an operation.

VLAN 1 is the Management VLAN by default. Therefore, all ports are assigned automatically to VLAN 1, and all ports are in the access mode. You do not need to create a VLAN 1, assign ports to it, or set the mode of each port. However, you must create VLANs 10 and 20, and you must assign ports 5 through 8 and ports 9 and 10 to each VLAN respectively.

Use the **range** command to assign ports 5 through 8 to VLAN 10:

```
Switch#config terminal
Switch(config)#interface range FastEthernet 0/5 - 8
Switch(config-if-range)switchport access vlan 10
% Access VLAN does not exist. Creating vlan 10
Switch(config-if-range)#^z
```

You created VLAN 10 at the same time you assigned ports 5 through 8 to it.

Issue a **show vlan** command to verify that VLAN 10 has been created and that ports 5 through 8 are assigned to it. The output should be similar to the following sample output:

```
Switch#show vlan

VLAN Name                             Status    Ports
---- -------------------------------- --------- -------------------------------
1    default                          active    Fa0/1, Fa0/2, Fa0/3, Fa0/4
                                                Fa0/11, Fa0/12, Fa0/13, Fa0/14
                                                Fa0/15, Fa0/16, Fa0/17, Fa0/18
                                                Fa0/19, Fa0/20, Fa0/21, Fa0/22
                                                Fa0/23, Fa0/24, Gi0/1, Gi0/2
10   VLAN0010                         active    Fa0/5, Fa0/6, Fa0/7, Fa0/8
1002 fddi-default                     active
1003 token-ring-default               active
1004 fddinet-default                  active
1005 trnet-default                    active

VLAN Type  SAID       MTU   Parent RingNo BridgeNo Stp  BrdgMode Trans1 Trans2
---- ----- ---------- ----- ------ ------ -------- ---- -------- ------ ------
1    enet  100001     1500  -      -      -        -    -        0      0
10   enet  100010     1500  -      -      -        -    -        0      0
1002 fddi  101002     1500  -      -      -        -    -        0      0
1003 tr    101003     1500  -      -      -        -    -        0      0
1004 fdnet 101004     1500  -      -      -        ieee -        0      0
1005 trnet 101005     1500  -      -      -        ibm  -        0      0

--output omitted--
```

Because you did not name VLAN 10, the switch automatically assigns a default name, which is VLAN0010.

Step 4

Create a VLAN without assigning ports to it at the same time. This involves a somewhat different process from Step 3. Enter the following VLAN database configuration mode from the privileged mode:

```
Switch#vlan database
Switch(vlan)#
```

Enter a question mark (**?**). The following output appears:

```
Switch(vlan)#?
VLAN database editing buffer manipulation commands:
  abort  Exit mode without applying the changes
  apply  Apply current changes and bump revision number
  exit   Apply changes, bump revision number, and exit mode
  no     Negate a command or set its defaults
  reset  Abandon current changes and reread current database
  show   Show database information
  vlan   Add, delete, or modify values associated with a single VLAN
  vtp    Perform VTP administrative functions.
```

Notice the highlighted vlan configuration option.

Create VLAN 20:

```
Switch(vlan)#vlan 20
VLAN 20 added:
    Name: VLAN0020
Switch(vlan)#
```

The VLAN is created immediately with a default name. To remove a VLAN, use the following command in the VLAN configuration mode:

```
Switch(vlan)#no vlan 20
```

You still need to assign ports to VLAN 20. Port assignment to a VLAN is an interface configuration operation. Exit VLAN configuration mode and enter interface configuration mode.

Exit from the VLAN configuration mode and use the **range** command to assign ports 9 and 10 to VLAN 20:

```
Switch(vlan)#exit
APPLY completed.
Exiting....
Switch#
Switch#config terminal
Switch(config)#interface range FastEthernet 0/9 , FastEthernet 0/10
Switch(config-if-range)#switchport access vlan 20
Switch(config-if-range)#^z
```

This time a comma (,) delimiter was used instead of a hyphen (–), which was used in Step 3. Make sure to insert a space before and after the comma.

Issue a **show vlan** command to verify the creation of VLAN 20 with ports 9 and 10 assigned to it. The output should be similar to the following sample output:

```
Switch#show vlan

VLAN Name                             Status    Ports
---- -------------------------------- --------- -------------------------------
1    default                          active    Fa0/1, Fa0/2, Fa0/3, Fa0/4
                                                Fa0/11, Fa0/12, Fa0/13, Fa0/14
                                                Fa0/15, Fa0/16, Fa0/17, Fa0/18
                                                Fa0/19, Fa0/20, Fa0/21, Fa0/22
                                                Fa0/23, Fa0/24, Gi0/1, Gi0/2
10   VLAN0010                         active    Fa0/5, Fa0/6, Fa0/7, Fa0/8
20   VLAN0020                         active    Fa0/9, Fa0/10
1002 fddi-default                     active
1003 token-ring-default               active
1004 fddinet-default                  active
1005 trnet-default                    active

VLAN Type  SAID       MTU   Parent RingNo BridgeNo Stp  BrdgMode Trans1 Trans2
---- ----- ---------- ----- ------ ------ -------- ---- -------- ------ ------
1    enet  100001     1500  -      -      -        -    -        0      0
10   enet  100010     1500  -      -      -        -    -        0      0
20   enet  100020     1500  -      -      -        -    -        0      0
1002 fddi  101002     1500  -      -      -        -    -        0      0
1003 tr    101003     1500  -      -      -        -    -        0      0
1004 fdnet 101004     1500  -      -      -        ieee -        0      0

VLAN Type  SAID       MTU   Parent RingNo BridgeNo Stp  BrdgMode Trans1 Trans2
---- ----- ---------- ----- ------ ------ -------- ---- -------- ------ ------
1005 trnet 101005     1500  -      -      -        ibm  -        0      0

--output omitted--
```

Step 5

Re-enter the VLAN configuration mode and issue a question mark (**?**):

```
Switch#vlan database
Switch(vlan)#?
VLAN database editing buffer manipulation commands:
  abort  Exit mode without applying the changes
  apply  Apply current changes and bump revision number
  exit   Apply changes, bump revision number, and exit mode
  no     Negate a command or set its defaults
```

```
  reset  Abandon current changes and reread current database
  show   Show database information
  vlan   Add, delete, or modify values associated with a single VLAN
  vtp    Perform VTP administrative functions.
```

Use the **vlan** option to name or rename a VLAN. For example, the following command renames VLAN 20 from its default name of VLAN0020 to Accounting.

```
Switch(vlan)#vlan 20 name Accounting
VLAN 20 modified:
     Name: Accounting
Switch(vlan)#
```

The **show** option allows users to view various settings before committing changes with the **apply** or **exit** options. Issue a **show ?** command and review the following output:

```
Switch(vlan)#show ?
  changes   Show the changes to the database since modification began (or since 'reset')
  current   Show the database installed when modification began (or since 'reset')
  proposed  Show the database as it would be modified if applied
  <cr>
```

Use the **abort** option to return to the privileged mode:

```
Switch(vlan)#abort
Aborting….
Switch#
```

Issue a **show running-config** command. The ports that were assigned to VLAN 10 and 20 indicate the VLAN to which the port has been assigned. The following is a partial sample output:

```
--output omitted--
!
interface FastEthernet0/1
!
interface FastEthernet0/2
!
interface FastEthernet0/3
!
interface FastEthernet0/4
!
interface FastEthernet0/5
 switchport access vlan 10
!
interface FastEthernet0/6
 switchport access vlan 10
!
interface FastEthernet0/7
 switchport access vlan 10
!
interface FastEthernet0/8
 switchport access vlan 10
!
interface FastEthernet0/9
 switchport access vlan 20
!
interface FastEthernet0/10
 switchport access vlan 20
!
interface FastEthernet0/11
!
interface FastEthernet0/12
!
--output omitted--
```

A port assignment to VLAN 1 is not indicated because VLAN 1 is the default.

You now have created static VLANs two different ways and assigned ports statically with the **range** command. You also have learned to name and rename VLANs.

Note: You must route traffic between VLANs. See Chapter 4, "Inter-VLAN Routing," to learn how.

Step 6

Prior to the next lab, disconnect all cables to avoid difficulties. Otherwise, inadvertent propagation of VLAN information via VLAN Trunking Protocol (VTP) might result.

Also, prepare for the next lab by removing all VLAN information and configurations. You need to delete the VLAN database, or vlan.dat, and startup configuration.

The VLAN information is saved in a flash file called vlan.dat. You must delete this file to remove the VLAN information. You can do this with the **delete flash:vlan.dat** or **delete vlan.dat** command:

```
Switch#delete flash:vlan.dat
Delete filename [vlan.dat]?
Delete flash:vlan.dat? [confirm]
Switch#
```

The **erase startup-config** command removes the VLAN configuration:

```
Switch#erase startup-config

Erasing the nvram filesystem will remove all files! Continue? [confirm]
[OK]
Erase of nvram: complete
Switch#
```

After you have erased the startup configuration and VLAN information, reload the switch:

```
Switch#reload
System configuration has been modified. Save? [yes/no]: n
Proceed with reload? [confirm]
```

After the switch reloads, it has the default VLAN information and configuration.

Lab 2.9.2: Catalyst 2950T and 3550 Series VTP Domain and VLAN Trunking

Estimated Time: 120 Minutes

Objective

Configure a VLAN trunk between two Cisco Catalyst WS-C2950T-24-EI switches and a Cisco Catalyst WS-C3550-24-EMI switch in the CLI mode. Figure 2-2 shows the topology for this lab.

Figure 2-2 Topology for Lab 2.9.2

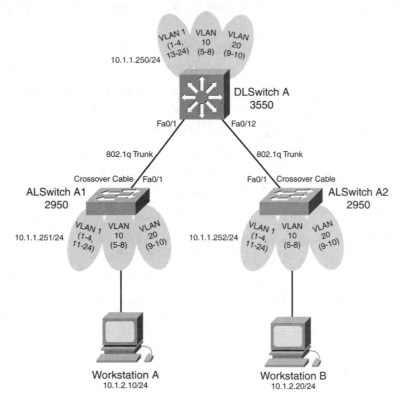

Scenario

VLANs must logically segment a network by function, team, or application regardless of the physical location of the users. End stations in a particular IP subnet often are associated with a specific VLAN. Trunking or connecting switches and VTP segment the network. VTP maintains configuration consistency by managing the addition, deletion, and renaming of VLANs on the entire network from a single central switch. VTP minimizes configuration inconsistencies that can cause problems such as duplicate VLAN names, incorrect VLAN-type specifications, and security violations.

The basic procedures for creating and maintaining trunks and VTP domains on the 2950T and 3550 switches are similar. Specific differences are addressed if necessary.

Step 1

Disconnect all cables to the switch, erase the startup configuration, erase the VLAN database, and reload the switch if necessary.

Cable the network devices according to Figure 2-2.

Use the information and procedures from the previous labs to do the following:

1. Name the switches **DLSwitchA**, **ALSwitchA1**, and **ALSwitchA2** respectively.

2. Configure cisco as the secret, console, and vty password on all the switches.

3. Assign the appropriate IP address to the Management VLAN 1 of each switch. Do not forget to enable the interface with the **no shutdown** command.

Step 2

Recall that a *VTP domain*, which is also called a *VLAN management domain*, consists of one or more trunked or interconnected switches that are under the administrative responsibility of a central switch. A switch can be in only one VTP domain with the same domain name. You can use the CLI, Cluster Management Suite (CMS) software, or Simple Network Management Protocol (SNMP) to make global VLAN configuration changes for a domain.

The default VTP mode for the 2950T and 3550 switches is the VTP Server mode. However, VLAN information is not propagated until a domain name is specified and learned through trunked ports. Table 2-1 describes the three VTP modes.

Table 2-1 Three VTP Modes

VTP Mode	Description
VTP Server	This is the default VTP mode. You can create, modify, and delete VLANs. You can specify other configuration parameters for all switches in the VTP domain. VTP servers advertise VLAN configurations to other switches in the same VTP domain and synchronize VLAN configurations with other switches based on advertisements received over trunk links. In VTP Server mode, you save VLAN configurations in NVRAM.
VTP Client	A VTP client behaves like a VTP server without the ability to create, change, or delete VLANs. In VTP Client mode, you save VLAN configurations in NVRAM.
VTP Transparent	Switches in VTP Transparent mode do not participate in VTP. The switch does not advertise its VLAN configuration and does not synchronize its VLAN configuration based on received advertisements. However, in VTP version two, transparent switches do forward VTP advertisements that they receive from the trunk interfaces of other switches. Therefore, you can create, modify, or delete local VLANs on a switch in the VTP Transparent mode. In VTP Transparent mode, you save VLAN configurations in NVRAM, but they are not advertised to other switches.

Issue a **show vtp status** command on any of the switches. The output should be similar to the following sample for DLSwitchA:

```
DLSwitchA#show vtp status
VTP Version                     : 2
Configuration Revision          : 0
Maximum VLANs supported locally : 1005
Number of existing VLANs        : 5
VTP Operating Mode              : Server
VTP Domain Name                 :
VTP Pruning Mode                : Disabled
VTP V2 Mode                     : Disabled
VTP Traps Generation            : Disabled
MD5 digest                      : 0xBF 0x86 0x94 0x45 0xFC 0xDF 0xB5 0x70
Configuration last modified by 0.0.0.0 at 0-0-00 00:00:00
Local updater ID is 10.1.1.250 on interface Vl1 (lowest numbered VLAN
interface found)
```

Because you made no VLAN configurations, all settings are the defaults. Notice that the VTP mode is Server. The number of existing VLANs is the five that are built in. The 3550 switch supports 1005 maximum VLANs locally. The 2950T switch supports 250. The Configuration Revision is 0, and the VTP version is 2. All switches must run the same VTP version.

The Configuration Revision number is important because the switch in the VTP Server mode that has the highest revision number propagates VLAN information over trunked ports. Every time you modify VLAN information and save it in the VLAN database or vlan.dat, the revision number increases by one when you exit from the VLAN configuration mode.

Multiple switches in the VTP domain can be in the VTP Server mode. You can use these switches to manage all other switches in the VTP domain. This is suitable for small-scale networks in which the VLAN information is stored easily in all switches. In a large network, you must determine which switches will make the best VTP servers. Set aside some of the more powerful switches and keep them as VTP servers. You can configure the other switches in the VTP domain as clients. The number of VTP servers should be consistent based on the amount of redundancy you desire in the network.

Note: To remove or delete all local VLAN configurations and to reset the revision number to 0, delete the VLAN database or vlan.dat. The steps for deleting the VLAN database were covered in the previous lab, "Catalyst 2950T and 3550 Series Static VLANs." Shut down the interfaces or disconnect all cables. From the privileged mode prompt, enter the **delete flash:vlan.dat** command, enter the **erase startup-config** command, and reload the switch.

Step 3

Enter the following VTP domain name in DLSwitchA to begin the VTP configuration:

```
DLSwitchA#vlan database
DLSwitchA(vlan)#vtp domain corp
Changing VTP domain name from NULL to corp
DLSwitchA(vlan)#exit
APPLY completed.
Exiting....
```

Issue a **show vtp status** command to verify that the VTP domain name is corp, the VTP mode is Server, and the Configuration Revision is 0, as shown in the following sample output. Because you enter only the VTP operating mode and domain name, the Configuration Revision is not affected and is still 0:

```
DLSwitchA#show vtp status
VTP Version                     : 2
Configuration Revision          : 0
Maximum VLANs supported locally : 1005
Number of existing VLANs        : 5
VTP Operating Mode              : Server
VTP Domain Name                 : corp
VTP Pruning Mode                : Disabled
VTP V2 Mode                     : Disabled
VTP Traps Generation            : Disabled
MD5 digest                      : 0xD3 0x8B 0x04 0xD2 0x2C 0x7B 0x29 0x05
Configuration last modified by 0.0.0.0 at 0-0-00 00:00:00
Local updater ID is 10.1.1.250 on interface Vl1 (lowest numbered VLAN interface found)
```

VLAN information is not propagated until a VTP domain name is specified and learned through trunked ports. The default settings for interfaces on the 2950T-24-EI and 3550-24-EMI switches are to trunk automatically when they are cabled appropriately. Therefore, VTP automatically propagates the corp VTP domain name to both ALSwitchA1 and ALSwitchA2.

Issue a **show vtp status** command on ALSwitchA1 and ALSwitchA2 to verify that the VTP domain name is corp, the VTP mode is Server, and the Configuration Revision is 0, as shown in the following ALSwitchA1 sample output:

```
ALSwitchA1#show vtp status
VTP Version                     : 2
Configuration Revision          : 0
Maximum VLANs supported locally : 250
Number of existing VLANs        : 5
VTP Operating Mode              : Server
VTP Domain Name                 : corp
VTP Pruning Mode                : Disabled
```

```
VTP V2 Mode                 : Disabled
VTP Traps Generation        : Disabled
MD5 digest                  : 0xD3 0x8B 0x04 0xD2 0x2C 0x7B 0x29 0x05
Configuration last modified by 0.0.0.0 at 0-0-00 00:00:00
Local updater ID is 10.1.1.251 on interface Vl1 (lowest numbered VLAN interface found)
```

Issue a **show interfaces FastEthernet 0/2 switchport** command on DLSwitchA and on ALSwitchA1 or ALSwitchA2 to view the default interface settings. The trunking-related items are highlighted:

```
DLSwitchA#show interfaces FastEthernet 0/2 switchport
Name: Fa0/2
Switchport: Enabled
Administrative Mode: dynamic desirable
Operational Mode: down
Administrative Trunking Encapsulation: negotiate
Negotiation of Trunking: On
Access Mode VLAN: 1 (default)
Trunking Native Mode VLAN: 1 (default)
Administrative private-vlan host-association: none
Administrative private-vlan mapping: none
Operational private-vlan: none
Trunking VLANs Enabled: ALL
Pruning VLANs Enabled: 2-1001

Protected: false
Unknown unicast blocked: disabled
Unknown multicast blocked: disabled

Voice VLAN: none (Inactive)
Appliance trust: none
```

```
ALSwitchA1#show interfaces FastEthernet 0/2 switchport
Name: Fa0/2
Switchport: Enabled
Administrative Mode: dynamic desirable
Operational Mode: down
Administrative Trunking Encapsulation: dot1q
Negotiation of Trunking: On
Access Mode VLAN: 1 (default)
Trunking Native Mode VLAN: 1 (default)
Administrative private-vlan host-association: none
Administrative private-vlan mapping: none
Operational private-vlan: none
Trunking VLANs Enabled: ALL
Pruning VLANs Enabled: 2-1001

Protected: false

Voice VLAN: none (Inactive)
Appliance trust: none
```

Issue a **show vlan** command on DLSwitchA and on ALSwitchA1 or ALSwitchA2. All ports except for those used as trunk ports are assigned to VLAN 1, as shown in the following sample output:

```
DLSwitchA#show vlan

VLAN Name                             Status    Ports
---- -------------------------------- --------- -------------------------------
1    default                          active    Fa0/1, Fa0/2, Fa0/3, Fa0/4
                                                Fa0/5, Fa0/6, Fa0/7, Fa0/8
                                                Fa0/9, Fa0/10, Fa0/13, Fa0/14
                                                Fa0/15, Fa0/16, Fa0/17, Fa0/18
                                                Fa0/19, Fa0/20, Fa0/21, Fa0/22
                                                Fa0/23, Fa0/24, Gi0/1, Gi0/2
```

```
1002 fddi-default                  active
1003 token-ring-default            active
1004 fddinet-default               active
1005 trnet-default                 active

--output omitted--
```

Notice that interfaces Fast Ethernet 0/11 and 0/12 are not in VLAN 1:

```
ALSwitchA1#show vlan

VLAN Name                      Status    Ports
---- ------------------------- --------- -------------------------------
1    default                   active    Fa0/2, Fa0/3, Fa0/4, Fa0/5
                                         Fa0/6, Fa0/7, Fa0/8, Fa0/9
                                         Fa0/10, Fa0/11, Fa0/12, Fa0/13
                                         Fa0/14, Fa0/15, Fa0/16, Fa0/17
                                         Fa0/18, Fa0/19, Fa0/20, Fa0/21
                                         Fa0/22, Fa0/23, Fa0/24, Gi0/1
                                         Gi0/2
1002 fddi-default              active
1003 token-ring-default        active
1004 fddinet-default           active
1005 trnet-default             active

VLAN Type  SAID   MTU   Parent RingNo BridgeNo Stp  BrdgMode Trans1 Trans2
---- ----- ------ ----- ------ ------ -------- ---- -------- ------ ------
1    enet  100001 1500  -      -      -        -    -        0      0
1002 fddi  101002 1500  -      -      -        -    -        0      0
1003 tr    101003 1500  -      -      -        -    srb      0      0
1004 fdnet 101004 1500  -      -      -        ieee -        0      0
1005 trnet 101005 1500  -      -      -        ibm  -        0      0

--output omitted--
```

Notice that interface Fast Ethernet 0/1 is not in VLAN 1.

Issue a **show interface FastEthernet 0/11 switchport** command on DLSwitchA and a **show interface FastEthernet 0/1 switchport** command on ALSwitchA1 or ALSwitchA2. Note the status of the highlighted items of the trunked interfaces:

```
DLSwitchA#show interfaces FastEthernet 0/11 switchport
Name: Fa0/11
Switchport: Enabled
Administrative Mode: dynamic desirable
Operational Mode: trunk
Administrative Trunking Encapsulation: negotiate
Operational Trunking Encapsulation: dot1q
Negotiation of Trunking: On
Access Mode VLAN: 1 (default)
Trunking Native Mode VLAN: 1 (default)
Administrative private-vlan host-association: none
Administrative private-vlan mapping: none
Operational private-vlan: none
Trunking VLANs Enabled: ALL
Pruning VLANs Enabled: 2-1001

Protected: false
Unknown unicast blocked: disabled
Unknown multicast blocked: disabled

Voice VLAN: none (Inactive)
Appliance trust: none
```

```
ALSwitchA1#show interfaces FastEthernet 0/1 switchport
Name: Fa0/1
Switchport: Enabled
Administrative Mode: dynamic desirable
Operational Mode: trunk
Administrative Trunking Encapsulation: dot1q
Operational Trunking Encapsulation: dot1q
Negotiation of Trunking: On
Access Mode VLAN: 1 (default)
Trunking Native Mode VLAN: 1 (default)
Administrative private-vlan host-association: none
Administrative private-vlan mapping: none
Operational private-vlan: none
Trunking VLANs Enabled: ALL
Pruning VLANs Enabled: 2-1001

Protected: false

Voice VLAN: none (Inactive)
Appliance trust: none
```

Another way to determine if ports are in the trunk mode is to issue the **show interface trunk** command. The following sample outputs are for DLSwitchA and ALSwitchA1:

```
DLSwitchA#show interfaces trunk

Port      Mode          Encapsulation  Status        Native vlan
Fa0/11    desirable     n-802.1q       trunking      1
Fa0/12    desirable     n-802.1q       trunking      1

Port      Vlans allowed on trunk
Fa0/11    1-4094
Fa0/12    1-4094

Port      Vlans allowed and active in management domain
Fa0/11    1
Fa0/12    1

Port      Vlans in spanning tree forwarding state and not pruned
Fa0/11    1
Fa0/12    1
```

```
ALSwitchA1#show interfaces trunk

Port      Mode          Encapsulation  Status        Native vlan
Fa0/1     desirable     802.1q         trunking      1

Port      Vlans allowed on trunk
Fa0/1     1-4094

Port      Vlans allowed and active in management domain
Fa0/1     1

Port      Vlans in spanning tree forwarding state and not pruned
Fa0/1
```

The **show vlan**, **show interfaces FastEthernet 0/# switchport**, and **show interfaces trunk** commands have trunked and verified the respective ports automatically. However, if a **show running-config** command is issued now, it does not show that the status of the respective ports is trunk. The following sample outputs are for DLSwitchA and ALSwitchA1:

```
DLSwitchA#show running-config
Building configuration...

Current configuration : 1595 bytes
```

```
!
--output omitted--
!
interface FastEthernet0/11
 no ip address
!
interface FastEthernet0/12
 no ip address
!
--output omitted—
```

```
ALSwitchA1#show running-config
Building configuration...

Current configuration : 1594 bytes
!
--output omitted--
!
!
interface FastEthernet0/1
 no ip address
!
--output omitted--
```

The trunk status of the respective trunk ports appears in the output of the **show running-config** command after you configure the ports manually as trunk ports.

Step 4

Remember that more than one switch can exist in the VTP Server mode. However, for this lab, DLSwitchA manages all switches in the VTP domain, so its VTP mode is left in the default Server mode. Change the VTP mode of ALSwitchA1 and ALSwitchA2 to the VTP Client mode:

```
ALSwitchA1#vlan database
ALSwitchA1(vlan)#vtp client
Setting device to VTP CLIENT mode.
ALSwitchA1(vlan)#exit
In CLIENT state, no apply attempted.
Exiting....
```

```
ALSwitchA2#vlan database
ALSwitchA2(vlan)#vtp client
Setting device to VTP CLIENT mode.
ALSwitchA2(vlan)#exit
In CLIENT state, no apply attempted.
Exiting....
```

You do not need to enter the VTP domain name corp because it is already propagated from DLSwitchA.

Issue a **show vtp status** command on ALSwitchA1 and ALSwitchA2 to verify that the VTP mode is Client. The Configuration Revision is still 0 on the three switches because only the VTP operating mode was entered:

```
ALSwitchA1#show vtp status
VTP Version                    : 2
Configuration Revision         : 0
Maximum VLANs supported locally : 250
Number of existing VLANs       : 5
VTP Operating Mode             : Client
VTP Domain Name                : corp
VTP Pruning Mode               : Disabled
VTP V2 Mode                    : Disabled
VTP Traps Generation           : Disabled
```

```
MD5 digest                        : 0xD3 0x8B 0x04 0xD2 0x2C 0x7B 0x29 0x05
Configuration last modified by 0.0.0.0 at 0-0-00 00:00:00
```

```
ALSwitchA2#show vtp status
VTP Version                      : 2
Configuration Revision           : 0
Maximum VLANs supported locally : 250
Number of existing VLANs         : 5
VTP Operating Mode               : Client
VTP Domain Name                  : corp
VTP Pruning Mode                 : Disabled
VTP V2 Mode                      : Disabled
VTP Traps Generation             : Disabled
MD5 digest                       : 0xD3 0x8B 0x04 0xD2 0x2C 0x7B 0x29 0x05
Configuration last modified by 0.0.0.0 at 0-0-00 00:00:00
```

Step 5

You need to create VLANs 10 and 20 and name them Accounting and Marketing. Assign ports statically to the respective VLANs. The VLAN configurations are necessary only on DLSwitchA because it manages the VTP domain and is in the VTP Server mode:

```
DLSwitchA#vlan database
DLSwitchA(vlan)#vlan 10 name Accounting
VLAN 10 added:
    Name: Accounting
DLSwitchA(vlan)#vlan 20 name Marketing
VLAN 20 added:
    Name: Marketing
DLSwitchA(vlan)#exit
APPLY completed.
Exiting....
```

Issue a **show vtp status** command on one of the switches. The Configuration Revision number increases from 0 to 1, as shown in the following sample output for DLSwitchA:

```
DLSwitchA#show vtp status
VTP Version                      : 2
Configuration Revision           : 1
Maximum VLANs supported locally : 1005
Number of existing VLANs         : 7
VTP Operating Mode               : Server
VTP Domain Name                  : corp
VTP Pruning Mode                 : Disabled
VTP V2 Mode                      : Disabled
VTP Traps Generation             : Disabled
MD5 digest                       : 0x13 0x72 0x7B 0x59 0x34 0xE0 0x8B 0x45
Configuration last modified by 10.1.1.250 at 3-1-93 00:28:52
Local updater ID is 10.1.1.250 on interface Vl1 (lowest numbered VLAN Interface found)
```

Assign ports to the respective VLANs on DLSwitchA:

```
DLSwitchA#configure terminal
DLSwitchA(config)#interface range FastEthernet 0/5 - 8
DLSwitchA(config-if-range)#switchport access vlan 10
DLSwitchA(config-if-range)#interface range FastEthernet 0/9 - 10
DLSwitchA(config-if-range)#switchport access vlan 20
DLSwitchA(config-if-range)#^z
```

You do not need to assign the other ports to VLAN 1 because that is the default VLAN to which the ports are assigned.

Issue the **show vlan** command on DLSwitchA to verify the configurations. The following sample output is shown:

```
DLSwitchA#show vlan

VLAN Name                             Status    Ports
---- -------------------------------- --------- -------------------------------
1    default                          active    Fa0/1, Fa0/2, Fa0/3, Fa0/4
                                                Fa0/13, Fa0/14, Fa0/15, Fa0/16
                                                Fa0/17, Fa0/18, Fa0/19, Fa0/20
                                                Fa0/21, Fa0/22, Fa0/23, Fa0/24
                                                Gi0/1, Gi0/2
10   Accounting                       active    Fa0/5, Fa0/6, Fa0/7, Fa0/8
20   Marketing                        active    Fa0/9, Fa0/10
1002 fddi-default                     active
1003 token-ring-default               active
1004 fddinet-default                  active
1005 trnet-default                    active

VLAN Type  SAID    MTU   Parent RingNo BridgeNo Stp  BrdgMode Trans1 Trans2
---- ----- ------- ----- ------ ------ -------- ---- -------- ------ ------
1    enet  100001  1500  -      -      -        -    -        0      0
10   enet  100010  1500  -      -      -        -    -        0      0
20   enet  100020  1500  -      -      -        -    -        0      0
1002 fddi  101002  1500  -      -      -        -    -        0      0
1003 tr    101003  1500  -      -      -        -    srb      0      0
1004 fdnet 101004  1500  -      -      -        ieee -        0      0


VLAN Type  SAID    MTU   Parent RingNo BridgeNo Stp  BrdgMode Trans1 Trans2
---- ----- ----- ------- ------ ------ -------- ---- -------- ------ ------
1005 trnet 101005 1500  -      -      -        ibm  -        0      0

Remote SPAN VLANs
-------------------------------------------------------------------------------


Primary Secondary Type             Ports
------- --------- ---------------- ------------------------------------------
```

Issue a **show vlan** command on ALSwitchA1 or ALSwitch2. VLAN 10 Accounting and VLAN 20 Marketing should be listed to indicate that VTP has propagated the information from DLSwitchA. The following sample output is for ALSwitchA1:

```
ALSwitchA1#show vlan

VLAN Name                             Status    Ports
---- -------------------------------- --------- -------------------------------
1    default                          active    Fa0/2, Fa0/3, Fa0/4, Fa0/5
                                                Fa0/6, Fa0/7, Fa0/8, Fa0/9
                                                Fa0/10, Fa0/11, Fa0/12, Fa0/13
                                                Fa0/14, Fa0/15, Fa0/16, Fa0/17
                                                Fa0/18, Fa0/19, Fa0/20, Fa0/21
                                                Fa0/22, Fa0/23, Fa0/24, Gi0/1
                                                Gi0/2
10   Accounting                       active
20   Marketing                        active
1002 fddi-default                     active
1003 token-ring-default               active
1004 fddinet-default                  active
1005 trnet-default                    active

VLAN Type  SAID    MTU   Parent RingNo BridgeNo Stp  BrdgMode Trans1 Trans2
---- ----- ------- ----- ------ ------ -------- ---- -------- ------ ------
1    enet  100001  1500  -      -      -        -    -        0      0
10   enet  100010  1500  -      -      -        -    -        0      0
20   enet  100020  1500  -      -      -        -    -        0      0
1002 fddi  101002  1500  -      -      -        -    -        0      0
```

```
VLAN Type  SAID    MTU   Parent RingNo BridgeNo Stp  BrdgMode Trans1 Trans2
---- ----- ------- ----- ------ ------ -------- ---- -------- ------ ------
1003 tr    101003  1500  -      -      -        -    srb      0      0
1004 fdnet 101004  1500  -      -      -        ieee -        0      0
1005 trnet 101005  1500  -      -      -        ibm  -        0      0

Remote SPAN VLANs
------------------------------------------------------------------------


Primary Secondary Type             Ports
------- --------- ---------------- ------------------------------------------
```

No VLANs were created locally on ALSwitchA1 and ALSwitchA2. Why do VLANs 10 and 20 appear in the preceding output?

_____

_____

_____

_____

Step 6

Use the following manual configurations to enable VTP so that VLAN configurations can be managed and propagated from DLSwitchA if the ports did not trunk automatically:

1. Enter the Ethernet trunk encapsulation type.

2. Configure the Fast Ethernet 0/11 and Fast Ethernet 0/12 interfaces as trunk ports.

3. Specify the native VLAN.

By default, interfaces on the 2950T-24-EI and 3550-24-EMI switches should trunk automatically when cabled and propagate VLAN information after you enter a domain name in a VTP server switch.

The 3550 switch supports three Ethernet trunk encapsulation types:

- Cisco proprietary Inter-Switch Link (ISL) protocol

- IEEE 802.1q

- Negotiate or default—This specifies that the interface negotiates with the neighboring interface to become an ISL, which is preferred, or an 802.1q trunk. This depends on the configuration and capabilities of the neighboring interface.

The 2950T switch does not support ISL. Because the 2950T switch supports only IEEE 802.1q, the 3550 switch automatically negotiates that encapsulation type through the trunk connection.

The negotiation of trunking is activated by default for both switches. As soon as a cable connection is present, the switches establish a trunk link.

VLAN 1 is the native VLAN by default, so you do not need to configure it. You can configure VLANs other than VLAN 1 as the Native VLAN. However, the native VLAN must be the same on trunked switches in 802.1q trunking.

In 802.1q trunking, all VLAN packets are tagged on the trunk link to indicate the VLAN to which they belong. The native VLAN packets are sent untagged on the trunk link.

Although trunking has been negotiated and established automatically, you need to configure the interfaces and native VLAN manually. Enter the following configurations on DLSwitchA:

```
DLSwitchA#configure terminal
DLSwitchA(config)#interface range FastEthernet 0/11 - 12
DLSwitchA(config-if-range)#switchport trunk encapsulation dot1q
```

```
DLSwitchA(config-if-range)#switchport mode trunk
DLSwitchA(config-if-range)#switchport trunk native vlan 1
DLSwitchA(config-if-range)#^z
```

Also configure ALSwitchA1 and ALSwitchA2 properly. Configure the Fast Ethernet 0/1 port as a trunk port for ALSwitchA1 and ALSwitchA2. Designate VLAN 1 as the native VLAN, which must be the same on all trunk links. Assign ports statically to the respective VLANs:

```
ALSwitchA1#configure terminal
ALSwitchA1(config)#interface FastEthernet 0/1
ALSwitchA1(config-if)#switchport mode trunk
ALSwitchA1(config-if)#switchport trunk native vlan 1
ALSwitchA1(config-if)#interface range FastEthernet 0/5 - 8
ALSwitchA1(config-if-range)#switchport access vlan 10
ALSwitchA1(config-if-range)#interface range FastEthernet 0/9 - 10
ALSwitchA1(config-if-range)#switchport access vlan 20
ALSwitchA1(config-if-range)#^z
```

```
ALSwitchA2#configure terminal
ALSwitchA2(config)#interface FastEthernet 0/1
ALSwitchA2(config-if)#switchport mode trunk
ALSwitchA2(config-if)#switchport trunk native vlan 1
ALSwitchA2(config-if)#interface range FastEthernet 0/5 - 8
ALSwitchA2(config-if-range)#switchport access vlan 10
ALSwitchA2(config-if-range)#interface range FastEthernet 0/9 - 10
ALSwitchA2(config-if-range)#switchport access vlan 20
ALSwitchA2(config-if-range)#^z
```

Step 7

Verify the configurations with various **show** commands on DLSwitchA. (Sample outputs are provided for comparison.)

Issue the **show vtp counters** command:

```
DLSwitchA#show vtp counters
VTP statistics:
Summary advertisements received     : 20
Subset advertisements received      : 4
Request advertisements received     : 2
Summary advertisements transmitted  : 16
Subset advertisements transmitted   : 6
Request advertisements transmitted  : 0
Number of config revision errors    : 0
Number of config digest errors      : 0
Number of V1 summary errors         : 0

VTP pruning statistics:

Trunk        Join Transmitted Join Received  Summary advts received from
                                             non-pruning-capable device
-----------  ---------------- -------------  ----------------------
Fa0/11            0                1              0
Fa0/12            0                1              0
```

1. Which ports on the DLSwitchA are the trunk ports?

Issue the **show interfaces** command on DLSwitchA for Fast Ethernet trunk ports 0/11 and 0/12. The output for Fast Ethernet 0/12 should be similar to the following output for Fast Ethernet 0/11:

```
DLSwitchA#show interfaces FastEthernet0/11 switchport
Name: Fa0/11
Switchport: Enabled
Administrative Mode: trunk
Operational Mode: trunk
Administrative Trunking Encapsulation: dot1q
Operational Trunking Encapsulation: dot1q
Negotiation of Trunking: On
Access Mode VLAN: 1 (default)
Trunking Native Mode VLAN: 1 (default)
Administrative private-vlan host-association: none
Administrative private-vlan mapping: none
Operational private-vlan: none
Trunking VLANs Enabled: ALL
Pruning VLANs Enabled: 2-1001

Protected: false
Unknown unicast blocked: disabled
Unknown multicast blocked: disabled

Voice VLAN: none (Inactive)
Appliance trust: none
```

2. What is the Ethernet trunk encapsulation type?

_____

3. What is the native VLAN?

_____

Issue the **show vtp counters**, **show interfaces FastEthernet 0/1 switchport**, and **show vlan** commands on ALSwitchA1 and ALSwitchA2. Output for ALSwitchA2 should be similar to the following sample output for ALSwitchA1:

```
ALSwitchA1#show vtp counters
VTP statistics:
Summary advertisements received     : 1543
Subset advertisements received      : 8
Request advertisements received     : 0
Summary advertisements transmitted  : 1473
Subset advertisements transmitted   : 16
Request advertisements transmitted  : 10
Number of config revision errors    : 0
Number of config digest errors      : 0
Number of V1 summary errors         : 0

VTP pruning statistics:

Trunk       Join Transmitted Join Received   Summary advts received from
                                             non-pruning-capable device
----------- ---------------- --------------- ---------------------------
Fa0/1       0                0               0

ALSwitchA1#show interfaces FastEthernet 0/1 switchport
Name: Fa0/1
Switchport: Enabled
Administrative Mode: trunk
Operational Mode: trunk
Administrative Trunking Encapsulation: dot1q
Operational Trunking Encapsulation: dot1q
Negotiation of Trunking: On
Access Mode VLAN: 1 (default)
```

```
Trunking Native Mode VLAN: 1 (default)
Administrative private-vlan host-association: none
Administrative private-vlan mapping: none
Operational private-vlan: none
Trunking VLANs Enabled: ALL
Pruning VLANs Enabled: 2-1001

Protected: false

Voice VLAN: none (Inactive)
Appliance trust: none

ALSwitchA1#show vlan

VLAN Name                             Status    Ports
---- -------------------------------- --------- -------------------------------
1    default                          active    Fa0/2, Fa0/3, Fa0/4, Fa0/11
                                                Fa0/12, Fa0/13, Fa0/14, Fa0/15
                                                Fa0/16, Fa0/17, Fa0/18, Fa0/19
                                                Fa0/20, Fa0/21, Fa0/22, Fa0/23
                                                Fa0/24, Gi0/1, Gi0/2
10   Accounting                       active    Fa0/5, Fa0/6, Fa0/7, Fa0/8
20   Marketing                        active    Fa0/9, Fa0/10
1002 fddi-default                     active
1003 token-ring-default               active
1004 fddinet-default                  active
1005 trnet-default                    active

VLAN Type  SAID   MTU  Parent RingNo BridgeNo Stp  BrdgMode Trans1 Trans2
---- ----- ------ ---- ------ ------ -------- ---- -------- ------ ------
1    enet  100001 1500 -      -      -        -    -        0      0
10   enet  100010 1500 -      -      -        -    -        0      0
20   enet  100020 1500 -      -      -        -    -        0      0
1002 fddi  101002 1500 -      -      -        -    -        0      0
1003 tr    101003 1500 -      -      -        -    srb      0      0
1004 fdnet 101004 1500 -      -      -        ieee -        0      0
1005 trnet 101005 1500 -      -      -        ibm  -        0      0

Remote SPAN VLANs
------------------------------------------------------------------------------

Primary Secondary Type             Ports
------- --------- ---------------- -----------------------------------------------
```

Output of the **show running-config** command shows the trunk status and trunk encapsulation type of the trunk ports. It also indicates whether the ports are in VLAN 10 or VLAN 20. Partial outputs for DLSwitchA and ALSwitchA1 are as follows:

```
DLSwitchA#show running-config
Building configuration...

Current configuration : 1879 bytes
!
--output omitted—
!
interface FastEthernet0/4
 no ip address
!
interface FastEthernet0/5
 switchport access vlan 10
 no ip address
!
interface FastEthernet0/6
 switchport access vlan 10
 no ip address
!
interface FastEthernet0/7
 switchport access vlan 10
 no ip address
```

```
!
interface FastEthernet0/8
 switchport access vlan 10
 no ip address
!
interface FastEthernet0/9
 switchport access vlan 20
 no ip address
!
interface FastEthernet0/10
 switchport access vlan 20
 no ip address
!
interface FastEthernet0/11
 switchport trunk encapsulation dot1q
 switchport mode trunk
 no ip address
!
interface FastEthernet0/12
 switchport trunk encapsulation dot1q
 switchport mode trunk
 no ip address
!
 output omitted
```

```
ALSwitchA1#show running-config
Building configuration...

Current configuration : 1779 bytes
!
 output omitted
!
interface FastEthernet0/1
 switchport mode trunk
 no ip address
!
interface FastEthernet0/2
 no ip address
!
interface FastEthernet0/3
 no ip address
!
interface FastEthernet0/4
 no ip address
!
interface FastEthernet0/5
 switchport access vlan 10
 no ip address
!
interface FastEthernet0/6
 switchport access vlan 10
 no ip address
!
interface FastEthernet0/7
 switchport access vlan 10
 no ip address
!
interface FastEthernet0/8
 switchport access vlan 10
 no ip address
!
interface FastEthernet0/9
 switchport access vlan 20
 no ip address
```

```
!
interface FastEthernet0/10
 switchport access vlan 20
 no ip address
!
interface FastEthernet0/11
 no ip address
!
--output omitted--
```

Step 8

Ping from Workstation A to Workstation B as a final test of the configuration. The ping should be successful.

Save the configurations for use in the next lab and retain the same switches and setup if possible.

Lab 2.9.3: Catalyst 2950T and 3550 Series VTP Pruning

Estimated Time: 60 Minutes

Objective

Configure VTP pruning between two Cisco Catalyst WS-C2950T-24-EI switches and a Cisco Catalyst WS-C3550-24-EMI switch using the CLI mode. Figure 2-3 shows a topology for this lab.

Figure 2-3 Topology for Lab 2.9.3

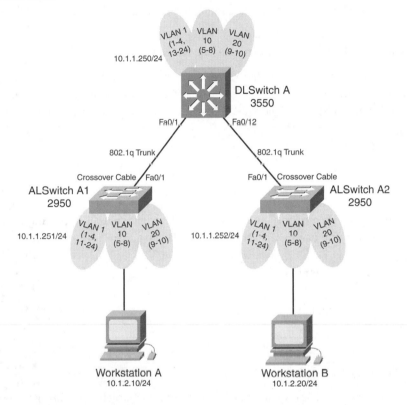

Scenario

In Lab 2.9.2, you configured a VTP trunk among a Cisco Catalyst WS-C3550-24-EMI, the DLSwitchA, and two Cisco Catalyst WS-C2950T-24-EI switches, which are indicated as ALSwitchA1 and ALSwitchA2. As a result, the switches flood broadcast, multicast, and unknown unicast traffic across the trunk link within the VTP domain. This happens even though receiving switches might discard them.

The network shown in Figure 2-3 has no devices connected to the Marketing VLAN 20. Therefore, flooded broadcast, multicast, and unknown unicast traffic for the Marketing VLAN 20 have no need to traverse the trunk link. VTP pruning allows the VTP to determine intelligently whether devices are present in a particular VLAN at the other end of a trunk link. By pruning, the VTP restricts flooded traffic to only those trunk links that the traffic must use to reach the destination devices. This results in increasing available bandwidth.

VTP pruning is disabled by default. It blocks unneeded, flooded traffic to VLANs on trunk ports that are included in the pruning-eligible list. Only VLANs that are included in the pruning-eligible list can be pruned. VLAN 1 is always ineligible for pruning. By default, VLANs 2 through 1001 are eligible for pruning on the Cisco Catalyst WS-C2950T-24-EI and WS-C3550-24-EMI trunk ports. If the VLANs are configured as ineligible for pruning, the flooding continues.

Notice that the basic procedures for VTP pruning on the 2950T and 3550 switches are the same.

Step 1

If you use the same switches and setup from Lab 2.9.2, verify connectivity with a ping between switches and between workstations. Then continue with Step 2.

If you use a different set of switches, ensure that no inappropriate VTP, VLAN information, or other configurations are present. Disconnect cables from the switches, and then power up the switches. Delete the startup configuration and the VLAN database (vlan.dat), and then reload the switches. Cable the lab according to the diagram shown, and then load the configurations from Lab 2.9.2.

Enable VLAN 1 on all switches with the **no shutdown** interface command.

The VTP and VLAN information that is retained in the VLAN database (vlan.dat) is not saved with the startup configuration. Therefore, if you do not use the switches from Lab 2.9.2 with this lab, load the previously saved configurations and settings into the respective switches that are to be used. The VTP domain name is not present; you must re-enter it to enable VTP:

```
DLSwitchA#vlan database
DLSwitchA(vlan)#vtp domain corp
Changing VTP domain name from NULL to corp
DLSwitchA(vlan)#exit
APPLY completed.
Exiting....
```

The accounting and marketing names created for VLAN 10 and VLAN 20 are absent also, but this does not have an impact on the completion of this lab. However, you can re-enter the names on DLSwitchA:

```
DLSwitchA#vlan database
DLSwitchA(vlan)#vlan 10 name Accounting
VLAN 10 added:
    Name: Accounting
DLSwitchA(vlan)#vlan 20 name Marketing
VLAN 20 added:
    Name: Marketing
DLSwitchA(vlan)#exit
APPLY completed.
Exiting....
```

All the switches are in the VTP Server mode. Again, this does not impact completion of this lab. However, you can reset ALSwitchA1 and ALSwitchA2 to the VTP Client mode:

```
ALSwitchA1#vlan database
ALSwitchA1(vlan)#vtp client
Setting device to VTP CLIENT mode.
ALSwitchA1(vlan)#exit
In CLIENT state, no apply attempted.
Exiting....
```

```
ALSwitchA2#vlan database
ALSwitchA2(vlan)#vtp client
Setting device to VTP CLIENT mode.
ALSwitchA2(vlan)#exit
In CLIENT state, no apply attempted.
Exiting....
```

Verify connectivity with a ping between switches and between workstations.

The sample outputs from this lab are based on the continuation of this lab from Lab 2.9.2 with the same switches and setup. If you use different switches with the Lab 2.9.2 configurations loaded, this output might appear slightly different. However, it will not impact successful completion of this lab.

Step 2

Issue the **show interfaces trunk** command on any of the switches to see the status of the VLANs when pruning is disabled. The following is sample output for DLSwitchA and ALSwitchA1:

```
DLSwitchA#show interfaces trunk

Port       Mode           Encapsulation  Status       Native vlan
Fa0/11     on             802.1q         trunking     1
Fa0/12     on             802.1q         trunking     1

Port       Vlans allowed on trunk
Fa0/11     1-4094
Fa0/12     1-4094

Port       Vlans allowed and active in management domain
Fa0/11     1,10,20
Fa0/12     1,10,20

Port       Vlans in spanning tree forwarding state and not pruned
Fa0/11     1,10,20
Fa0/12     1,10,20

ALSwitchA1#show interfaces trunk

Port       Mode           Encapsulation  Status       Native vlan
Fa0/1      on             802.1q         trunking     1

Port       Vlans allowed on trunk
Fa0/1      1-4094

Port       Vlans allowed and active in management domain
Fa0/1      1,10,20
Port       Vlans in spanning tree forwarding state and not pruned
Fa0/1      1,10,20
```

Notice that VLANs 1, 10, and 20 are all active in the VTP management domain.

1. Which VLANs are not pruned?

_____

2. Which VLAN and switch currently have workstations that are connected?

_____

_____

_____

Enabling VTP pruning on a VTP server enables pruning for the entire VTP domain. Therefore, you need to enable VTP pruning only on DLSwitchA, as shown in the following:

```
DLSwitchA#vlan database
DLSwitchA(vlan)#vtp pruning
Pruning switched ON
DLSwitchA(vlan)#exit
APPLY completed.
Exiting....
```

Note: To disable VTP pruning, use the **no vtp pruning** VLAN database configuration mode command.

On any of the switches, verify that VTP pruning is enabled with the **show vtp status** command. The following is sample output for DLSwitchA:

```
DLSwitchA#show vtp status
VTP Version                     : 2
Configuration Revision          : 2
Maximum VLANs supported locally : 1005
Number of existing VLANs        : 7
VTP Operating Mode              : Server
VTP Domain Name                 : corp
VTP Pruning Mode                : Enabled
VTP V2 Mode                     : Disabled
VTP Traps Generation            : Disabled
MD5 digest                      : 0x02 0xF1 0xDF 0xD4 0x61 0xBA 0x5E 0x18
Configuration last modified by 10.1.1.250 at 3-1-93 01:17:55
Local updater ID is 10.1.1.250 on interface Vl1 (lowest numbered VLAN interface
found)
```

Step 3

Issue the **show interfaces trunk** command on all the switches to see the status of the VLANs with pruning enabled. The following shows sample outputs from this command:

```
DLSwitchA#show interfaces trunk

Port        Mode        Encapsulation  Status        Native vlan
Fa0/11      on          802.1q         trunking      1
Fa0/12      on          802.1q         trunking      1

Port        Vlans allowed on trunk
Fa0/11      1-4094
Fa0/12      1-4094

Port        Vlans allowed and active in management domain
Fa0/11      1,10,20
Fa0/12      1,10,20

Port        Vlans in spanning tree forwarding state and not pruned
Fa0/11      1,10
Fa0/12      1,10
```

```
ALSwitchA1#show interfaces trunk

Port        Mode        Encapsulation  Status        Native vlan
Fa0/1       on          802.1q         trunking      1

Port        Vlans allowed on trunk
Fa0/1       1-4094

Port        Vlans allowed and active in management domain
Fa0/1       1,10,20

Port        Vlans in spanning tree forwarding state and not pruned
Fa0/1       1,10
```

```
ALSwitchA2#show interfaces trunk
```

```
Port        Mode            Encapsulation  Status     Native vlan
Fa0/1       on              802.1q         trunking   1

Port        Vlans allowed on trunk
Fa0/1       1-4094

Port        Vlans allowed and active in management domain
Fa0/1       1,10,20

Port        Vlans in spanning tree forwarding state and not pruned
Fa0/1       1,10
```

1. How is the output from Step 3, with pruning enabled, different from Step 2, with pruning disabled? Why?

2. If no devices are connected to ports in VLAN 1, why is it not pruned?

Step 4

Unplug the workstation from VLAN 10 on ALSwitchA2. Then plug the workstation into port 9 or 10 on VLAN 20. Now a workstation is connected to VLAN 10 on ALSwitchA1 and VLAN 20 on ALSwitchA2. No workstations are connected to DLSwitchA. Issue the **show interfaces trunk** command on all switches and examine the output. It might take a minute or two for the switches to adjust to the change. Sample outputs are shown as follows:

```
DLSwitchA#show interfaces trunk

Port        Mode            Encapsulation  Status     Native vlan
Fa0/11      on              802.1q         trunking   1
Fa0/12      on              802.1q         trunking   1

Port        Vlans allowed on trunk
Fa0/11      1-4094
Fa0/12      1-4094

Port        Vlans allowed and active in management domain
Fa0/11      1,10,20
Fa0/12      1,10,20

Port        Vlans in spanning tree forwarding state and not pruned
Fa0/11      1,10
Fa0/12      1,20

ALSwitchA1#show interfaces trunk

Port        Mode            Encapsulation  Status     Native vlan
Fa0/1       on              802.1q         trunking   1

Port        Vlans allowed on trunk
Fa0/1       1-4094

Port        Vlans allowed and active in management domain
Fa0/1       1,10,20

Port        Vlans in spanning tree forwarding state and not pruned
Fa0/1       1,20

ALSwitchA2#show interfaces trunk
```

```
Port        Mode            Encapsulation  Status       Native vlan
Fa0/1       on              802.1q         trunking     1

Port        Vlans allowed on trunk
Fa0/1       1-4094

Port        Vlans allowed and active in management domain
Fa0/1       1,10,20

Port        Vlans in spanning tree forwarding state and not pruned
Fa0/1       1,10
```

Examine the pruning status, which is highlighted in the sample output, of the trunk ports in each switch. What is the result of pruning on each switch with the changes that you made in Step 4?

_____

_____

_____

_____

_____

_____

Step 5

Unplug the workstation from VLAN 20 on ALSwitchA2. Plug the workstation into a port in VLAN 10, using ports 5 through 8. VLAN 10 now has workstations on both ALSwitchA1 and ALSwitchA2.

Verify connectivity with a ping between the workstations.

You can execute various commands to view trunking and pruning status and activity for informational and troubleshooting purposes. The commands you use in these Chapter 2 labs are as follows:

show vtp status

show vtp counters

show interfaces switchport

show interfaces trunk

Issue the commands on any of the switches. Then observe and examine the output. Another useful command is the **debug sw-vlan vtp pruning** command.

Execute the **debug sw-vlan vtp pruning** command on any of the switches and observe the output. After observing the output for a few minutes, use the **undebug all** command to turn off debugging.

Save the configurations for use in the next lab. If possible, retain the same switches and setup.

Lab 2.9.4: Catalyst 2950T and 3550 Series Intra-VLAN Security

Objective

Configure intra-VLAN security with VLAN access control lists (VACLs or VLAN maps) using the CLI mode. Figure 2-4 shows the topology for this lab.

Figure 2-4 Topology for Lab 2.9.4

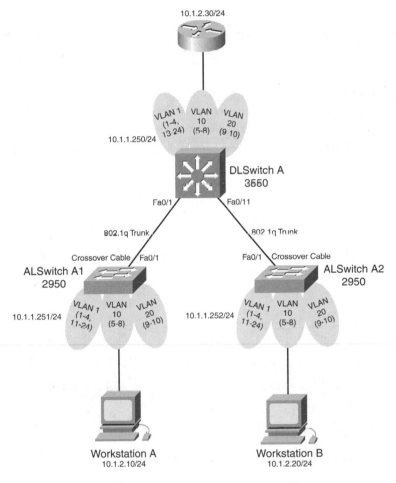

Scenario

This lab covers how to configure basic network security on a switch by using VACLs (or VLAN maps). The 3550 switch supports two types of Access Control Lists (ACLs):

- **IP ACLs**—Filters IP traffic, including TCP, User Datagram Protocol (UDP), Internet Group Management Protocol (IGMP), and Internet Control Message Protocol (ICMP).

- **Ethernet ACLs**—Filter non-IP traffic. The 2950 switch supports only IP ACLs.

The 3550 switch supports two applications of ACLs to filter traffic:

- **Router ACLs**—Access control routed traffic between VLANs. The enhanced multiplayer switch image is required for this to work. You can apply router ACLs on switch virtual interfaces (SVIs), on physical Layer 3 interfaces, and on Layer 3

EtherChannel interfaces. Router ACLs are applied on interfaces for specific directions, whether inbound or outbound. Note that the 2950 switch supports only port ACLs, a type of ACL applied to Layer 2 switch ports.

- **VLAN Access Control Lists (VACLs) or VLAN maps**—Access control all packets, bridged and routed. You can use VLAN maps to filter traffic among devices in the same VLAN. The enhanced image is not required to create or apply VLAN maps. VLAN maps are configured to provide access control, which is based on Layer 3 addresses for IP. Unsupported protocols are access controlled through MAC addresses using Ethernet access control entries (ACEs).

When you apply a VLAN map to a VLAN, all packets that enter the VLAN —whether the packets are routed or bridged—are checked against the VLAN map. Packets can enter the VLAN through a switch port. They also can enter through a routed port after they are routed.

VLAN maps can access control all traffic. You can apply VLAN maps on the switch to all packets that are routed into or out of a VLAN or are bridged within a VLAN. VLAN maps are used strictly for security packet filtering. Unlike router ACLs, input and output do not define VLAN maps.

You can configure VLAN maps to match Layer 3 addresses for IP traffic. All non-IP protocols are access controlled through MAC addresses and EtherType using MAC VLAN maps. MAC VLAN maps do not access control IP traffic. You can enforce VLAN maps only on packets that are going through the switch. You cannot enforce VLAN maps on traffic between hosts on a hub or on another switch connected to this switch.

With VLAN maps, forwarding of packets is either permitted or denied, depending on the action specified in the map.

Step 1

You can use the Catalyst 3550 switch and configuration used in Lab 2.9.3 for DLSwitchA for this lab.

To ensure that no inappropriate VTP, VLAN, or other configurations are present, disconnect any cables from the switches that are to be used for ALSwitchA1 and ALSwitchA2, power up the switches, and delete the startup configuration and VLAN database (vlan.dat). Then reload the switches and cable the lab according to Figure 2-4.

For both AL switches, do the following:

- Configure the appropriate switch name.

- Configure cisco as the enable secret, console, and vty password.

- Configure interface Fast Ethernet 0/1 as a trunk port with dot1q as the trunk encapsulation.

- Assign the appropriate ports to VLAN 10 and 20 respectively.

- Configure the appropriate IP address for VLAN 1.

Enable VLAN 1 on all switches with the **no shutdown** interface command.

If you are not using the same DLSwitchA from Lab 2.9.3 and loading the configuration into a different switch, enter the VTP domain name to enable VTP and pruning. Then re-enter the VLAN names as follows:

```
DLSwitchA#vlan database
DLSwitchA(vlan)#vtp domain corp
Changing VTP domain name from NULL to corp
DLSwitchA(vlan)#vtp pruning
Pruning switched ON
DLSwitchA(vlan)#vlan 10 name Accounting
VLAN 10 added:
    Name: Accounting
DLSwitchA(vlan)#vlan 20 name Marketing
VLAN 20 added:
    Name: Marketing
DLSwitchA(vlan)#exit
APPLY completed.
Exiting....
```

Although it is not absolutely necessary, set ALSwitchA1 and ALSwitchA2 to the VTP Client mode by issuing the following commands:

```
ALSwitchA1#vlan database
ALSwitchA1(vlan)#vtp client
Setting device to VTP CLIENT mode.
ALSwitchA1(vlan)#exit
In CLIENT state, no apply attempted.
Exiting....
```

```
ALSwitchA2#vlan database
ALSwitchA2(vlan)#vtp client
Setting device to VTP CLIENT mode.
ALSwitchA2(vlan)#exit
In CLIENT state, no apply attempted.
Exiting....
```

Verify connectivity with a ping between switches and between workstations.

Step 2

Connect a router to port 5 of the DLSwitchA to simulate a file server and configure it as follows:

```
Router#configure terminal
Router(config)#hostname Server
Server(config)#ip http server
Server(config)#interface FastEthernet0/0
Server(config-if)#ip address 10.1.2.30 255.255.255.0
Server(config-if)#no shutdown
Server(config-if)#line console 0
Server(config-line)#password cisco
Server(config-line)#login
Server(config-line)#line vty 0 4
Server(config-line)#password cisco
Server(config-line)#login
Server(config-line)#^z
```

Verify connectivity with a ping among the Management VLANs of the switches, among workstations, and among the workstations and router. All ping attempts should be successful.

Step 3

Issue the following in DLSwitchA to deny ICMP ping access from Workstation A to the server (10.1.2.30):

```
DLSwitchA#configure terminal

DLSwitchA(config)#ip access-list extended map
DLSwitchA(config-ext-nacl)#deny icmp host 10.1.2.10 host 10.1.2.30 echo
DLSwitchA(config-ext-nacl)#permit ip any any
DLSwitchA(config-ext-nacl)#^z
DLSwitchA#
```

Configure the VACL (VLAN map) and apply it to VLAN 10:

```
DLSwitchA#configure terminal
DLSwitchA(config)#vlan access-map map 10
DLSwitchA(config-access-map)#match ip address map
DLSwitchA(config-access-map)#exit
DLSwitchA(config)#vlan filter map vlan-list 10
DLSwitchA(config)#^z
DLSwitchA#
```

Note: No action is specified because the default, forward, is acceptable.

The ICMP ping traffic from Workstation A to the server should be blocked now.

Test the ACL with a ping from Workstation A to the server (10.1.2.30). The ping should fail.

1. Should a ping from the server to Workstation A (10.1.2.10) be successful? Why?

_____

_____

_____

_____

Verify with a ping from the server to Workstation A (10.1.2.10).

2. Should a ping from the server to Workstation B (10.1.2.20) be successful? Why?

_____

_____

_____

_____

Verify with a ping from the server to Workstation B (10.1.2.20).

3. Should a ping from Workstation A to Workstation B and another ping back from Workstation B to Workstation A be successful? Why?

_____

_____

Verify with a ping from Workstation A (10.1.2.10) to Workstation B (10.1.2.20) or with a ping from Workstation B (10.1.2.20) to Workstation A (10.1.2.10).

Step 4

Issue the following command to remove the first VACL from DLSwitchA. Then create another one that will deny Telnet and HTTP access to the server from Workstation B:

```
DLSwitchA#configure terminal
DLSwitchA(config)#no ip access-list extended map
DLSwitchA(config)#no vlan access-map map 10

DLSwitchA(config)#ip access-list extended map
DLSwitchA(config-ext-nacl)#deny tcp host 10.1.2.20 host 10.1.2.30 eq telnet
DLSwitchA(config-ext-nacl)#deny tcp host 10.1.2.20 host 10.1.2.30 eq www
DLSwitchA(config-ext-nacl)#permit ip any any
DLSwitchA(config-ext-nacl)#exit
DLSwitchA(config)#vlan access-map map 10
DLSwitchA(config-access-map)#match ip address map
DLSwitchA(config-access-map)#^z
DLSwitchA#
```

You do not need to reapply the access list.

A ping from Workstation A to the server (10.1.2.30) should be successful now, because the first access list is no longer applicable. Verify this with a ping.

Step 5

Test the new VACL. Attempt to telnet from Workstation B to the server (10.1.2.30), and then open a web browser and attempt to access the server (10.1.2.30). Both attempts should fail.

1. Should a ping from Workstation B to the server (10.1.2.30) be successful? Why?

_____

_____

Verify with a ping from Workstation B to the server (10.1.2.30).

2. Should Telnet and HTTP access to the server (10.1.2.30) from Workstation A (10.1.2.10) be successful? Why?

_____

_____

Verify by telnetting into the server (10.1.2.30) from Workstation A. Then open a browser in Workstation A and access the server (10.1.2.30) by way of HTTP.

Intra-VLAN security with VACLs or VLAN maps has been successfully configured.

Note: Refer to the *Catalyst 3550 Multilayer Switch Software Configuration Guide* and the *Catalyst 2950 Desktop Switch Software Configuration Guide* for more information about configuring network security on the Cisco Catalyst 3550 and 2950 switches.

Chapter 3

Spanning Tree Protocol (STP)

Lab 3.10.1: Spanning Tree Protocol (STP) Default Behavior

Estimated Time: 60 Minutes

Objective

In this lab, you observe the default behavior of STP. Figure 3-1 shows the topology for this lab.

Figure 3-1 Topology for Lab 3.10.1

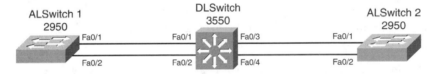

Scenario

You have just installed three switches. The distribution layer switch is a Catalyst 3550 and the access layer switches are both Catalyst 2950. Redundant uplinks exist between the access layer and the distribution layer. Because of the possibility of bridging loops, spanning tree logically removes any redundant links.

Step 1

Erase all switch configurations and vlan.dat files before you cable the lab. If cables are already attached, remove them prior to starting. This prevents VLAN Trunking Protocol (VTP) from reinstating previous VLAN configurations. After you have removed the VLAN database and startup configurations, power-cycle the switch or issue the **reload** command. Cable and configure the two switches as shown in Figure 3-1 with a host name, enable password, and console security.

Console into DLSwitch and enter the following commands:

```
Switch>enable
Switch#configure terminal
Switch(config)#hostname DLSwitch
DLSwitch(config)#enable secret class
DLSwitch(config)#line console 0
DLSwitch(config-line)#password cisco
DLSwitch(config-line)#login
```

Console into ALSwitch1 and enter the following commands:

```
Switch>enable
Switch#configure terminal
Switch(config)#hostname ALSwitch1
ALSwitch1(config)#enable secret class
```

```
ALSwitch1(config)#line console 0
ALSwitch1(config-line)#password cisco
ALSwitch1(config-line)#login
```

Console into the ALSwitch2 and enter the following commands:

```
Switch>enable
Switch# configure terminal
Switch(config)#hostname ALSwitch2
ALSwitch2(config)#enable secret class
ALSwitch2(config)#line console 0
ALSwitch2(config-line)#password cisco
ALSwitch2(config-line)#login
```

Step 2

Use crossover Cat 5 cables to make the connections because the switches are like devices:

1. Connect a cable from Fast Ethernet 0/1 on DLSwitch to Fast Ethernet 0/1 ALSwitch1.

2. Connect a cable from Fast Ethernet 0/2 on DLSwitch to Fast Ethernet 0/2 ALSwitch1.

3. Connect a cable from Fast Ethernet 0/3 on DLSwitch to Fast Ethernet 0/1 ALSwitch2.

4. Connect a cable from Fast Ethernet 0/4 on DLSwitch to Fast Ethernet 0/2 ALSwitch2.

After you connect the cables and the switch detects the redundant links, spanning tree is initiated.

By default, spanning tree runs on every port. When a new link becomes active, the port goes through the listening, learning, and forwarding states before it becomes active. During this period, the switch discovers whether it is connected to another switch or an end-user device.

If another switch is detected, the two switches begin creating a spanning tree. One of the switches is elected as the root of the tree. Then an agreement is established as to which links to keep active and which links to disable if multiple links exist.

Which type of frame does STP use to communicate with other switches?

Note: The results in this lab vary. Spanning-tree operation is based on the MAC address of the switches.

Observe the LEDs on the switch to check the status of the link. A bright green light indicates an active link. An amber light indicates an inactive link.

Step 3

Verify STP with the **show spanning-tree** command on the DLSwitch:

```
DLSwitch#show spanning-tree

VLAN0001
  Spanning tree enabled protocol ieee
  Root ID    Priority    32769
             Address     0009.430f.a400
             Cost        19
             Port        3 (FastEthernet0/3)
             Hello Time  2 sec  Max Age 20 sec  Forward Delay 15 sec

  Bridge ID  Priority    32769  (priority 32768 sys-id-ext 1)
             Address     000a.b701.f700
             Hello Time  2 sec  Max Age 20 sec  Forward Delay 15 sec
             Aging Time 300
```

```
Interface      Port ID                   Designated              Port ID
Name           Prio.Nbr     Cost Sts     Cost Bridge ID          Prio.Nbr
-------------- --------- ---------- --- ------- ------------------- --------
Fa0/1          128.1         19 FWD       19 32769 000a.b701.f700 128.1
Fa0/2          128.2         19 FWD       19 32769 000a.b701.f700 128.2
Fa0/3          128.3         19 FWD        0 32769 0009.430f.a400 128.1
Fa0/4          128.4         19 BLK        0 32769 0009.430f.a400 128.2
```

Console into ALSwitch1. Issue the **show spanning-tree** command:

```
ALSwitch1#show spanning-tree
VLAN0001
  Spanning tree enabled protocol ieee
  Root ID    Priority    32769
             Address     0009.430f.a400
             Cost        38
             Port        1 (FastEthernet0/1)
             Hello Time  2 sec  Max Age 20 sec  Forward Delay 15 sec

  Bridge ID  Priority    32769  (priority 32768 sys-id-ext 1)
             Address     000a.8afc.dd80
             Hello Time  2 sec  Max Age 20 sec  Forward Delay 15 sec
             Aging Time 300

Interface      Port ID                   Designated              Port ID
Name           Prio.Nbr     Cost Sts     Cost Bridge ID          Prio.Nbr
-------------- --------- ---------- --- ------- ------------------- --------
Fa0/1          128.1         19 FWD       19 32769 000a.b701.f700 128.1
Fa0/2          128.2         19 BLK       19 32769 000a.b701.f700 128.2
```

Console into ALSwitch2. Issue the **show spanning-tree** command:

```
ALSwitch2#show spanning-tree

VLAN0001
  Spanning tree enabled protocol ieee
  Root ID    Priority    32769
             Address     0009.430f.a400
             This bridge is the root
             Hello Time  2 sec  Max Age 20 sec  Forward Delay 15 sec

  Bridge ID  Priority    32769  (priority 32768 sys-id-ext 1)
             Address     0009.430f.a400
             Hello Time  2 sec  Max Age 20 sec  Forward Delay 15 sec
             Aging Time 300

Interface      Port ID                   Designated              Port ID
Name           Prio.Nbr     Cost Sts     Cost Bridge ID          Prio.Nbr
-------------- --------- ---------- --- ------- ------------------- --------
Fa0/1          128.1         19 FWD        0 32769 0009.430f.a400 128.1
Fa0/2          128.2         19 FWD        0 32769 0009.430f.a400 128.2
```

Notice that between two switches, one of the two ports is set to blocking. Blocking can occur on the access layer switch or the distribution layer switch. If all ports have their default settings, the higher MAC address of the two ports is set to blocking.

The switch port is in a blocking state because it detected two links between the same switches. This results in a bridge loop if the switch did not logically disable one link.

After you review the spanning-tree output, answer the following questions:

1. Which switch is the root of the spanning tree?

_____

2. How can you identify the root switch?

3. Why was that switch selected as the root?

_____

_____

_____

4. What caused the one port to be in a blocking state over another?

_____

_____

5. What caused one link to be blocked over another?

_____

Step 4

Create a diagram of the spanning-tree topology for VLAN 1. With Cisco Catalyst switches, each VLAN has a different spanning-tree state. Identify the root bridge, root ports, and designated ports.

In this lab, you observed the default operation of spanning tree. Because you specified no bridge priorities, the switch with the lowest MAC address was elected as the root. You changed no link priorities, so the link with the lowest cost became the active link. If costs were equal, the lowest port number broke the tie.

In Lab 3.10.3, you modify the default STP behavior so that spanning tree works according to the specifications.

Lab 3.10.2: Use Network Inspector to Observe STP Behavior

Estimated Time: 120 Minutes

Objective

In this lab, you observe STP behavior with the Network Inspector (NI) switch trace feature. Figure 3-2 shows the topology for this lab.

Figure 3-2 Topology for Lab 3.10.2

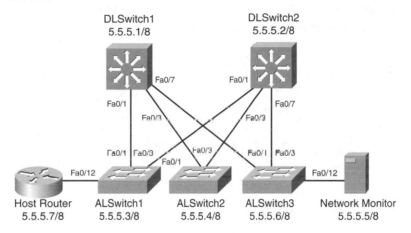

Scenario

You have just installed a new switched network, and you must monitor the STP behavior. Fluke NI has a trace feature that can track the path that data takes over the network.

The network design is shown here.

Switch	VTP Domain	VTP Mode
DLSwitch1	CORP	Server
DLSwitch2	CORP	Client
ALSwitch1	CORP	Client
ALSwitch2	CORP	Client
ALSwitch3	CORP	Client

The VLAN configuration information is shown here.

VLAN ID	VLAN Name	VLAN Subnet	DLSwitch	ALSwitch
1	Native	5.0.0.0/8	All ports	All ports
Trunk				802.1Q

Device	DLSwitch1	DLSwitch2	ALSwitch1	ALSwitch2	ALSwitch3	NI	Host Router
IP Address	5.5.5.1/8	5.5.5.2/8	5.5.5.3/8	5.5.5.4/8	5.5.5.6/8	5.5.5.5/8	5.5.5.7/8

Step 1

Erase all switch configurations and vlan.dat files before you cable the lab. If cables are attached, remove them prior to starting. Doing so prevents VTP from reinstating previous VLAN configurations. After you have removed the VLAN database and startup configurations, power-cycle the switch or issue the **reload** command. Cable the lab according to Figure 3-2.

Before you configure the switches, delete the vlan.dat database file and power-cycle each switch. Then erase the startup configuration on each switch and issue the **reload** command:

```
DLSwitch1#delete flash
Delete filename [flash]?
Enter vlan.dat at the Delete prompt.
DLSwitch1#erase start
Switch#reload
```

Note: Do not save the configuration changes when prompted.

Configure the host name, passwords, and Telnet access to all the switches. Use interface VLAN 1 to configure the IP address of all the switches.

Step 2

Configure the trunking interfaces.

Create a trunk link between the switches. On the DLSwitch1 and DLSwitch2, set the port to trunking with the 802.1Q encapsulation.

Note: If an error is received, it is because the port is set to auto encapsulation. Fix the error by entering the **switchport mode trunk** command after the **switchport trunk encapsulation dot1q** command.

```
DLSwitch1(config)#interface FastEthernet 0/1
DLSwitch1(config-if)#switchport mode trunk
DLSwitch1(config-if)#switchport trunk encapsulation dot1q
DLSwitch1(config)#interface FastEthernet 0/3
DLSwitch1(config-if)#switchport mode trunk
DLSwitch1(config-if)#switchport trunk encapsulation dot1q
DLSwitch1(config)#interface FastEthernet 0/7
DLSwitch1(config-if)#switchport mode trunk
DLSwitch1(config-if)#switchport trunk encapsulation dot1q
DLSwitch1(config-if)#^Z
```

```
DLSwitch2(config)#interface FastEthernet 0/1
DLSwitch2(config-if)#switchport mode trunk
DLSwitch2(config-if)#switchport trunk encapsulation dot1q
DLSwitch2(config)#interface FastEthernet 0/3
DLSwitch2(config-if)#switchport mode trunk
DLSwitch2(config-if)#switchport trunk encapsulation dot1q
DLSwitch2(config)#interface FastEthernet 0/7
DLSwitch2(config-if)#switchport mode trunk
```

```
DLSwitch2(config-if)#switchport trunk encapsulation dot1q
DLSwitch2(config-if)#^Z
```

The access layer switches do not need the encapsulation to be configured. It defaults to 802.1Q. Some IOS versions have no other options:

```
ALSwitch1(config)#interface FastEthernet0/1
ALSwitch1(config-if)#switchport mode trunk
ALSwitch1(config)#interface FastEthernet 0/3
ALSwitch1(config-if)#switchport mode trunk
ALSwitch1(config-if)#^Z
```

```
ALSwitch2(config)#interface fastethernet 0/1
ALSwitch2(config-if)#switchport mode trunk
ALSwitch2(config-if)# ALSwitch2(config)#interface fastethernet 0/3
ALSwitch2(config-if)#switchport mode trunk
ALSwitch2(config-if)#^Z
```

```
ALSwitch3(config)#interface fastethernet 0/1
ALSwitch3(config-if)#switchport mode trunk
ALSwitch3(config)#interface fastethernet 0/3
ALSwitch3(config-if)#switchport mode trunk
ALSwitch3(config-if)#^Z
```

Verify the trunk configuration with the **show vtp counters** command:

```
DLSwitch1#show vtp counters
VTP statistics:
Summary advertisements received    : 0
Subset advertisements received     : 0
Request advertisements received    : 0
Summary advertisements transmitted : 0
Subset advertisements transmitted  : 0
Request advertisements transmitted : 0
Number of config revision errors   : 0
Number of config digest errors     : 0
Number of V1 summary errors        : 0

VTP pruning statistics:

Trunk          Join Transmitted Join Received    Summary advts received from
                                                 non-pruning-capable device
-------------- ---------------- ---------------- ---------------------------
Fa0/1                 0                0                    0
Fa0/3                 0                0                    0
Fa0/7                 0                0                    0
```

Verify the configuration on all the switches.

Step 3

Configure the VLAN database on DLSwitch1 and DLSwitch2.

Create the VLAN database on DLSwitch1. Place the switch in VTP Server mode:

```
DLSwitch1#vlan database
DLSwitch1(vlan)#vtp domain CORP
DLSwitch1(vlan)#vtp server
DLSwitch1(vlan)#exit
```

Use the **show vtp status** command to verify the configuration.

On the DLSwitch2, create the VLAN database. Place the switch in VTP Client mode:

```
DLSwitch2#vlan database
DLSwitch2(vlan)#vtp client
DLSwitch2(vlan)#exit
```

Use the **show vtp status** command to verify the configuration.

Step 4

Configure the VLAN database on the access layer switches. Place them in Client mode:

```
ALSwitch1(vlan)#vtp client
ALSwitch1(vlan)#exit
```

```
ALSwitch2(vlan)#vtp client
ALSwitch2(vlan)#exit
```

```
ALSwitch3(vlan)#vtp client
ALSwitch3(vlan)#exit
```

Verify the vtp configuration with the **show vtp status** command on all the switches.

Step 5

Configure DLSwitch1 as the root bridge.

Change the root bridge priority to 4096 on DLSwitch1, which is less than the default priority of 32768:

```
DLSwitch1(config)#spanning-tree vlan 1 priority 4096
```

Verify that DLSwitch1 is the root bridge with the **show spanning-tree** command:

```
DLSwitch1#show spanning-tree

VLAN0001
  Spanning tree enabled protocol ieee
  Root ID    Priority    4097
             Address     000b.be4f.bc00
             This bridge is the root
             Hello Time   2 sec  Max Age 20 sec  Forward Delay 15 sec

  Bridge ID  Priority    4097   (priority 4096 sys-id-ext 1)
             Address     000b.be4f.bc00
             Hello Time   2 sec  Max Age 20 sec  Forward Delay 15 sec
             Aging Time 300

Interface     Port ID                        Designated            Port ID
Name          Prio.Nbr    Cost Sts  Cost Bridge ID            Prio.Nbr
------------- -------- ---------- --- ------- ------------------- --------
Fa0/1         128.1         19 FWD     0  4097 000b.be4f.bc00 128.1
Fa0/3         128.3         19 FWD     0  4097 000b.be4f.bc00 128.3
Fa0/7         128.7         19 FWD     0  4097 000b.be4f.bc00 128.7
```

Step 6

Configure the HostRouter, which is acting only as a host device. You will use it as an end device to which to trace:

```
Router(config)#hostname HostRouter
HostRouter(config)#interface fa0/0
HostRouter(config-if)#ip address 5.5.5.7 255.0.0.0
HostRouter(config-if)#no shutdown
HostRouter(config-if)#exit
```

Step 7

You can use Fluke NI to monitor the behavior of the switched network. Monitoring is important in successful network management. For this lab, use the switch trace feature to monitor STP.

Run Fluke NI console from the Start menu or from a desktop shortcut. The screen should look like Figure 3-3.

Figure 3-3 NI Console

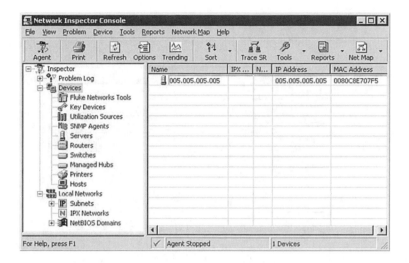

First, you must define a community string. A public community string might be defined by default. For security purposes, it is highly recommended that you select a different community string. Click the **Agent** tab at the top of the console to get the screen that is shown in Figure 3-4.

Figure 3-4 NI Agent Manager

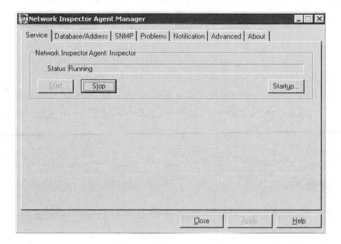

Then click on the **SNMP** tab, as shown in Figure 3-5. Type **cisco** as an alternative community string. You might have to enter **cisco** as the default Simple Network Management Protocol (SNMP) community string on older versions of NI.

Figure 3-5 SNMP Tab

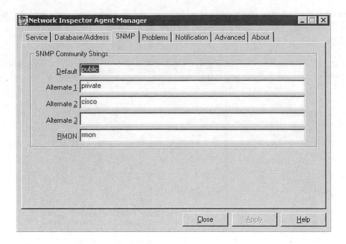

Click the **Apply** button at the bottom of the screen. A prompt appears stating that the changes will take effect the next time you start the service.

Now you must stop and start the service. Click the **Service** tab at the top of the screen, and click the **Stop** button. Click **Yes** when prompted to confirm the action. Then click **Start** to start the service. Starting the service might take a few seconds.

Connect the computer that is running Network Monitor to ALSwitch3 to port Fast Ethernet 0/12. This completes the setup of the Network Monitor.

Step 8

You must configure SNMP on all the devices so that the Network Monitor can find them. Define the SNMP community with the **snmp-server community** command. You must define the SNMP server host IP address with the **snmp-server host** command for a device to send SNMP traps to the Network Monitor. Enable SNMP by typing these global configuration commands on all the devices:

```
snmp-server community cisco ro
snmp-server host 5.5.5.5 cisco
```

The **ro** defines "read only" for the SNMP server. This prevents the SNMP server from making changes on the device.

This is a good time to take a break. It takes a few minutes for the Fluke NI to find all the devices.

Step 9

The Network Monitor finds all the devices and displays them in the main window. The screen should look like Figure 3-6.

Network Monitor displays the host name, IP address, MAC address, and type of device on the right side of the screen. If the device type does not appear, change it by right-clicking the device and selecting **Modify Type**. If the device's IP address is displayed instead of the host name, enter the following command on the device, which sends the host name to the Network Monitor:

```
snmp-server chassis-id [device_hostname]
```

Next, start the switch trace. Select host 5.5.5.5 by clicking it and highlighting it. This is the starting device for the trace. Then click the **Trace SR** button on top of the screen, as shown in Figure 3-7, or right-click and then left-click the **Trace SwitchRoute** option.

Figure 3-6 NI Console with All Devices Displayed

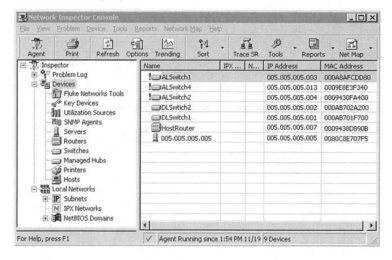

Figure 3-7 Trace SR Button

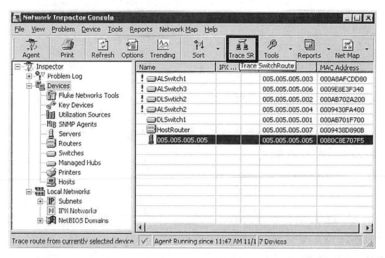

On the next screen, choose the HostRouter as the ending device for the trace, as shown in Figure 3-8.

Figure 3-8 HostRouter as the Ending Device for the Trace

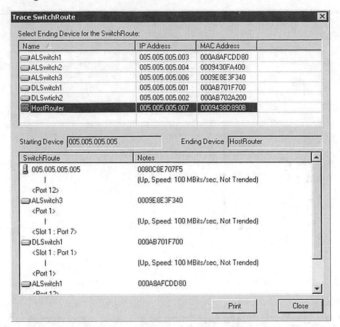

Notice all the devices in the trace display and the entrance and exit ports of the trace through all the devices. This a great tool to observe STP behavior.

1. Why did the trace go through DLSwitch1 instead of DLSwitch2?

_____

Now try a trace from ALSwitch2 to DLSwitch2.

2. Did the trace go through DLSwitch1?

_____

Step 10

Change the root bridge to DLSwitch2 and observe STP behavior.

On DLSwitch1, enter the following command to change the spanning-tree priority:

```
DLSwitch1(config)#no spanning-tree vlan 1 priority 4096
```

On DLSwitch2, enter the following command to change the spanning-tree priority:

```
DLSwitch2(config)#spanning-tree vlan 1 priority 4096
```

Verify that DLSwitch2 became the root bridge with the **show spanning-tree** command:

```
DLSwitch2#show spanning-tree

VLAN0001
  Spanning tree enabled protocol ieee
  Root ID    Priority    4097
             Address     000a.b702.a200
             This bridge is the root
             Hello Time   2 sec  Max Age 20 sec  Forward Delay 15 sec
```

```
Bridge ID  Priority    4097   (priority 4096 sys-id-ext 1)
           Address     000a.b702.a200
           Hello Time   2 sec  Max Age 20 sec  Forward Delay 15 sec
           Aging Time 15

Interface      Port ID                Designated              Port ID
Name           Prio.Nbr   Cost Sts   Cost Bridge ID           Prio.Nbr
-------------- --------- ---------- --- ------- ------------------- --------
Fa0/1          128.1          19 FWD       0  4097 000a.b702.a200 128.1
Fa0/3          128.3          19 FWD       0  4097 000a.b702.a200 128.3
Fa0/7          128.7          19 FWD       0  4097 000a.b702.a200 128.7
```

Wait a few minutes while Network Monitor is updated with the new spanning-tree topology.

Now try a trace from host 5.5.5.5 to the HostRouter.

1. Did the trace go though DLSwitch1 or DLSwitch2? Why?

_____

Try a trace from ALSwitch1 to DLSwitch1, as shown in Figure 3-9.

Figure 3-9 Trace from ALSwitch1 to DLSwitch1

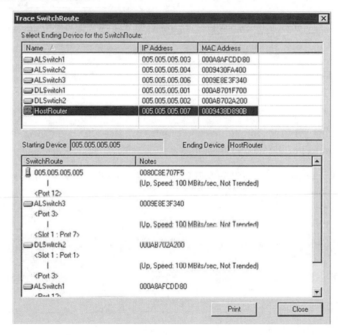

ALSwitch1 and DLSwitch1 are connected directly. However, the trace still goes through DLSwitch2. STP always sends frames to the root bridge before sending them to the destination switch.

Now do a trace from ALSwitch2 to DLSwitch1, as shown in Figure 3-10.

Figure 3-10 Trace from ALSwitch2 to DLSwitch1

2. Did the trace go through DLSwitch2?

Network Monitor is a great tool that provides an overview of a network. Use it to chart the data flow of the network. You can make changes to the configuration to get the desired results.

You also can use the switch trace feature of Network Monitor with all the labs. This is another way to verify the network behavior.

Lab 3.10.3: Advanced PVST+ Configuration

Estimated Time: 60 Minutes

Objective

In this lab, you modify the default per-VLAN spanning tree plus (PVST+) configuration to control the spanning-tree behavior. Figure 3-11 shows the topology for this lab.

Figure 3-11 Topology for Lab 3.10.3

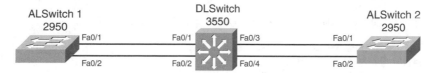

Scenario

You have just installed a switched network. By default, Cisco IOS Software uses per-VLAN spanning tree (PVST). The network administrator wants the distribution layer switch to be the root spanning-tree switch. He wants to use port priorities to control which links are elected as active. You can decrease convergence time by adjusting the spanning-tree timers.

Step 1

You can use the same setup and basic configurations from Lab 3.10.1 for this lab. If necessary, disconnect the cables, clear the configurations by deleting the vlan.dat and startup configuration files, power-cycle the switches, and re-enter the basic configurations into each switch as follows:

- Configure host names for the respective switches according to Figure 3-11.

- Configure all switches with the secret password—class.

- Configure all switches with the login console password—cisco.

- Connect the switches according to Figure 3-11.

Remember that the output for each switch is different from the sample outputs in relation to MAC addresses and which switch is the root bridge.

Console into the DLSwitch. View the spanning-tree output:

```
DLSwitch#show spanning-tree

VLAN0001
  Spanning tree enabled protocol ieee
  Root ID    Priority    32769
             Address     0009.430f.a400
             Cost        19
             Port        3 (FastEthernet0/3)
             Hello Time   2 sec  Max Age 20 sec  Forward Delay 15 sec

  Bridge ID  Priority    32769  (priority 32768 sys-id-ext 1)
             Address     000a.b701.f700
             Hello Time   2 sec  Max Age 20 sec  Forward Delay 15 sec
             Aging Time 300

Interface       Port ID                  Designated          Port ID
Name            Prio.Nbr   Cost Sts    Cost Bridge ID        Prio.Nbr
```

```
-------------- -------- --------- --- -------- -------------------- --------
Fa0/1           128.1       19 FWD    19 32769 000a.b701.f700 128.1
Fa0/2           128.2       19 FWD    19 32769 000a.b701.f700 128.2
Fa0/3           128.3       19 FWD     0 32769 0009.430f.a400 128.1
Fa0/4           128.4       19 BLK     0 32769 0009.430f.a400 128.2
```

Console into the ALSwitch1. View the spanning-tree output:

```
ALSwitch1#show spanning-tree

VLAN0001
  Spanning tree enabled protocol ieee
  Root ID    Priority    32769
             Address     0009.430f.a400
             Cost        38
             Port        1 (FastEthernet0/1)
             Hello Time  2 sec  Max Age 20 sec  Forward Delay 15 sec

  Bridge ID  Priority    32769  (priority 32768 sys-id-ext 1)
             Address     000a.8afc.dd80
             Hello Time  2 sec  Max Age 20 sec  Forward Delay 15 sec
             Aging Time 300

Interface       Port ID                    Designated              Port ID
Name            Prio.Nbr    Cost Sts   Cost Bridge ID              Prio.Nbr
-------------- -------- --------- --- ------- -------------------- --------
Fa0/1           128.1       19 FWD    19 32769 000a.b701.f700 128.1
Fa0/2           128.2       19 BLK    19 32769 000a.b701.f700 128.2
```

Console into the ALSwitch2. View the spanning-tree output:

```
ALSwitch2#show spanning-tree

VLAN0001
  Spanning tree enabled protocol ieee
  Root ID    Priority    32769
             Address     0009.430f.a400
             This bridge is the root
             Hello Time  2 sec  Max Age 20 sec  Forward Delay 15 sec

  Bridge ID  Priority    32769  (priority 32768 sys-id-ext 1)
             Address     0009.430f.a400
             Hello Time  2 sec  Max Age 20 sec  Forward Delay 15 sec
             Aging Time 300

Interface       Port ID                    Designated              Port ID
Name            Prio.Nbr    Cost Sts   Cost Bridge ID              Prio.Nbr
-------------- -------- --------- --- ------- -------------------- --------
Fa0/1           128.1       19 FWD     0 32769 0009.430f.a400 128.1
Fa0/2           128.2       19 FWD     0 32769 0009.430f.a400 128.2
```

In the previous sample outputs, note that ALSwitch2 is the root bridge, and the active links between the switches have the lower port numbers.

Step 2

Configure the DLSwitch to be the primary root bridge. This lowers the bridge priority automatically.

The switch with the lower Bridge ID (BID) determines the root bridge priority. The BID consists of the root bridge priority and the MAC address assigned to the switch. The BID is not a real number. The root bridge priority is expressed in decimal form, and the MAC address is expressed in HEX. The default bridge priority has a value of 32768. The current root bridge in the previous sample output is ALSwitch2 because it has a lower MAC address.

The root bridge priority is at the beginning of the BID. The bridge priority is a large number. The root bridge priority always determines the length of the BID because the MAC address is a fixed length.

Newer Cisco switches default to PVST. VLAN 1 is used for this configuration. The available priority value range is 0 to 61440 in increments of 4096. The default value is 32768. The lower the number, the more likely the switch will be chosen as the root switch. Valid priority values are 0, 4096, 8192, 12288, 16384, 20480, 24576, 28672, 32768, 36864, 40960, 45056, 49152, 53248, 57344, and 61440. All other values are rejected.

For Catalyst 3550 switches with the extended system ID release 12.1(8)EA1 and later, you can use the **spanning-tree vlan 1 root primary** command to set the switch priority to 24576. If all other switches in the VLAN have the default priority, this switch becomes the root bridge for VLAN 1.

Console into the DLSwitch. Configure it to be the primary root bridge, as shown here, even if it is already the root bridge:

```
DLSwitch(config)#spanning-tree vlan 1 root primary
 vlan 1 bridge priority set to 24576
 vlan 1 bridge max aging time unchanged at 20
 vlan 1 bridge hello time unchanged at 2
 vlan 1 bridge forward delay unchanged at 15
```

With the **show spanning-tree** command, verify that the DLSwitch either is or became the root bridge and that the bridge priority changed to 24577, as shown in the sample output:

```
DLSwitch#show spanning-tree

VLAN0001
  Spanning tree enabled protocol ieee
  Root ID    Priority    24577
             Address     000a.b701.f700
             This bridge is the root
             Hello Time   2 sec  Max Age 20 sec  Forward Delay 15 sec

  Bridge ID  Priority    24577  (priority 24576 sys-id-ext 1)
             Address     000a.b701.f700
             Hello Time   2 sec  Max Age 20 sec  Forward Delay 15 sec
             Aging Time 300

Interface      Port ID                 Designated                Port ID
Name           Prio.Nbr    Cost Sts    Cost Bridge ID            Prio.Nbr
-------------- -------- --------- --- ------- -------------------- --------
Fa0/1          128.1         19 FWD    0 24577 000a.b701.f700 128.1
Fa0/2          128.2         19 FWD    0 24577 000a.b701.f700 128.2
Fa0/3          128.3         19 FWD    0 24577 000a.b701.f700 128.3
Fa0/4          128.4         19 FWD    0 24577 000a.b701.f700 128.4
```

Notice that all the port statuses are forwarding. All ports on a root bridge become designated ports. Designated ports are always in the forwarding state.

Console into the ALSwitch1. Verify the spanning-tree status:

```
ALSwitch1#show spanning-tree
VLAN0001
  Spanning tree enabled protocol ieee
  Root ID    Priority    24577
             Address     000a.b701.f700
             Cost        19
             Port        1 (FastEthernet0/1)
             Hello Time   2 sec  Max Age 20 sec  Forward Delay 15 sec

  Bridge ID  Priority    32769  (priority 32768 sys-id-ext 1)
             Address     000a.8afc.dd80
             Hello Time   2 sec  Max Age 20 sec  Forward Delay 15 sec
             Aging Time 300

Interface      Port ID                 Designated                Port ID
Name           Prio.Nbr    Cost Sts    Cost Bridge ID            Prio.Nbr
-------------- -------- --------- --- ------- -------------------- --------
Fa0/1          128.1         19 FWD    0 24577 000a.b701.f700 128.1
Fa0/2          128.2         19 BLK    0 24577 000a.b701.f700 128.2
```

Notice that the root bridge priority is now 24577.

Console into ALSwitch2. Verify the spanning-tree status:

```
ALSwitch2#show spanning-tree

VLAN0001
  Spanning tree enabled protocol ieee
  Root ID    Priority    24577
             Address     000a.b701.f700
             Cost        19
             Port        1 (FastEthernet0/1)
             Hello Time  2 sec  Max Age 20 sec  Forward Delay 15 sec

  Bridge ID  Priority    32769  (priority 32768 sys-id-ext 1)
             Address     0009.430f.a400
             Hello Time  2 sec  Max Age 20 sec  Forward Delay 15 sec
             Aging Time 300

Interface      Port ID                    Designated              Port ID
Name           Prio.Nbr    Cost Sts       Cost Bridge ID          Prio.Nbr
-------------- -------- --------- ---      ------- ------------------ --------
Fa0/1          128.1          19 FWD         0 24577 000a.b701.f700 128.3
Fa0/2          128.2          19 BLK         0 24577 000a.b701.f700 128.4
```

Step 3

Force interface Fast Ethernet 0/2 to be the active link between DLSwitch and ALSwitch1. The active link is currently interface Fast Ethernet 0/1.

Console into ALSwitch1. Verify the current port status:

```
ALSwitch1#show spanning-tree

VLAN0001
  Spanning tree enabled protocol ieee
  Root ID    Priority    24577
             Address     000a.b701.f700
             Cost        19
             Port        1 (FastEthernet0/1)
             Hello Time  2 sec  Max Age 20 sec  Forward Delay 15 sec

  Bridge ID  Priority    32769  (priority 32768 sys-id-ext 1)
             Address     000a.8afc.dd80
             Hello Time  2 sec  Max Age 20 sec  Forward Delay 15 sec
             Aging Time 300

Interface      Port ID                    Designated              Port ID
Name           Prio.Nbr    Cost Sts       Cost Bridge ID          Prio.Nbr
-------------- -------- --------- ---      ------- ------------------ --------
Fa0/1          128.1          19 FWD         0 24577 000a.b701.f700 128.1
Fa0/2          128.2          19 BLK         0 24577 000a.b701.f700 128.2
```

The higher number port, which is fa 0/2, is in a blocking state. Both links have port costs of 19.

1. How is port path cost determined?

Configure port cost to force interface Fast Ethernet 0/2 to become the active uplink. As with the bridge priority, the lower cost is preferred when selecting the active link. Set the link that is currently blocked to a cost of 1 and the other link to a cost of 100. Note that you can change either value to produce the desired results.

Change the port cost on the ALSwitch1:

```
ALSwitch1(config-if)#interface fastethernet 0/1
ALSwitch1(config-if)#spanning-tree cost 100
ALSwitch1(config-if)#interface fastethernet 0/2
ALSwitch1(config-if)#spanning-tree cost 1
```

Verify that the port cost and interface status have changed, as shown in the sample output:

```
ALSwitch1#show spanning-tree

VLAN0001
  Spanning tree enabled protocol ieee
  Root ID    Priority    24577
             Address     000a.b701.f700
             Cost        19
             Port        2 (FastEthernet0/2)
             Hello Time   2 sec  Max Age 20 sec  Forward Delay 15 sec

  Bridge ID  Priority    32769  (priority 32768 sys-id-ext 1)
             Address     000a.8afc.dd80
             Hello Time   2 sec  Max Age 20 sec  Forward Delay 15 sec
             Aging Time 300

Interface       Port ID                      Designated              Port ID
Name            Prio.Nbr      Cost Sts     Cost Bridge ID            Prio.Nbr
--------------- --------- ---------- --- ------- ------------------- --------
Fa0/1           128.1         100 BLK        0 24577 000a.b701.f700 128.1
Fa0/2           128.2           1 FWD        0 24577 000a.b701.f700 128.2
```

2. What changed?

Console into DLSwitch and configure the same changes for consistency:

```
DLSwitch(config-if)#interface fastethernet 0/1
DLSwitch(config-if)#spanning-tree cost 100
DLSwitch(config-if)#interface fastethernet 0/2
DLSwitch(config-if)#spanning-tree cost 1
```

Use the **show spanning-tree** command to view STP configuration changes:

```
DLSwitch#show spanning-tree


VLAN0001

  Spanning tree enabled protocol ieee

  Root ID    Priority    24577

             Address     000a.b701.f700

             This bridge is the root

             Hello Time   2 sec  Max Age 20 sec  Forward Delay 15 sec


  Bridge ID  Priority    24577  (priority 24576 sys-id-ext 1)

             Address     000a.b701.f700

             Hello Time   2 sec  Max Age 20 sec  Forward Delay 15 sec

             Aging Time 300
```

```
Interface      Port ID                      Designated              Port ID
Name           Prio.Nbr      Cost Sts       Cost Bridge ID          Prio.Nbr
-------------- -------- ---------- ---       ------- ------------------- --------

Fa0/1          128.1        100 FWD            0 24577 000a.b701.f700 128.1

Fa0/2          128.2          1 FWD            0 24577 000a.b701.f700 128.2

Fa0/3          128.3         19 FWD            0 24577 000a.b701.f700 128.3

Fa0/4          128.4         19 FWD            0 24577 000a.b701.f700 128.4
```

You have forced interface Fast Ethernet 0/2 to become the active link.

Step 4

PVST+ is enabled automatically on 802.1Q trunks. No user configuration is required. PVST+ does not affect the external spanning-tree behavior on access ports and Inter-Switch Link (ISL) trunks. Cisco IOS supports a maximum of 128 spanning-tree instances.

Console into DLSwitch. Add additional VLANs and then use the **show spanning-tree** command to monitor spanning-tree behavior:

```
DLSwitch#vlan database
DLSwitch(vlan)#vlan 10 name Accounting
VLAN 10 added:
    Name: Accounting
DLSwitch(vlan)#vlan 20 name Marketing
VLAN 20 added:
    Name: Marketing
DLSwitch(vlan)#exit
APPLY completed.
Exiting....

DLSwitch#show spanning-tree

VLAN0001
  Spanning tree enabled protocol ieee
  Root ID    Priority    24577
             Address     000a.b701.f700
             This bridge is the root
             Hello Time   2 sec  Max Age 20 sec  Forward Delay 15 sec

  Bridge ID  Priority    24577  (priority 24576 sys-id-ext 1)
             Address     000a.b701.f700
             Hello Time   2 sec  Max Age 20 sec  Forward Delay 15 sec
             Aging Time 300

Interface      Port ID                      Designated              Port ID
Name           Prio.Nbr      Cost Sts       Cost Bridge ID          Prio.Nbr
-------------- -------- ---------- ---       ------- ------------------- --------
Fa0/1          128.1        100 FWD            0 24577 000a.b701.f700 128.1
Fa0/2          128.2          1 FWD            0 24577 000a.b701.f700 128.2
Fa0/3          128.3         19 FWD            0 24577 000a.b701.f700 128.3
Fa0/4          128.4         19 FWD            0 24577 000a.b701.f700 128.4


VLAN0010
  Spanning tree enabled protocol ieee
  Root ID    Priority    32778
             Address     0009.430f.a400
             Cost        19
             Port        3 (FastEthernet0/3)
             Hello Time   2 sec  Max Age 20 sec  Forward Delay 15 sec
```

```
    Bridge ID  Priority    32778  (priority 32768 sys-id-ext 10)
               Address     000a.b701.f700
               Hello Time   2 sec  Max Age 20 sec  Forward Delay 15 sec
               Aging Time 300

Interface     Port ID                      Designated              Port ID
Name          Prio.Nbr    Cost Sts    Cost Bridge ID              Prio.Nbr
------------- --------- --------- --- ------- ------------------- --------
Fa0/1         128.1       100 FWD       19 32778 000a.b701.f700 128.1
Fa0/2         128.2         1 FWD       19 32778 000a.b701.f700 128.2
Fa0/3         128.3        19 FWD        0 32778 0009.430f.a400 128.1
Fa0/4         128.4        19 BLK        0 32778 0009.430f.a400 128.2


VLAN0020
  Spanning tree enabled protocol ieee
  Root ID    Priority    32788
             Address     0009.430f.a400
             Cost        19
             Port        3 (FastEthernet0/3)
             Hello Time   2 sec  Max Age 20 sec  Forward Delay 15 sec

    Bridge ID  Priority    32788  (priority 32768 sys-id-ext 20)
               Address     000a.b701.f700
               Hello Time   2 sec  Max Age 20 sec  Forward Delay 15 sec
               Aging Time 300

Interface     Port ID                      Designated              Port ID
Name          Prio.Nbr    Cost Sts    Cost Bridge ID              Prio.Nbr
------------- --------- --------- --- ------- ------------------- --------
Fa0/1         128.1       100 FWD       19 32788 000a.b701.f700 128.1
Fa0/2         128.2         1 FWD       19 32788 000a.b701.f700 128.2
Fa0/3         128.3        19 FWD        0 32788 0009.430f.a400 128.1
Fa0/4         128.4        19 BLK        0 32788 0009.430f.a400 128.2
```

Now three instances of spanning tree exist, but DLSwitch might not be the root bridge for all the VLANs as in the previous sample output. However, port cost is effective on all VLANs because it is applied to the interface.

Step 5

You can adjust the STP hello timers to decrease the convergence time. Use the **diameter** keyword to specify the Layer 2 network diameter. The diameter is the maximum number of switch hops between any two end stations in the Layer 2 network. When you specify the network diameter, the switch automatically sets an optimal hello time, forward-delay time, and maximum-age time for the network. This can reduce STP convergence time significantly. Use the **hello** keyword to override the automatically calculated hello time.

Use the **show spanning-tree vlan 1 bridge** command to check the current STP timers:

```
DLSwitch#show spanning-tree vlan 1 bridge
                                       Hello  Max  Fwd
Vlan                     Bridge ID     Time   Age  Dly  Protocol
--------------- -------------------------------- ----- --- --- --------
VLAN0001        24577 (24576,1) 000a.b701.f700   2    20  15   ieee
```

Use the **spanning-tree vlan 1 root primary diameter** command to change the timer:

```
DLSwitch(config)#spanning-tree vlan 1 root primary diameter 2
% This switch is already the root bridge of the VLAN0001 spanning tree
 vlan 1 bridge priority unchanged at 24576
 vlan 1 bridge max aging time set to 10
 vlan 1 bridge hello time unchanged at 2
 vlan 1 bridge forward delay set to 7
```

Use the **show spanning-tree vlan 1 bridge** command to check the current STP timers:

```
DLSwitch#show spanning-tree vlan 1 bridge
                                       Hello  Max  Fwd
Vlan                     Bridge ID     Time   Age  Dly  Protocol
---------------  ------------------------------  -----  ---  ---  --------
VLAN0001         24577 (24576,1) 000a.b701.f700    2    10    7   ieee
```

Only the forward delay and the max aging times were changed. You should use the **spanning-tree vlan 1 root primary** command with the **diameter** option to change the STP timers. Do not change default STP timers without careful consideration. If you do change them, do so only from the root bridge. You can use the following commands to change the STP timers:

> **spanning-tree vlan** *vlan-id* **hello-time** *seconds*
>
> **spanning-tree vlan** *vlan-id* **forward-time** *seconds*
>
> **spanning-tree vlan** *vlan-id* **max-age** *seconds*

Lab 3.10.4: Implementing MST

Estimated Time: 120 Minutes

Objective

In this lab, you implement Multiple Spanning Tree (MST) in a switched network. Figure 3-12 shows the topology for this lab.

Figure 3-12 Topology for Lab 3.10.4

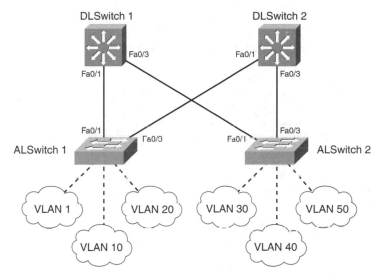

Scenario

PVST is the default STP behavior. However, it has two disadvantages. First, PVST is a Cisco proprietary protocol, so it cannot work with other vendor products. Second, PVST creates spanning-tree instances for every VLAN, which can be processor intensive. You will implement MST to reduce the processor utilization, and you will provide load balancing over the distribution layer switches.

The design is shown here.

Catalyst Type	Switch	VTP Domain	VTP Mode
3550	DLSwitch1	CORP	Server
3550	DLSwitch2	CORP	Client
2950	ALSwitch1	CORP	Client
2950	ALSwitch2	CORP	Client

Step 1

Do not cable the lab until you have erased all switch configurations and vlan.dat files and reloaded the switches:

```
switch#delete flash:vlan.dat
Delete filename [vlan.dat]?
Delete flash:vlan.dat? [confirm]
```

```
switch#
switch#erase startup-config
Erasing the nvram filesystem will remove all files! Continue? [confirm]
DLSwitchA#reload

System configuration has been modified. Save? [yes/no]:n
Proceed with reload? [confirm]
```

Cable the lab according to Figure 3-12. You must use crossover Cat 5 cables because the devices are similar.

Configure the host name and passwords on all switches.

Step 2

Create a trunk link between the switches. Set the port to trunking with 802.1Q encapsulation on DLSwitch1 and DLSwitch2 and then verify the configurations with the **show interfaces trunk** command on both switches.

Note: An error might appear because the port is set to auto encapsulation. If this occurs, enter the **switchport mode trunk** command after the **switchport trunk encapsulation dot1q** command.

```
DLSwitch1(config)#interface fastethernet 0/1
DLSwitch1(config-if)#switchport trunk encapsulation dot1q
DLSwitch1(config-if)#switchport mode trunk
DLSwitch1(config-if)#exit
DLSwitch1(config)#interface fastethernet 0/3
DLSwitch1(config-if)#switchport trunk encapsulation dot1q
DLSwitch1(config-if)#switchport mode trunk
DLSwitch1(config-if)#exit
```

```
DLSwitch2(config)#interface fastethernet 0/1
DLSwitch2(config-if)#switchport trunk encapsulation dot1q
DLSwitch2(config-if)#switchport mode trunk
DLSwitch2(config-if)#exit
DLSwitch2(config)#interface fastethernet 0/3
DLSwitch2(config-if)#switchport trunk encapsulation dot1q
DLSwitch2(config-if)#switchport mode trunk
DLSwitch2(config-if)#exit
```

The 2950 switches do not need the encapsulation to be configured. These switches default to 802.1Q. Some IOS versions do not include other options. Console into each access layer switch and configure trunking. Then verify the configurations with the **show interfaces trunk** command on both switches:

```
ALSwitch1(config)#interface fastethernet 0/1
ALSwitch1(config-if)#switchport mode trunk
ALSwitch1(config-if)#exit
ALSwitch1(config)#interface fastethernet 0/3
ALSwitch1(config-if)#switchport mode trunk
ALSwitch1(config-if)#exit
```

```
ALSwitch2(config)#interface fastethernet 0/1
ALSwitch2(config-if)#switchport mode trunk
ALSwitch2(config-if)#exit
ALSwitch2(config)#interface fastethernet 0/3
ALSwitch2(config-if)#switchport mode trunk
ALSwitch2(config-if)#exit
```

Step 3

Configure the VLAN database on DLSwitch1.

Create the VLANs on the DLSwitch1 and place the switch in VTP Server mode. Name the VLANs as shown here:

```
DLSwitch1#vlan database
DLSwitch1(vlan)#vtp domain CORP
DLSwitch1(vlan)#vtp server
DLSwitch1(vlan)#vlan 10 name Accounting
VLAN 10 modified:
    Name: Accounting
DLSwitch1(vlan)#vlan 20 name Marketing
VLAN 20 modified:
    Name: Marketing
DLSwitch1(vlan)#vlan 30 name Engineering
VLAN 30 added:
    Name: Engineering
DLSwitch1(vlan)#vlan 40 name HumanResource
VLAN 40 added:
    Name: HumanResource
DLSwitch1(vlan)#vlan 50 name GraphicDesign
VLAN 50 added:
    Name: GraphicDesign
DLSwitch1(vlan)#exit
```

Use the **show vlan** command to verify the configuration:

```
DLSwitch1#show vlan
VLAN Name                             Status    Ports
---- -------------------------------- --------- -------------------------------
1    default                          active    Fa0/2, Fa0/4, Fa0/5, Fa0/6
                                                Fa0/7, Fa0/8, Fa0/9, Fa0/10
                                                Fa0/11, Fa0/12, Fa0/13, Fa0/14
                                                Fa0/15, Fa0/16, Fa0/17, Fa0/18
                                                Fa0/19, Fa0/20, Fa0/21, Fa0/22
                                                Fa0/23, Fa0/24, Gi0/1, Gi0/2
10   Accounting                       active
20   Marketing                        active
30   Engineering                      active
40   HumanResource                    active
50   GraphicDesign                    active
1002 fddi-default                     active
1003 token-ring-default               active
1004 fddinet-default                  active
1005 trnet-default                    active

VLAN Type  SAID    MTU   Parent RingNo BridgeNo Stp  BrdgMode Trans1 Trans2
---- ----- ------- ----- ------ ------ -------- ---- -------- ------ ------
1    enet  100001  1500  -      -      -        -    -        0      0
10   enet  100010  1500  -      -      -        -    -        0      0
20   enet  100020  1500  -      -      -        -    -        0      0
30   enet  100030  1500  -      -      -        -    -        0      0
40   enet  100040  1500  -      -      -        -    -        0      0
50   enet  100050  1500  -      -      -        -    -        0      0
1002 fddi  101002  1500  -      -      -        -    -        0      0
1003 tr    101003  1500  -      -      -        -    srb      0      0
1004 fdnet 101004  1500  -      -      -        ieee -        0      0
1005 trnet 101005  1500  -      -      -        ibm  -        0      0

Remote SPAN VLANs
-------------------------------------------------------------------------------

Primary Secondary Type            Ports
------- --------- --------------- ------------------------------------------
```

Verify the trunk configuration on each switch with the **show vtp status** and **show vtp counters** commands:

```
DLSwitch1#show vtp status
VTP Version                       : 2
Configuration Revision            : 5
Maximum VLANs supported locally   : 1005
Number of existing VLANs          : 10
VTP Operating Mode                : Server
VTP Domain Name                   : CORP
VTP Pruning Mode                  : Disabled
VTP V2 Mode                       : Disabled
VTP Traps Generation              : Disabled
MD5 digest                        : 0xF2 0xB3 0x19 0x9B 0x2E 0xD3 0xE0 0xD5
Configuration last modified by 0.0.0.0 at 3-1-93 09:14:16
Local updater ID is 0.0.0.0 (no valid interface found)

DLSwitch1#show vtp counter
VTP statistics:
Summary advertisements received    : 225
Subset advertisements received     : 8
Request advertisements received    : 0
Summary advertisements transmitted : 234
Subset advertisements transmitted  : 27
Request advertisements transmitted : 2
Number of config revision errors   : 0
Number of config digest errors     : 0
Number of V1 summary errors        : 0


VTP pruning statistics:

Trunk         Join Transmitted Join Received    Summary advts received from
                                                non-pruning-capable device
------------- ---------------- ---------------- ---------------------------
Fa0/1              0                0                   0
Fa0/3              0                0                   0
```

Verify the configuration on all remaining switches.

Step 4

Console into DLSwitch2 and each access layer switch. Then configure the VTP mode to Client from the vlan database configuration mode, as shown in this generic example:

```
Switch#vlan database
Switch(vlan)#vtp client
Switch(vlan)#exit
```

Verify the VLAN configuration on all the switches with the **show vlan** command:

```
DLSwitch1#show vlan

VLAN Name                     Status    Ports
---- ------------------------ --------- -------------------------------
1    default                  active    Fa0/2, Fa0/4, Fa0/5, Fa0/6
                                        Fa0/7, Fa0/8, Fa0/9, Fa0/10
                                        Fa0/11, Fa0/12, Gi0/1, Gi0/2

10   Accounting               active
20   Marketing                active
30   Engineering              active
40   HumanResource            active
50   GraphicDesign            active
1002 fddi-default             active
1003 token-ring-default       active
1004 fddinet-default          active
1005 trnet-default            active
```

```
VLAN Type   SAID    MTU   Parent RingNo BridgeNo Stp  BrdgMode Trans1 Trans2
---- -----  ------  ----- ------ ------ -------- ---- -------- ------ ------
1    enet   100001  1500  -      -      -        -    -        0      0
10   enet   100010  1500  -      -      -        -    -        0      0
20   enet   100020  1500  -      -      -        -    -        0      0
30   enet   100030  1500  -      -      -        -    -        0      0
40   enet   100040  1500  -      -      -        -    -        0      0
50   enet   100050  1500  -      -      -        -    -        0      0

VLAN Type   SAID    MTU   Parent RingNo BridgeNo Stp  BrdgMode Trans1 Trans2
---- -----  ------  ----- ------ ------ -------- ---- -------- ------ ------
1002 fddi   101002  1500  -      -      -        -    -        0      0
1003 tr     101003  1500  -      -      -        -    srb      0      0
1004 fdnet  101004  1500  -      -      -        ieee -        0      0
1005 trnet  101005  1500  -      -      -        ibm  -        0      0

Remote SPAN VLANs
------------------------------------------------------------------------------


Primary Secondary Type          Ports
------- --------- ------------- ------------------------------------------------
```

Step 5

Verify the default behavior of STP. Use the **show spanning-tree** command on all the switches:

```
ALSwitch2#show spanning-tree

VLAN0001
  Spanning tree enabled protocol ieee
  Root ID    Priority    32769
             Address     0009.430f.a400
             This bridge is the root
             Hello Time   2 sec  Max Age 20 sec  Forward Delay 15 sec

  Bridge ID  Priority    32769  (priority 32768 sys-id-ext 1)
             Address     0009.430f.a400
             Hello Time   2 sec  Max Age 20 sec  Forward Delay 15 sec
             Aging Time 300

Interface    Port ID                   Designated              Port ID
Name         Prio.Nbr    Cost Sts      Cost Bridge ID          Prio.Nbr
------------ --------    --------- --- ---------- -------------------- --------
Fa0/1        128.1        19 FWD        0 32769 0009.430f.a400 128.1
Fa0/3        128.3        19 FWD        0 32769 0009.430f.a400

--Output Omitted--
```

1. Which switch became the root bridge and why?

_____

_____

2. Do all the VLANS have the same root bridge?

_____

This is not the most efficient behavior of spanning tree. Every VLAN has an instance of spanning tree.

Step 6

Multiple Spanning Tree Protocol (MST) uses Rapid Spanning Tree Protocol (RSTP) for rapid convergence. MST enables you to group VLANs into a spanning-tree instance. Each instance has a spanning-tree topology that is independent of the other spanning-tree instances. This architecture provides multiple forwarding paths for data traffic and enables load balancing. It also reduces the number of spanning-tree instances that are required to support numerous VLANs.

MST regions are used to partition the network. All switches in the same region must have the same VLAN-to-instance mapping, the same configuration revision number, and the same name.

MST groups a few VLANs into one spanning-tree instance, unlike PVST, which has a spanning-tree instance for every VLAN. This reduces the number of spanning-tree processes that are required and enhances the switch performance. MST supports 16 instances, numbered 0 through 15.

You configure MST in the MST configuration mode. You enable it in the global configuration mode.

Enter the MST configuration mode to configure MST on DLSwitch1. Map VLAN 1 through VLAN 50 to spanning-tree instance 1:

```
DLSwitch1(config)#spanning-tree mst configuration
DLSwitch1(config-mst)#instance 1 vlan 1-50
```

Name the MST region region1:

```
DLSwitch1(config-mst)#name region1
```

Configure the MST revision number:

```
DLSwitch1(config-mst)#revision 1
```

Verify the configuration with the **show pending** command:

```
DLSwitch1(config-mst)#show pending
Pending MST configuration
Name      [region1]
Revision  1
Instance  Vlans mapped
--------  -----------------------------------------------------------
0         51-4094
1         1-50
--------------------------------------------------------------------
```

The **exit** command applies the changes and returns the prompt to global configuration mode:

```
DLSwitch1(config-mst)#exit
DLSwitch1(config)#
```

You must enable MST after configuration.

Note: Traffic sometimes is disrupted when you change spanning-tree modes because all spanning-tree instances are stopped for the previous mode and restarted in the new mode:

```
DLSwitch1(config)#spanning-tree mode mst
```

Use the **show spanning-tree** command to view spanning-tree configuration:

```
DLSwitch1#show spanning-tree

MST00
   Spanning tree enabled protocol MST
   Root ID    Priority    32768
              Address     000a.b701.f700
              This bridge is the root
              Hello Time   2 sec  Max Age 20 sec  Forward Delay 15 sec
```

```
    Bridge ID  Priority    32768  (priority 32768 sys-id-ext 0)
               Address     000a.b701.f700
               Hello Time   2 sec  Max Age 20 sec  Forward Delay 15 sec
               Aging Time 0

Interface   Port ID                     Designated             Port ID
Name        Prio.Nbr     Cost Sts       Cost Bridge ID         Prio.Nbr
----------- -------- --------- ---  --------- ------------------- --------
Fa0/1       128.1         100 FWD         0 32768 000a.b701.f700 128.1
Fa0/3       128.3      200000 FWD         0 32768 000a.b701.f700 128.3


MST01
  Spanning tree enabled protocol MST
  Root ID    Priority    32769
             Address     000a.b701.f700
             This bridge is the root
             Hello Time   2 sec  Max Age 20 sec  Forward Delay 15 sec

   Bridge ID  Priority    32769  (priority 32768 sys-id-ext 1)
              Address     000a.b701.f700
              Hello Time   2 sec  Max Age 20 sec  Forward Delay 15 sec
              Aging Time 0

Interface   Port ID                     Designated             Port ID
Name        Prio.Nbr     Cost Sts       Cost Bridge ID         Prio.Nbr
----------- -------- --------- ---  --------- ------------------- --------
Fa0/1       128.1         100 FWD         0 32769 000a.b701.f700 128.1
Fa0/3       128.3      200000 FWD         0 32769 000a.b701.f700 128.3
```

Notice only two instances of spanning tree exist. The 0 instance was created by default, and the 1 instance was configured. The DLSwitch1 became the root bridge because it is the only switch that is running MST.

Use the following commands to configure and enable the remaining switches for MST:

```
DLSwitch2(config)#spanning-tree mst configuration
DLSwitch2(config-mst)#instance 1 vlan 1-50
DLSwitch2(config-mst)#name region1
DLSwitch2(config-mst)#revision 1
DLSwitch2(config-mst)#exit
DLSwitch2(config)#spanning-tree mode mst
```

```
ALSwitch2(config)#spanning-tree mst configuration
ALSwitch2(config-mst)#instance 1 vlan 1-50
ALSwitch2(config-mst)#name region1
ALSwitch2(config-mst)#revision 1
ALSwitch2(config-mst)#exit
ALSwitch2(config)#spanning-tree mode mst
```

```
ALSwitch1(config)#spanning-tree mst configuration
ALSwitch1(config-mst)#instance 1 vlan 1-50
ALSwitch1(config-mst)#name region1
ALSwitch1(config-mst)#revision 1
ALSwitch1(config-mst)#exit
ALSwitch1(config)#spanning-tree mode mst
```

Use the **show spanning-tree** command to verify spanning tree:

```
ALSwitch2#show spanning-tree

MST00
  Spanning tree enabled protocol MST
  Root ID    Priority    32768
             Address     0009.430f.a400
             This bridge is the root
             Hello Time   2 sec  Max Age 20 sec  Forward Delay 15 sec
```

```
Bridge ID  Priority    32768  (priority 32768 sys-id-ext 0)
           Address     0009.430f.a400
           Hello Time   2 sec  Max Age 20 sec  Forward Delay 15 sec
           Aging Time 0

Interface    Port ID                     Designated              Port ID
Name         Prio.Nbr    Cost Sts      Cost Bridge ID            Prio.Nbr
------------ --------- --------- ---   --------- ------------------- --------
Fa0/1        128.1       200000 FWD        0 32768 0009.430f.a400 128.1
Fa0/3        128.3       200000 FWD        0 32768 0009.430f.a400 128.3

MST01
  Spanning tree enabled protocol MST
  Root ID   Priority    32769
            Address     0009.430f.a400
            This bridge is the root
            Hello Time   2 sec  Max Age 20 sec  Forward Delay 15 sec

  Bridge ID  Priority    32769  (priority 32768 sys-id-ext 1)
             Address     0009.430f.a400
             Hello Time   2 sec  Max Age 20 sec  Forward Delay 15 sec
             Aging Time 0

Interface    Port ID                     Designated              Port ID
Name         Prio.Nbr    Cost Sts      Cost Bridge ID            Prio.Nbr
------------ --------- --------- ---   --------- ------------------- --------
Fa0/1        128.1       200000 FWD        0 32769 0009.430f.a400 128.1
Fa0/3        128.3       200000 FWD        0 32769 0009.430f.a400 128.3
```

Notice that in the previous sample output, the ALSwitch2 has become the root bridge.

Note: Whichever switch was the root bridge in Step 5 should resume being the root bridge.

Now the MST is configured on the network.

Step 7

Configure the distribution layer switch as the root bridge to make the network more efficient.

To configure a switch to become the root, use the **spanning-tree mst** *instance-id* **root** global configuration command. This changes the switch priority from the default value of 32768 to a significantly lower value. With the lowest root priority, this switch becomes the root switch for the specified spanning-tree instance.

When you enter this command, the switch checks the switch priorities of the root switches. The switch sets its own priority for the specified instance to 24576 because of the extended system ID support. If any root switch for the specified instance has a switch priority lower than 24576, the switch sets its own priority to 4096 less than the lowest switch priority.

Enter the following command on DLSwitch1:

```
DLSwitch1(config)#spanning-tree mst 1 root primary
mst 1 bridge priority set to 24576
```

Use the show **spanning-tree mst** *instance-number* command to view the changes.

```
DLSwitch1#show spanning-tree mst 1

###### MST01        vlans mapped:   1-50
Bridge      address 000a.b701.f700  priority  24577 (24576 sysid 1)
Root        this switch for MST01

Interface       role state cost       prio type
--------------- ---- ----- ---------  ---- ---------------------------------
Fa0/1           desg FWD   100        128  P2P
Fa0/3           desg FWD   200000     128  P2P
```

The DLSwitch1 is now the root bridge with a priority of 24576. Use the **spanning-tree mst 1 priority** command to set the MST root priority manually. The **spanning-tree mst 1 root primary** command configures the lowest priority dynamically.

Step 8

Configure DLSwitch2 as the secondary root to create fault tolerance in the network. DLSwitch2 acts as a backup root bridge if the primary root bridge fails.

When you configure a Catalyst 3550 switch that supports the extended system ID as the secondary root, you modify the spanning-tree switch priority from the default value of 32768 to 28672:

```
DLSwitch2(config)#spanning-tree mst 1 root secondary
mst 1 bridge priority set to 28672
```

Use the **show spanning-tree mst 1** command to view the STP priority:

```
DLSwitch2#show spanning-tree mst 1

###### MST01        vlans mapped:    1-50
Bridge      address 000a.b702.a200  priority  28673 (28672 sysid 1)
Root        address 000a.b701.f700  priority  24577 (24576 sysid 1)
            port    Fa0/1           cost      200100              rem hops 18

Interface       role state cost      prio type
--------------- ---- ----- --------- ---- -------------------------------
Fa0/1           root FWD   200000    120  P2P
Fa0/3           altn BLK   200000    128  P2P
```

Disconnect DLSwitch1 from the network and monitor. DLSwitch2 becomes the root bridge. Enter the **show spanning-tree mst 1** command on DLSwitch2:

```
DLSwitch2#show spanning-tree mst 1

###### MST01        vlans mapped:    1-50
Bridge      address 000a.b702.a200  priority  28673 (28672 sysid 1)
Root        this switch for MST01

Interface       role state cost      prio type
--------------- ---- ----- --------- ---- -------------------------------
Fa0/1           desg FWD   200000    128  P2P
Fa0/3           desg FWD   200000    128  P2P
```

DLSwitch2 is now the root bridge. Reconnect DLSwitch1 into the network.

Step 9

Group VLANs 30 through 60 into a second MST instance to provide load balancing.

One of the advantages of MST is that it permits load balancing. When you group VLANs into separate MST instances, a different root bridge is chosen for each MST instance.

Enter the following commands on all switches:

```
DLSwitch1(config)#spanning-tree mst configuration
DLSwitch1(config-mst)#instance 2 vlan 30-60
DLSwitch1(config-mst)#exit
```

Configure DLSwitch2 to become the root for MST instance 2:

```
DLSwitch2(config)#spanning-tree mst 2 root primary
```

Use the **show spanning-tree mst** command to monitor the change. DLSwitch1 is the root bridge for VLANs 1 to 29, and DLSwitch2 is the root bridge for VLANs 30 to 60.

Load balancing has been achieved.

Lab 3.10.5: Configuring Fast EtherChannel

Estimated Time: 90 Minutes

Objective

In this lab, you provide more bandwidth between Ethernet switches. Two 100-Mb full-duplex links combine to form a full duplex 200-Mb link for a total of 400 Mbps bandwidth. Figure 3-13 shows the topology for this lab.

Figure 3-13 Topology for Lab 3.10.5

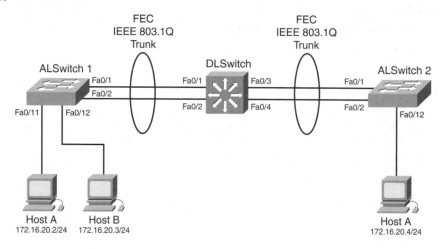

Scenario

The uplink from the distribution layer switch to the access layer switch has been saturated with bandwidth-intensive applications. The users in VLAN 20 who are served by the access layer switches need more bandwidth. Instead of purchasing new switches with Gigabit Ethernet capability, you will configure Fast EtherChannel (FEC). FEC is the Cisco method of scaling bandwidth for 100-Mb Ethernet links.

You will add a second 100-Mb Ethernet link between the distribution layer and the access layer switches. Then you will configure the switches to operate as one logical link.

The network design is shown here.

Catalyst Type	Switch	VTP Domain	VTP Mode
3550	DLSwitch	CORP	Server
2950	ALSwitch1	CORP	Client
2950	ALSwitch2	CORP	Client

The VLAN configuration information is shown here.

VLAN ID	VLAN Name	VLAN Subnet	DLSwitch	ALSwitch1	ALSwitch2
1	Native	172.16.1.0/24	All ports	Gb0/1-2 Fa0/1-4	Gb0/1-2 Fa0/1-4
10	Accounting	172.16.10.0/24		Fa0/5-8	Fa0/5-8
20	Marketing	172.16.20.0/24		Fa0/9-12	FA0/9-12
Trunk			802.1Q	802.1Q	802.1Q

Step 1

Wait until all switch configurations and vlan.dat files have been erased and switches have been reloaded before cabling the equipment.

Cable the lab according to Figure 3-13. You must use crossover Cat 5 cables because the devices are similar.

Configure the host name, passwords, and Telnet access on all the switches. Configure the interface VLAN 1 IP address on each switch and configure the IP address on each host.

Step 2

Configure the VTP domain CORP and create and name VLAN 10 and VLAN 20 on the DLSwitch. The 3550 switch defaults to the VTP Server mode, so you do not need to configure it. However, if necessary, the command to enable the Server mode is **vtp server** in the vlan database configuration mode:

```
DLSwitch#vlan database
DLSwitch(vlan)#vtp domain CORP
DLSwitch(vlan)#vlan 10 name Accounting
DLSwitch(vlan)#vlan 20 name Marketing
DLSwitch(vlan)#exit
```

Configure ALSwitch1 and ALSwitch2 as VTP clients and assign ports to the respective VLANs in each switch, as shown in the previous configuration table. You can use the **interface range** command to configure several interfaces at the same time. You must configure the interfaces to join the domain in Client mode:

```
ALSwitch1(vlan)#vtp client
ALSwitch1(vlan)#exit


ALSwitch1(config)#interface range fastethernet 0/5 - 8
ALSwitch1(config-if-range)#switchport mode access
ALSwitch1(config-if-range)#switchport access vlan 10
ALSwitch1(config-if-range)#exit
ALSwitch1(config)#interface range fastethernet 0/9 - 12
ALSwitch1(config-if-range)#switchport mode access
ALSwitch1(config-if-range)#switchport access vlan 20
ALSwitch1(config-if-range)#exit
```

Configure the VLAN database on ALSwitch2:

```
ALSwitch2(vlan)#vtp client
ALSwitch2(vlan)#exit
```

Place the ports on ALSwitch2 into the proper VLAN:

```
ALSwitch2(config)#interface range fastethernet 0/5 - 8
ALSwitch1(config-if-range)#switchport mode access
ALSwitch2(config-if-range)#switchport access vlan 10
ALSwitch2(config-if-range)#exit
ALSwitch2(config)#interface range fastethernet 0/9 - 12
ALSwitch1(config-if-range)#switchport mode access
ALSwitch2(config-if-range)#switchport access vlan 20
ALSwitch2(config-if-range)#exit
```

Step 3

Configure the ports that connect the switches to trunk mode.

Configure ports Fast Ethernet 0/1, 0/2, 0/3, and 0/4 on the DLSwitch.

Note: The encapsulation in some IOS versions might be set to auto, which does not allow the user to set the switchport mode to trunking. If this is the case, you need to configure the encapsulation first.

```
DLSwitch(config)#interface range fastethernet 0/1 - 4
DLSwitch(config-if-range)#switchport trunk encapsulation dot1q
DLSwitch(config-if-range)#switchport mode trunk
DLSwitch(config-if-range)#^Z
```

Configure ports Fast Ethernet 0/1 and Fast Ethernet 0/2 on ALSwitch1:

```
ALSwitch1(config)#interface range fastethernet 0/1 - 2
ALSwitch1(config-if-range)#switchport mode trunk
ALSwitch1(config-if-range)#^Z
```

Configure ports Fast Ethernet 0/1 and Fast Ethernet 0/2 on ALSwitch2:

```
ALSwitch2(config)#interface range fastethernet 0/1 - 2
ALSwitch2(config-if-range)#switchport mode trunk
ALSwitch2(config-if-range)#^Z
```

Step 4

An EtherChannel is composed of individual FEC or Gigabit EtherChannel (GEC) links, which are bundled into a single logical link, as shown in Figure 3-13. GEC provides full-duplex bandwidth of up to 16 Gbps between a switch and another switch or host.

FEC allows you to combine eight 100-Mbps full duplex links for a 1.6-Gbps full duplex link.

You must configure the Ethernet switches to treat two physical links as one logical link.

Configure DLSwitch to combine ports Fast Ethernet 0/1 and 0/2 into one logical channel:

```
DLSwitch(config)#interface range fastethernet 0/1 - 2
DLSwitch(config-if-range)#channel-group 1 mode desirable
DLSwitch(config-if-range)#^Z
```

Configure DLSwitch to combine ports Fast Ethernet 0/3 and 0/4 into another logical channel:

```
DLSwitch(config)#interface range fastethernet 0/3 - 4
DLSwitch(config-if-range)#channel-group 2 mode desirable
DLSwitch(config-if-range)#^Z
```

Configure ALSwitch1 to combine ports 0/1 and 0/2 into one logical channel:

```
ALSwitch1(config)#interface range fastethernet 0/1 - 2
ALSwitch1(config-if-range)#channel-group 1 mode desirable
ALSwitch1(config-if-range)#^Z
```

Configure the ALSwitch2 to combine ports 0/1 and 0/2 into one logical channel:

```
ALSwitch2(config)#interface range fastethernet 0/1 - 2
ALSwitch2(config-if-range)#channel-group 1 mode desirable
ALSwitch2(config-if-range)#^Z
```

The disadvantage of using FEC is that up to eight Fast Ethernet ports are unavailable for clients. When GEC is available, FEC is an expensive way to increase bandwidth. You can use EtherChannel technology with Gigabit links to create multi-gigabit logical links.

Step 5

Use the **show etherchannel summary** command to verify the fast EtherChannel connection:

```
DLSwitch#show etherchannel summary

Flags:  D - down          P - in port-channel
        I - stand-alone s - suspended
        R - Layer3       S - Layer2
        u - unsuitable for bundling
        U - port-channel in use
        d - default port
Group Port-channel  Ports
-----+------------+-----------------------------------------------------
1      Po1(SU)     Fa0/1(P)   Fa0/2(P)
2      Po2(SU)     Fa0/3(P)   Fa0/4(P)

DLSwitch#show etherchannel brief
               Channel-group listing:
               ----------------------

Group: 1
----------
Group state = L2
Ports: 2   Maxports = 8
Port-channels: 1 Max Port-channels = 1

Group: 2
----------
Group state = L2
Ports: 2   Maxports = 8
Port-channels: 1 Max Port-channels = 1
```

Step 6

Verify the port aggregation protocol (PAgP) operation.

The PAgP facilitates the automatic creation of EtherChannels by exchanging packets between Ethernet interfaces. By using PAgP, the switch learns the identity of partners that are capable of supporting PAgP and learns the capabilities of each interface. It then dynamically groups similarly configured interfaces into a single logical link, channel, or aggregate port. These interfaces are grouped based on hardware, administrative, and port parameter constraints. For example, PAgP groups the interfaces with the same speed, duplex, native VLAN, VLAN range, trunking status, and trunking type. After grouping the links into an EtherChannel, PAgP adds the group to the spanning tree as a single switch port.

Use the **show pagp neighbor** command on DLSwitch to verify PagP operation:

```
DLSwitch#show pagp neighbor
Flags: S - Device is sending Slow hello. C - Device is in Consistent state.
       A - Device is in Auto mode.       P - Device learns on physical port.
Channel group 1 neighbors
         Partner            Partner        Partner         Partner Group
Port     Name               Device ID      Port      Age  Flags   Cap.
Fa0/1    ALSwitch1          000a.8afc.dd80 Fa0/1     27s  SC      10001
Fa0/2    ALSwitch1          000a.8afc.dd80 Fa0/2      7s  SC      10001

Channel group 2 neighbors
         Partner            Partner        Partner         Partner Group
Port     Name               Device ID      Port      Age  Flags   Cap.
Fa0/3    ALSwitch2          0009.e8e3.f340 Fa0/1     14s  SC      10001
Fa0/4    ALSwitch2          0009.e8e3.f340 Fa0/2     20s  SC      10001
```

1. How is it shown that PAgP is operational?

_____

Use **show pagp ?** and some of the other **show** commands for EtherChannel and PAgP.

Step 7

Configure and monitor EtherChannel load balancing.

EtherChannel balances the traffic load across the links in a channel. It accomplishes this by reducing part of the binary pattern formed from the addresses in the frame to a numerical value that selects one of the links in the channel. EtherChannel load balancing can use either source MAC or destination MAC address forwarding.

Execute the **show etherchannel load-balance** command on the DLSwitch:

```
DLSwitch#show etherchannel load-balance
Source MAC address
```

The load balancing decision is based on source MAC address by default.

The remainder of this step requires the transfer of files between hosts to observe the load balancing. View the port lights on DLSwitch to determine which source MAC address is used.

Verify the default behavior by transferring a TFTP file from Host A to Host C.

1. Observe the lights on the DLSwitch. Which links were used?

_____

2. Transfer a file from Host B to Host C. Were the same links used as in the previous question between the two hosts?

_____

_____

3. Transfer a file from Host C to Host A. Which links did the file transfer use?

_____

_____

4. Transfer a file from Host C to Host B. Were the same links used as in the previous file transfer?

_____

_____

Step 8

Configure and monitor destination MAC address load balancing.

Configure the DLSwitch for load balancing based on the destination MAC address:

```
DLSwitch(config)#port-channel load-balance dst-mac
```

Verify destination MAC address load balancing with the **show etherchannel load-balance** command:

```
DLSwitch#show etherchannel load-balance
Destination MAC address
```

Verify the default behavior by transferring a TFTP file from Host A to Host C.

1. Observe the lights on the switch. Which link(s) did the file transfer over?

_____

_____

2. Transfer a file from Host B to Host C. Was the file transferred over the same link(s) as in the previous file transfer?

_____

_____

3. Transfer a file from Host C to Host A. Which link(s) did the file transfer use?

_____

_____

4. Transfer a file from Host C to Host B. Were the same links used as in the previous file transfer?

_____

_____

_____

Lab 3.10.6: Per-VLAN Spanning-Tree Load Balancing

Estimated Time: 90 Minutes

Objective

In this lab, you modify the default behavior of spanning tree for VLAN load balancing using Cisco IOS commands. Figure 3-14 shows the topology for this lab.

Figure 3-14 Topology for Lab 3.10.6

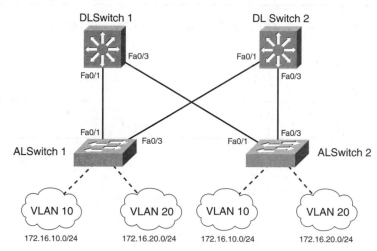

Scenario

Two distribution-layer and two access layer switches have been installed. The network administrator wants to ensure that the access layer switches do not become the root bridge for spanning tree. The distribution layer switch serves this function. The network administrator also wants to provide per VLAN load balancing. DLSwitch1 will need to become the root bridge for VLAN 10, and DLSwitch2 will need to become the root bridge for VLAN 20.

The network design is shown here.

Catalyst Type	Switch	VTP Domain	VTP Mode
3550	DLSwitch1	CORP	Server
3550	DLSwitch2	CORP	Client
2950	ALSwitch1	CORP	Client
2950	ALSwitch2	CORP	Client

The VLAN configuration information is shown here.

VLAN ID	VLAN Name	VLAN Subnet	DLSwitch1	DLSwitch2	ALSwitch1	ALSwitch2
1	Native	172.16.1.0	Fa0/1-10	Fa0/1-10	Fa0/1-4 Fa0/13 – 24	Fa0/1-4 Fa0/13 - 24
10	Accounting	172.16.10.0	Fa0/11-20	Fa0/11-20	Fa0/5-8	Fa0/5-8
20	Marketing	172.16.20.0	Fa0/21-24	Fa0/21-24	Fa0/9-12	Fa0/9-12
Trunk		802.1Q	802.1Q	802.1Q	802.1Q	802.1Q

Step 1

Do not cable the lab until you have erased all switch configurations and vlan.dat files and reloaded the switches.

Cable the lab according to Figure 3-14.

Configure the host name, passwords, and Telnet access on all the switches. Configure the interface VLAN 1 IP address on each switch.

Observe the default behavior of STP using the **show spanning-tree** command on all switches.

1. Which switch became the root bridge and why?

2. What command did you use to view the root bridge?

Step 2

Configure the trunking interfaces to create a trunk link between the switches. Set the port to trunking with 802.1Q encapsulation on DLSwitch1 and DLSwitch2.

Note: If an error is received because the port is set to auto encapsulation, enter the **switchport mode trunk** command after the **switchport trunk encapsulation dot1q** command.

```
DLSwitch1(config)#interface range fastethernet 0/1 , fastethernet 0/3
DLSwitch1(config-if-range)#switchport trunk encapsulation dot1q
DLSwitch1(config-if-range)#switchport mode trunk
DLSwitch1(config-if-range)#^Z
```

```
DLSwitch2(config)#interface range fastethernet 0/1 , fastethernet 0/3
DLSwitch2(config-if-range)#switchport trunk encapsulation dot1q
DLSwitch2(config-if-range)#switchport mode trunk
DLSwitch2(config-if-range)#^Z
```

You do not need to configure the encapsulation for the 2950 switches. These switches default to 802.1Q. Some IOS versions do not offer other options. Console into each access level switch and configure trunking:

```
ALSwitch1(config)#interface range fastethernet 0/1 , fastethernet 0/3
ALSwitch1(config-if-range)#switchport mode trunk
ALSwitch1(config-if-range)#^Z
```

```
ALSwitch2(config)#interface range fastethernet 0/1 , fastethernet 0/3
ALSwitch2(config-if-range)#switchport mode trunk
ALSwitch2(config-if-range)#^Z
```

Step 3

Console into DLSwitch1 and configure the vtp domain CORP, Server mode, and appropriate VLANs and names:

```
DLSwitch1#vlan database
DLSwitch1(vlan)#vtp domain CORP
DLSwitch1(vlan)#vtp server
DLSwitch1(vlan)#vlan 10 name Accounting
DLSwitch1(vlan)#vlan 20 name Marketing
DLSwitch1(vlan)#exit
```

Verify the trunk configuration with the **show vtp status** and **show vtp counters** commands:

```
DLSwitch1#show vtp status
VTP Version                     : 2
Configuration Revision          : 1
Maximum VLANs supported locally : 1005
Number of existing VLANs        : 7
VTP Operating Mode              : Server
VTP Domain Name                 : CORP
VTP Pruning Mode                : Disabled
VTP V2 Mode                     : Disabled
VTP Traps Generation            : Disabled
MD5 digest                      : 0xB4 0x57 0x1A 0x95 0x99 0x85 0x6D 0x49
Configuration last modified by 0.0.0.0 at 3-1-93 00:13:27
Local updater ID is 0.0.0.0 (no valid interface found)

DLSwitch1#show vtp counters
VTP statistics:
Summary advertisements received   : 32
Subset advertisements received    : 2
Request advertisements received   : 3
Summary advertisements transmitted : 44
Subset advertisements transmitted  : 3
Request advertisements transmitted : 0
Number of config revision errors  : 0
Number of config digest errors    : 0
Number of V1 summary errors       : 0


VTP pruning statistics:

Trunk        Join Transmitted Join Received    Summary advts received from
                                               non-pruning-capable device
------------ ---------------- ---------------- ---------------------------
Fa0/1               0                0                   0
Fa0/3               0                1                   0
```

Assign ports to the respective VLANs in DLSwitch1, as shown in the following code. You can use the **interface range** command to configure several interfaces at the same time:

```
DLSwitch1(config)#interface range fastethernet 0/11 - 20
DLSwitch1(config-if-range)#switchport mode access
DLSwitch1(config-if-range)#switchport access vlan 10
DLSwitch1(config)#interface range fastethernet 0/21 - 24
DLSwitch1(config-if-range)#switchport mode access
DLSwitch1(config-if-range)#switchport access vlan 20
```

Configure DLSwitch2 as a VTP client and assign ports to the respective VLANs, as shown in the following code. You can use the **interface range** command to configure several interfaces at the same time:

```
DLSwitch2#vlan database
DLSwitch2(vlan)#vtp client
DLSwitch2(vlan)#exit
DLSwitch2#config terminal
DLSwitch2(config)#interface range fastethernet 0/11 - 20
DLSwitch2(config-if-range)#switchport mode access
DLSwitch2(config-if-range)#switchport access vlan 10
DLSwitch2(config-if-range)#interface range fastethernet 0/21 - 24
DLSwitch2(config-if-range)#switchport mode access
DLSwitch2(config-if-range)#switchport access vlan 20
DLSwitch2(config-if-range)#^Z
```

Step 4

Configure ALSwitch1 and ALSwitch2 as VTP clients and assign ports to the respective VLANs in each switch, as shown here. You can use the **interface range** command to configure several interfaces at the same time:

```
ALSwitch1#vlan database
ALSwitch1(vlan)#vtp client
ALSwitch1(vlan)#exit
ALSwitch1#config terminal
ALSwitch1(config)#interface range fastethernet 0/5 - 8
ALSwitch1(config-if-range)#switchport mode access
ALSwitch1(config-if-range)#switchport access vlan 10
ALSwitch1(config-if-range)#interface range fastethernet 0/9 - 12
ALSwitch1(config-if-range)#switchport mode access
ALSwitch1(config-if-range)#switchport access vlan 20
ALSwitch1(config-if-range)#^Z
```

```
ALSwitch2#vlan database
ALSwitch2(vlan)#vtp client
ALSwitch2(vlan)#exit
ALSwitch2#config terminal
ALSwitch2(config)#interface range fastethernet 0/5 - 8
ALSwitch2(config-if-range)#switchport mode access
ALSwitch2(config-if-range)#switchport access vlan 10
ALSwitch2(config-if-range)#interface range fastethernet 0/9 - 12
ALSwitch2(config-if-range)#switchport mode access
ALSwitch2(config-if-range)#switchport access vlan 20
ALSwitch2(config-if-range)#^Z
```

Console into each switch and verify the VTP and VLAN configurations with the **show vtp status** and **show vlan** commands.

Step 5

Verify the default behavior of STP. Use the **show spanning-tree** command on all the switches:

```
ALSwitch2#show spanning-tree

VLAN0001
  Spanning tree enabled protocol ieee
  Root ID    Priority    32769
             Address     0009.430f.a400
             This bridge is the root
             Hello Time   2 sec  Max Age 20 sec  Forward Delay 15 sec

  Bridge ID  Priority    32769  (priority 32768 sys-id-ext 1)
             Address     0009.430f.a400
             Hello Time   2 sec  Max Age 20 sec  Forward Delay 15 sec
             Aging Time 300

Interface       Port ID                 Designated              Port ID
Name            Prio.Nbr    Cost Sts    Cost Bridge ID          Prio.Nbr
```

```
-------------- -------- -------- --- --------- ------------------ ----
Fa0/1          128.1             19 FWD        0 32769 0009.430f.a400 128.1
Fa0/3          128.3             19 FWD        0 32769 0009.430f.a400 128.3

VLAN0010
  Spanning tree enabled protocol ieee
  Root ID    Priority    32778
             Address     0009.430f.a400
             This bridge is the root
             Hello Time   2 sec  Max Age 20 sec  Forward Delay 15 sec

  Bridge ID  Priority    32778  (priority 32768 sys-id-ext 10)
             Address     0009.430f.a400
             Hello Time   2 sec  Max Age 20 sec  Forward Delay 15 sec
             Aging Time 300

Interface      Port ID                  Designated              Port ID
Name           Prio.Nbr    Cost Sts     Cost Bridge ID          Prio.Nbr
-------------- -------- --------- --- -------- ------------------ --------
Fa0/1          128.1             19 FWD        0 32778 0009.430f.a400 128.1
Fa0/3          128.3             19 FWD        0 32778 0009.430f.a400 128.3

VLAN0020
  Spanning tree enabled protocol ieee
  Root ID    Priority    32788
             Address     0009.430f.a400
             This bridge is the root
             Hello Time   2 sec  Max Age 20 sec  Forward Delay 15 sec

  Bridge ID  Priority    32788  (priority 32768 sys-id-ext 20)
             Address     0009.430f.a400
             Hello Time   2 sec  Max Age 20 sec  Forward Delay 15 sec
             Aging Time 300

Interface      Port ID                  Designated              Port ID
Name           Prio.Nbr    Cost Sts     Cost Bridge ID          Prio.Nbr
-------------- -------- --------- --- -------- ------------------ --------
Fa0/1          128.1             19 FWD        0 32788 0009.430f.a400 128.1
Fa0/3          128.3             19 FWD        0 32788 0009.430f.a400 128.3
```

1. Which switch became the root bridge and why?

_____

2. Did all the VLANs have the same root bridge?

_____

_____

This is not the most efficient behavior of spanning tree. In the previous sample output, ALSwitch2 became the root bridge. That means all traffic will go through ALSwitch2 even if it is not the best path to the destination. It would be more efficient to set a distribution layer switch as the root bridge.

Step 6

Set a distribution layer switch as the root bridge to increase network efficiency. To further increase efficiency, split the load between the two distribution layer switches. DLSwitch1 becomes the root bridge for VLAN 10, and DLSwitch2 becomes the root bridge for VLAN 20.

Cisco switches use PVST by default. The range for the priority value is 0 to 61440 in increments of 4096. The default value is 32768. The lower the number, the more likely the switch will be chosen as the root bridge. Valid priority values are 0, 4096,

8192, 12288, 16384, 20480, 24576, 28672, 32768, 36864, 40960, 45056, 49152, 53248, 57344, and 61440. All other values are rejected.

Change the root bridge priority for DLSwitch1 on VLAN 10 to 4096 to force DLSwitch1 to be the root bridge:

```
DLSwitch1(config)#spanning-tree vlan 10 priority 4096
```

Use the **show spanning-tree** command to verify which switch is the root bridge:

```
DLSwitch1#show spanning-tree

VLAN0001
  Spanning tree enabled protocol ieee
  Root ID    Priority    32769
             Address     0009.430f.a400
             Cost        19
             Port        3 (FastEthernet0/3)
             Hello Time  2 sec  Max Age 20 sec  Forward Delay 15 sec

   Bridge ID  Priority    32769  (priority 32768 sys-id-ext 1)
              Address     000a.b701.f700
              Hello Time  2 sec  Max Age 20 sec  Forward Delay 15 sec
              Aging Time 300

Interface      Port ID                    Designated              Port ID
Name           Prio.Nbr      Cost Sts     Cost Bridge ID          Prio.Nbr
------------   --------   --------- ---  ------- ------------------ --------
Fa0/1          128.1         19 FWD       19 32769 000a.b701.f700 128.1
Fa0/3          128.3         19 FWD        0 32769 0009.430f.a400 128.1

VLAN0010
  Spanning tree enabled protocol ieee
  Root ID    Priority    4106
             Address     000a.b701.f700
             This bridge is the root
             Hello Time  2 sec  Max Age 20 sec  Forward Delay 15 sec

   Bridge ID  Priority    4106  (priority 4096 sys-id-ext 10)
              Address     000a.b701.f700
              Hello Time  2 sec  Max Age 20 sec  Forward Delay 15 sec
              Aging Time 300

Interface      Port ID                    Designated              Port ID
Name           Prio.Nbr      Cost Sts     Cost Bridge ID          Prio.Nbr
------------   --------   --------- ---  ------- ------------------ --------
Fa0/1          128.1         19 FWD        0  4106 000a.b701.f700 128.1
Fa0/3          128.3         19 FWD        0  4106 000a.b701.f700 128.3

VLAN0020
  Spanning tree enabled protocol ieee
  Root ID    Priority    32788
             Address     0009.430f.a400
             Cost        19
             Port        3 (FastEthernet0/3)
             Hello Time  2 sec  Max Age 20 sec  Forward Delay 15 sec

   Bridge ID  Priority    32788  (priority 32768 sys-id-ext 20)
              Address     000a.b701.f700
              Hello Time  2 sec  Max Age 20 sec  Forward Delay 15 sec
              Aging Time 300

Interface      Port ID                    Designated              Port ID
Name           Prio.Nbr      Cost Sts     Cost Bridge ID          Prio.Nbr
------------   --------   --------- ---  ------- ------------------ --------
Fa0/1          128.1         19 FWD       19 32788 000a.b701.f700 128.1
Fa0/3          128.3         19 FWD        0 32788 0009.430f.a400 128.1
```

Notice that the root bridge priority changed only for VLAN 10, and DLSwitch1 is the root bridge.

You will configure DLSwitch2 as the root bridge for VLAN 20. You can configure a switch to be the root using the **spanning-tree vlan** *vlan-id* **root primary** command. This sets the default root priority to 24576. If a switch has a lower priority than 24576, this command sets the priority to 4096 lower than the lowest priority to guarantee that the switch will become root:

```
DLSwitch2(config)#spanning-tree vlan 20 root primary
vlan 20 bridge priority set to 24576
vlan 20 bridge max aging time unchanged at 20
vlan 20 bridge hello time unchanged at 2
vlan 20 bridge forward delay unchanged at 15
```

Verify the change with the **show spanning-tree vlan 20** command:

```
DLSwitch2#show spanning-tree vlan 20

VLAN0020
  Spanning tree enabled protocol ieee
  Root ID    Priority    24596
             Address     000a.b702.a200
             This bridge is the root
             Hello Time   2 sec  Max Age 20 sec  Forward Delay 15 sec

  Bridge ID  Priority    24596  (priority 24576 sys-id-ext 20)
             Address     000a.b702.a200
             Hello Time   2 sec  Max Age 20 sec  Forward Delay 15 sec
             Aging Time 300

Interface      Port ID                     Designated            Port ID
Name           Prio.Nbr    Cost Sts     Cost Bridge ID          Prio.Nbr
-------------- --------- ---------- --- ------- ------------------- --------
Fa0/1          128.1          19 FWD        0 24596 000a.b702.a200 128.1
Fa0/3          128.3          19 FWD        0 24596 000a.b702.a200 128.3
```

The root bridge priority has changed to 24576, and DLSwitch2 has become the root bridge.

All traffic that originates from VLAN 10 and crosses the distribution layer is forwarded to DLSwitch1. All traffic from VLAN 20 that crosses the distribution layer is forwarded to DLSwitch2.

Lab 3.10.7: Port Level Tuning to Control STP Behavior

Estimated Time: 120 Minutes

Objective

In this lab, you use PortFast, UplinkFast, Bridge Protocol Data Unit (BPDU) guard, Root guard, and UniDirectional Link Detection (UDLD) to control STP behavior on a port. Figure 3-15 shows the topology for this lab.

Figure 3-15 Topology for Lab 3.10.7

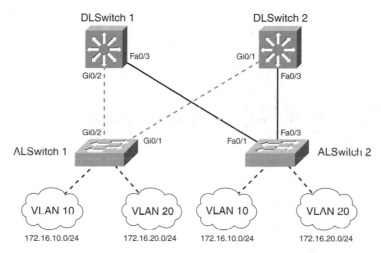

Note: This lab uses fiber connections between the ALSwitch1 and DLSwitch1 and DLSwitch2. If the available equipment does not have fiber connections, use Cat 5 crossover cables between the Gigabit Ethernet interfaces. However, you cannot follow exactly instructions and tasks for Steps 8 (UplinkFast) and 11 (UDLD), and certain results will not be as indicated or expected.

Scenario

A new redundant switched network has just been implemented. The default behavior of STP has created some undesirable results. The ports take up to 50 seconds to reach forwarding state, which prevents Dynamic Host Configuration Protocol (DHCP) clients from receiving an IP address during normal bootup. You will use PortFast to prevent this problem in the future.

Enabling PortFast can create a security risk in a switched network. A port that you configure with PortFast goes into blocking state if it receives a BPDU. An unauthorized device can send BPDUs into the PortFast interface and set a port to blocking. When the port is in blocking state, it accepts all BPDUs. This could lead to false STP information that enters the switched network and could cause unexpected STP behavior. You will use Bridge Guard Data Unit (BGDU) to prevent unauthorized BPDUs from entering the switched network through PortFast-enabled ports.

When the active uplink between the two switches is broken, it takes the redundant link 30 seconds to complete the spanning-tree process before bringing up the backup, or blocked, link. This results in a temporary network outage for users. You must use UplinkFast to reduce STP convergence time.

ALSwitch2 is connected with a slower and less reliable connection. The network administrator wants to prevent the ALSwitch2 from becoming the root bridge or from being in the path to the root bridge. Avoid ALSwitch2 as much as possible. You will use root guard to prevent ALSwitch2 from becoming the root bridge.

ALSwitch1 is connected to the distribution layer with Gigabit Ethernet links. If the transmit or receive link in a fiber cable is disconnected or cut, it could lead to a unidirectional link. Unidirectional links can transmit or receive data, but not both. Unidirectional links have an adverse effect on the network. Use the UDLD protocol to prevent unidirectional links from occurring.

The network design is shown here.

Catalyst Type	Switch	VTP Domain	VTP Mode
3550	DLSwitch1	CORP	Server
3550	DLSwitch2	CORP	Client
2950	ALSwitch1	CORP	Client
2950	ALSwitch2	CORP	Client

The VLAN configuration information is shown here.

VLAN ID	VLAN Name	VLAN Subnet	DLSwitch1 and DLSwitch2	ALSwitch1 and ALSwitch2
1	Native	172.16.1.0/24	All ports	Gi0/1-2 Fa0/1-4 Fa0/12-24
10	Accounting	172.16.10.0/24		Fa0/5-8
20	Marketing	172.16.20.0/24		FA0/9-12
Trunk		802.1Q	802.1Q	802.1Q

Step 1

Do not cable the lab until you have erased all switch configurations and vlan.dat files and reloaded the switches.

Cable the lab according to Figure 3-15. You must use crossover Cat 5 cables because the devices are similar. Use fiber cable among ALSwitch1, DLSwitch1, and DLSwitch2 if the switches support the media.

Configure the host name, passwords, and Telnet access to all the switches. Configure the interface VLAN 1 IP address on each switch.

Step 2

Observe the default behavior of STP using the **show spanning-tree** command on all switches.

1. Which switch became the root bridge?

_____

2. What command was used to find the root bridge?

_____

Step 3

Configure the trunking interfaces to create a trunk link between the switches. Set the port to trunking with 802.1Q encapsulation on DLSwitch1 and DLSwitch2.

Note: An error might appear because the port is set to auto encapsulation. If this occurs, enter the **switchport mode trunk** command after the **switchport trunk encapsulation dot1q** command:

```
DLSwitch1(config)#interface range gigabitethernet 0/2 , fastethernet 0/3
DLSwitch1(config-if-range)#switchport trunk encapsulation dot1q
DLSwitch1(config-if-range)#switchport mode trunk
DLSwitch1(config-if-range)#^Z
```

```
DLSwitch2(config)#interface range gigabitethernet 0/1 , fastethernet 0/3
DLSwitch2(config-if-range)#switchport trunk encapsulation dot1q
DLSwitch2(config-if-range)#switchport mode trunk
DLSwitch2(config-if-range)#^Z
```

You do not need to configure the encapsulation on the 2950 switches. These switches default to 802.1Q. Some IOS versions do not offer other options. Console into each access layer switch and configure trunking:

```
ALSwitch1(config)#interface range gigabitethernet 0/1 , gigabitethernet 0/2
ALSwitch1(config-if-range)#switchport mode trunk
ALSwitch1(config-if-range)#^Z
```

```
ALSwitch2(config)#interface range fastethernet 0/1 , fastethernet 0/3
ALSwitch2(config-if-range)#switchport mode trunk
ALSwitch2(config-if-range)#^Z
```

Verify the trunk configuration on each switch with the **show interfaces trunk** command.

Step 4

Console into DLSwitch1 and configure the vtp domain CORP, Server mode, and appropriate VLANs and names:

```
DLSwitch1#vlan database
DLSwitch1(vlan)#vtp domain CORP
DLSwitch1(vlan)#vtp server
DLSwitch1(vlan)#vlan 10 name Accounting
DLSwitch1(vlan)#vlan 20 name Marketing
DLSwitch1(vlan)#exit
```

Configure DLSwitch2 as a VTP client:

```
DLSwitch2#vlan database
DLSwitch2(vlan)#vtp client
DLSwitch2(vlan)#exit
```

Step 5

Configure ALSwitch1 and ALSwitch2 as VTP clients and assign ports to the respective VLANs in each switch. You can use the **interface range** command to configure several interfaces at the same time:

```
ALSwitch1#vlan database
ALSwitch1(vlan)#vtp client
ALSwitch1(vlan)#exit
ALSwitch1#config terminal
ALSwitch1(config)#interface range fastethernet 0/5 - 8
ALSwitch1(config-if-range)#switchport access vlan 10
ALSwitch1(config-if-range)#interface range fastethernet 0/9 - 12
ALSwitch1(config-if-range)#switchport access vlan 20
ALSwitch1(config-if-range)#^Z
```

```
ALSwitch2#vlan database
ALSwitch2(vlan)#vtp client
```

```
ALSwitch2(vlan)#exit
ALSwitch2#config terminal
ALSwitch2(config)#interface range fastethernet 0/5 - 8
ALSwitch2(config-if-range)#switchport mode access
ALSwitch2(config-if-range)#switchport access vlan 10
ALSwitch2(config-if-range)#interface range fastethernet 0/9 - 12
ALSwitch2(config-if-range)#switchport mode access
ALSwitch2(config-if-range)#switchport access vlan 20
ALSwitch2(config-if-range)#^Z
```

Console into each switch and verify the VTP and VLAN configurations with the **show vtp status** and **show vlan** commands.

Step 6

Configure DLSwitch1 as the root bridge.

Change the root bridge priority for each VLAN on DLSwitch1 to 4096:

```
DLSwitch1(config)#spanning-tree vlan 1 priority 4096
DLSwitch1(config)#spanning-tree vlan 10 priority 4096
DLSwitch1(config)#spanning-tree vlan 20 priority 4096
```

Verify that DLSwitch1 is the root bridge for each VLAN with the **show spanning-tree** command:

```
DLSwitch1#show spanning-tree

VLAN0001
  Spanning tree enabled protocol ieee
  Root ID    Priority    4097
             Address     000a.b701.f700
             This bridge is the root
             Hello Time   2 sec  Max Age 20 sec  Forward Delay 15 sec

  Bridge ID  Priority    4097   (priority 4096 sys-id-ext 1)
             Address     000a.b701.f700
             Hello Time   2 sec  Max Age 20 sec  Forward Delay 15 sec
             Aging Time 300

Interface      Port ID                    Designated              Port ID
Name           Prio.Nbr    Cost Sts       Cost Bridge ID          Prio.Nbr
------------   --------  --------- ---  --------- ------------------- --------
Fa0/3          128.3         19 FWD         0  4097 000a.b701.f700 128.3
Gi0/2          128.26         4 FWD         0  4097 000a.b701.f700 128.26


VLAN0010
  Spanning tree enabled protocol ieee
  Root ID    Priority    4106
             Address     000a.b701.f700
             This bridge is the root
             Hello Time   2 sec  Max Age 20 sec  Forward Delay 15 sec

  Bridge ID  Priority    4106   (priority 4096 sys-id-ext 10)
             Address     000a.b701.f700
             Hello Time   2 sec  Max Age 20 sec  Forward Delay 15 sec
             Aging Time 300

Interface      Port ID                    Designated              Port ID
Name           Prio.Nbr    Cost Sts       Cost Bridge ID          Prio.Nbr
------------   --------  --------- ---  --------- ------------------- --------
Fa0/3          128.3         19 FWD         0  4106 000a.b701.f700 128.3
Gi0/2          128.26         4 FWD         0  4106 000a.b701.f700 128.26


VLAN0020
  Spanning tree enabled protocol ieee
  Root ID    Priority    4116
             Address     000a.b701.f700
             This bridge is the root
```

```
          Hello Time   2 sec  Max Age 20 sec  Forward Delay 15 sec

  Bridge ID  Priority    4116   (priority 4096 sys-id-ext 20)
             Address     000a.b701.f700
             Hello Time   2 sec  Max Age 20 sec  Forward Delay 15 sec
             Aging Time 300

Interface    Port ID               Designated             Port ID
Name         Prio.Nbr    Cost Sts  Cost Bridge ID         Prio.Nbr
------------ --------- ---------- --- ---------- -------------------- --------
 Fa0/3       128.3         19 FWD      0  4116 000a.b701.f700 128.3
 Gi0/2       128.26         4 FWD      0  4116 000a.b701.f700 128.26
```

Step 7

Observe the default behavior of spanning tree. Connect a workstation to any of the switch ports on either access layer switch and turn on the workstation. After the operating system initializes the network interface card (NIC), the port turns yellow. The port is now active and starting the spanning-tree process. Watch the workstation boot up and watch the color of the link light. The workstation should make it through most of the startup before the link turns green and active. This is where DHCP has the opportunity to get an IP address while spanning tree is in listening and learning state.

It should take about 30 seconds for a new device to become active in a port.

Configure PortFast on the switch ports.

Configure Fast Ethernet ports 0/5 through 12 for PortFast on the access layer switches:

```
ALSwitch1(config)#interface range fastethernet 0/5 - 12
ALSwitch1(config-if-range)#spanning-tree portfast
```

Caution: Enable PortFast only on ports that are connected to a single host. If hubs, concentrators, switches, and bridges are connected to the interface when PortFast is enabled, temporary bridging loops can occur.

Configure PortFast on eight interfaces with the **range** command. Note that PortFast is effective only when the interfaces are in a non-trunking mode:

```
ALSwitch2(config)#interface range fastethernet 0/5 - 12
ALSwitch2(config-if-range)#spanning-tree portfast
```

Verify that PortFast is operating on the access layer switches.

Remove the workstation from the switch and plug it into any port that is configured with PortFast. The port should become active immediately. The access layer switch indicator light turns green without the yellow learning and listening period. Use the **show spanning-tree** command to check the state of each link.

1. How can PortFast create bridging loops?

Step 8

Observe what happens when the status of an uplink changes.

Remove the uplink cable between ALSwitch1 and DLSwitch1 while monitoring the backup link port. Observe whether the light on the switch is indicating a yellow blocked port, or use the **show spanning-tree** command.

It should take about 30 seconds for the backup uplink ports to become active. Reconnect the cable between ALSwitch1 and DLSwitch1.

UplinkFast is now enabled on ALSwitch2:

```
ALSwitch2(config)#spanning-tree uplinkfast
```

Use the following command to verify the UplinkFast configuration:

```
ALSwitch2#show spanning-tree summary total

Root bridge for: none.
Extended system ID is enabled.
PortFast BPDU Guard is disabled
EtherChannel misconfiguration guard is enabled
UplinkFast is enabled
BackboneFast is disabled
Default pathcost method used is short

Name                   Blocking Listening Learning Forwarding STP Active
---------------------- -------- --------- -------- ---------- ----------
3 vlans                     0         0        0        3          3

Station update rate set to 150 packets/sec.

UplinkFast statistics
---------------------
Number of transitions via uplinkFast (all VLANs)        : 0
Number of proxy multicast addresses transmitted (all VLANs) : 0
```

Disconnect the cable between ALSwitch1 and DLSwitch2 while monitoring the backup uplink port. The backup port should come up in less than 10 seconds.

Step 9

Use the global configuration mode to enable the BPDU guard feature on ALSwitch1:

```
ALSwitch1(config)#spanning-tree portfast bpduguard
```

When the BPDU guard feature is enabled on the switch, STP shuts down PortFast-enabled interfaces that receive BPDUs instead of putting them into a blocking state. PortFast-enabled interfaces do not receive BPDUs in a valid configuration. The receipt of a BPDU by a PortFast-enabled interface indicates an invalid configuration, such as the connection of an unauthorized device. The BPDU guard feature blocks BPDUs by placing the interface in the ErrDisable state. The BPDU guard feature provides a secure response to invalid configurations because the interface must be placed back in service manually.

Configure port Fast Ethernet 0/1 on ALSwitch1 to access mode with PortFast enabled:

```
ALSwitch1(config)#interface fastethernet 0/1
ALSwitch1(config-if)#switchport mode access
ALSwitch1(config-if)#spanning-tree portfast
ALSwitch1(config-if)#exit
```

Connect a cable between Fast Ethernet 0/1 on ALSwitch1 and Fast Ethernet 0/1 on DLSwitch1.

The following error should appear:

```
05:31:56: %SPANTREE-2-RX_PORTFAST: Received BPDU on PortFast
  enabled port. Disabling FastEthernet0/1.
05:31:56: %PM-4-ERR_DISABLE: bpduguard error detected on Fa0/1,
  putting Fa0/1 in err-disable state
05:31:57: %LINEPROTO-5-UPDOWN: Line protocol on Interface FastEthernet0/1, changed
  state to down
```

The switch receives the error and shuts down the port. This protects the switch from accepting false BPDUs.

Step 10

Prevent ALSwitch2 from becoming the root or from being in the path to the root.

The Layer 2 network of a service provider (SP) can include many connections to switches that the SP does not own. STP can reconfigure itself in this type of topology and select a customer switch as the STP root switch. You can configure the root-guard feature on interfaces that connect to switches outside of the customer network. You can use STP calculations to identify an interface in the customer network as the root port. Root guard places this interface in the root-inconsistent or blocked state to prevent the customer switch from becoming the root switch or from being in the path to the root.

Disable UplinkFast because you cannot use it with root guard:

```
ALSwitch2(config)#no spanning-tree uplinkfast
```

Configure all the DLSwitch1 and DLSwitch2 ports that connect to ALSwitch2 with root guard:

```
DLSwitch1(config)#interface fastethernet 0/3
DLSwitch1(config-if)#spanning-tree guard root
DLSwitch1(config-if)#exit
```

```
DLSwitch2(config)#interface fastethernet 0/3
DLSwitch2(config-if)#spanning-tree guard root
DLSwitch2(config-if)#exit
```

Configure ALSwitch2 with a lower STP priority than DLSwitch1 for VLAN 1. ALSwitch2 becomes the root for VLAN1 without root guard:

```
ALSwitch2(config)#spanning-tree vlan 1 priority 0
```

Issue the **show spanning-tree** command on DLSwitch1.

DLSwitch1 is still the root bridge for VLAN 1 on ALSwitch1 and DLSwitch2. Root guard prevented ALSwtch2 from becoming the root bridge.

Interface Fast Ethernet 0/3 on both the DLSwitch1 and DLSwitch2 are in the blocking state for VLAN 1, which essentially prevents VLAN 1 traffic from traversing the ALSwitch2 links.

Step 11

Disconnect one of the fiber connectors between ALSwitch1 and DLSwitch1. Observe the line status on the switches. A unidirectional link has just been created.

A unidirectional link occurs when the neighbor receives traffic that the local device sends, but the local device does not receive traffic from the neighbor. This indicates that the transmit or receive part of the connection is broken. This can be caused by a cut or disconnected cable.

UDLD is a Layer 2 protocol that enables devices that are connected through fiber-optic or twisted-pair Ethernet cables to monitor the physical configuration of the cables and detect a unidirectional link.

All connected devices must support UDLD for the protocol to identify and disable unidirectional links. When UDLD detects a unidirectional link, it shuts down the affected port and sends out an alert. Unidirectional links can cause a variety of problems, including spanning-tree topology loops.

Reconnect the transmit or receive cable to the switch.

Enable UDLD with the global configuration command **udld enable** on DLSwitch1, DLSwitch2, and ALSwitch1.

Note: This command affects only fiber-optic interfaces. Use the **udld** interface configuration command to enable UDLD on other interface types.

```
ALSwitch1(config)#udld enable
DLSwitch1(config)#udld enable
DLSwitch2(config)#udld enable
```

Disconnect one of the fiber connecters between ALSwitch1 and DLSwitch1. Observe what happens to the line status on the two switches.

UDLD administratively shuts down the port.

Chapter 4

Inter-VLAN Routing

Estimated Time: 90 Minutes

Objective

In this lab, you configure an external router to route inter-VLAN traffic. An external router that utilizes subinterfaces for inter-VLAN routing is also called *Router-on-a-Stick*. Figure 4-1 shows the topology for this lab.

Figure 4-1 Topology for Lab 4.3.1

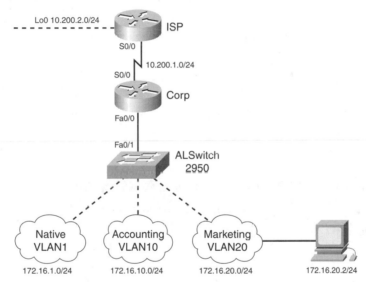

Scenario

Network loads and management issues require the segmentation of a network from a single broadcast domain into three functional areas. You can accomplish this by implementing VLANs throughout the switched network. The VLAN names are Accounting and Marketing for the users and the default names for the native network management VLAN.

After you decide on the subnet ranges and VLAN Trunking Protocol (VTP) configuration, you use a Cisco 2600 series router to implement Inter-VLAN routing. Inter-VLAN routing allows individuals and servers on the VLANs to exchange information. The 2600 Series WAN router already facilitates a WAN connection to the ISP and a 100-Mb Ethernet private zone. Because only one Ethernet connection is available on a private network, you must configure the router using the Router-on-a-Stick method to support Inter-VLAN routing.

The VTP design information is shown here:

VTP Domain	VTP Mode
CORP	Server

The VLAN configuration information is shown here:

VLAN ID	VLAN Name	VLAN Subnet	VLAN Gateway	Switch Ports
1	Default (Native)	172.16.1.0	172.16.1.1/24	Fa0/2-4 Fa0/13-24
10	Accounting	172.16.10.0	172.16.10.1/24	Fa0/5-8
20	Marketing	172.16.20.0	172.16.20.1/24	FA0/9-12
Trunk				Fa0/1 802.1Q

The 2600 Interface configuration information is shown here:

Interface	IP Address	VLAN
Fast Ethernet 0/0.1	172.16.1.1	1 Native
Fast Ethernet 0/0.10	172.16.10.1	10
Fast Ethernet 0/0.20	172.16.20.1	20
Serial0/0	10.200.1.2	

Step 1

Do not cable the lab until you have erased the router configurations, switch configurations, and switch vlan.dat file.

Delete the VLAN database if it exists on any switches, and clear the configuration:

```
switch#delete flash:vlan.dat
Delete filename [vlan.dat]?
Delete flash:vlan.dat? [confirm]
switch#
switch#erase startup-config
Erasing the nvram filesystem will remove all files! Continue? [confirm]
switch#reload

System configuration has been modified. Save? [yes/no]:n
Proceed with reload? [confirm]
```

Cable the lab according to Figure 4-1.

Step 2

Configure ISP for communication with the CORP router:

```
Router(config)#hostname ISP
ISP(config)#interface Loopback0
ISP(config-if)#ip address 10.200.2.1 255.255.255.0
```

```
ISP(config)#interface Serial0/0
ISP(config-if)#ip address 10.200.1.1 255.255.255.0
ISP(config-if)#clockrate 56000
ISP(config-if)#no shutdown
ISP(config)#ip route 172.16.0.0 255.255.0.0 10.200.1.2
```

The ISP router is not part of the main network. The static route provides a path back to the local network.

Configure the CORP router to communicate with the ISP router:

```
Router(config)#hostname CORP
CORP(config)#interface Serial0/0
CORP(config-if)#ip address 10.200.1.2 255.255.255.0
CORP(config-if)#no shutdown
CORP(config-if)#exit
CORP(config-if)#ip route 10.200.2.0 255.255.255.0 10.200.1.1
CORP(config)#exit
```

Verify the connectivity between the ISP and CORP routers.

1. How did you verify the connectivity?

Step 3

Set the duplex mode to full and enable the interface.

The router must now use the same trunking protocol to communicate with the switch. The two primary trunking protocols are the Cisco proprietary Inter-Switch Link (ISL) and 802.1q, or dot1q. This lab uses Dot1q trunking:

```
CORP(config)#interface fastethernet 0/0
CORP(config-if)#full-duplex
CORP(config-if)#no shutdown
```

You cannot configure the native VLAN on a subinterface for Cisco IOS releases that are earlier than 12.1(3)T. You need to configure the native VLAN IP address on the physical interface. You can configure other VLAN traffic on subinterfaces. Cisco IOS releases 12.1(3)T and later support native VLAN configuration on a subinterface with the **encapsulation** *encapsulation vlan_id* **native** command. You use this technique in the lab configuration.

Create a subinterface for each VLAN. Enable each subinterface with the proper trunking protocol and tie it to a particular VLAN with the **encapsulation** command.

Assign an IP address to each subinterface that hosts on the VLAN can use for a default gateway.

VLAN 1 Interface

```
CORP(config)#interface fastethernet 0/0.1
CORP(config-subif)#description Management VLAN 1
CORP(config-subif)#encapsulation dot1q 1 native
CORP(config-subif)#ip address 172.16.1.1 255.255.255.0
```

VLAN 10 Interface

```
CORP(config)#interface fastethernet 0/0.10
CORP(config-subif)#description Accounting VLAN 10
CORP(config-subif)#encapsulation dot1q 10
CORP(config-subif)#ip address 172.16.10.1 255.255.255.0
```

VLAN 20 Interface

```
CORP(config)#interface fastethernet 0/0.20
CORP(config-subif)#description Marketing VLAN 20
CORP(config-subif)#encapsulation dot1q 20
CORP(config-subif)#ip address 172.16.20.1 255.255.255.0
```

Use the **show ip interface brief** command to verify proper interface configuration and status.

Step 4

Configure the host name, password, and Telnet access for the switch:

```
Switch(config)#hostname ALSwitch
ALSwitch(config)#enable secret cisco
ALSwitch(config)#line vty 0 15
ALSwitch(config-line)#password cisco
ALSwitch(config-line)#login
ALSwitch(config-line)#exit
```

Create a virtual interface on the switch for VLAN 1 and assign an IP address. This becomes the IP address for the switch. Set this switch to 172.16.1.2 because the router gateway address is set to 172.16.1.1:

```
ALSwitch(config)#interface VLAN 1
ALSwitch(config-if)#ip address 172.16.1.2 255.255.255.0
ALSwitch(config-if)#no shutdown
ALSwitch(config-if)#exit
```

Create a default gateway to pass packets to the interface on the Management VLAN router:

```
ALSwitch(config)#ip default-gateway 172.16.1.1
```

1. Why do you use the **ip default-gateway** command?

Step 5

Configure the switch for trunking and assign VLANs as specified in the table at the beginning of this lab.

Set the interface that is connected to the router to trunk with the router. The router is already set to trunk with the VLAN sub-interfaces. The default encapsulation is 802.1Q. Therefore, you do not need the **switchport trunk encapsulation dot1q** command:

```
ALSwitch(config)#interface fastethernet 0/1
ALSwitch(config-if)#switchport mode trunk
```

Look at the interface and CDP information to verify that the trunking is working properly:

```
ALSwitch#show interface fastethernet 0/1 switchport
ALSwitch#show cdp neighbors detail
```

1. What is the IP address of the neighbor?

Place the ports in the correct VLAN and configure PortFast:

```
ALSwitch(config)#interface range fastethernet 0/5 - 8
ALSwitch(config-if)#switchport access vlan 10
ALSwitch(config-if)#spanning-tree portfast
ALSwitch(config)#interface range fastethernet 0/9 - 12
ALSwitch(config-if)#switchport access vlan 20
ALSwitch(config-if)#spanning-tree portfast
```

Step 6

Verify the configuration and host access after you complete the configuration of the switch and router.

Ensure that the workstation is connected to a port on the switch that is set to VLAN 20, such as port 9. You should set the workstation IP address to 172.16.20.2/24, with a gateway of 172.16.20.1.

Ping the following addresses from a command prompt on the workstation:

```
C:\>ping 172.16.20.1
C:\>ping 172.16.1.2
C:\>ping 10.200.1.1
C:\>ping 10.200.1.2
C:\>ping 10.200.2.1
```

If a ping fails, return to the router and switch and take corrective action.

Step 7

Verify that you can manage the switch from a workstation on VLANs 10 or 20. The workstation traffic must leave the VLAN at the router to connect to the switch. The router forwards the traffic to the switch management VLAN. The process is repeated in reverse for switch traffic that is destined for the workstation.

Telnet to the switch from the DOS command prompt on the workstation. Log in with the **cisco** password:

```
C:\>telnet 172.16.1.2
```

1. Did the Telnet work?

Lab 4.3.2: Inter-VLAN Routing with the Internal Route Processor

Estimated Time: 90 Minutes

Objective

In this lab, you configure Inter-VLAN routing using a switch that has an internal route processor. Figure 4-2 shows a topology for this lab.

Figure 4-2 Topology for Lab 4.3.2

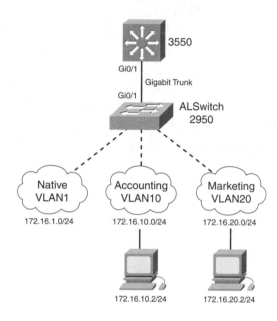

Scenario

The network-switching equipment currently includes a 3550 distribution layer switch and a 2950 access switch. The network is segmented into three functional VLANs for better network management. The VLANs include Accounting and Marketing for the users, and the default name is used for the native VLAN network management. After you have determined the subnet ranges and VTP configuration, implement Inter-VLAN routing. Inter-VLAN routing allows individuals and servers on the virtual LANs to exchange information. You use the internal route processor for routing on the 3550 and establish VLAN trunking over a gigabit Ethernet link to the 2950.

The VTP design information is shown here.

Switch	VTP Domain	VTP Mode
DLSwitch	CORP	Server
ALSwitch	CORP	Client

The VLAN configuration information is shown here.

VLAN ID	VLAN Name	VLAN Subnet	DLSwitch	ALSwitch Ports
1	Default (Native)	172.16.1.0	Fa0/1-4 Gi0/2	Fa0/1-4 Gi0/2
10	Accounting	172.16.10.0	Fa0/5-14	Fa0/5-8
20	Marketing	172.16.20.0	Fa0/15-24	FA0/9-12
Trunk			Gi0/1 802.1Q	Gi0/1 802.1Q

The internal router processor interface configuration information is shown here.

Interface	IP Address	VLAN
VLAN1	172.16.1.1	1 Native
VLAN10	172.16.10.1	10
VLAN 20	172.16.20.1	20

Step 1

Do not cable the lab until you have erased all switch configurations and vlan.dat files.

Delete the VLAN database if it exists on any switches, and clear the configuration:

```
switch#delete flash:vlan.dat
Delete filename [vlan.dat]?
Delete flash:vlan.dat? [confirm]
switch#
switch#erase startup-config
Erasing the nvram filesystem will remove all files! Continue? [confirm]
DLSwitchA#reload

System configuration has been modified. Save? [yes/no]:n
Proceed with reload? [confirm]
```

Cable the lab according to Figure 4-2.

Configure the host name, passwords, and Telnet access on the switches.

Step 2

Configure the VLANs on DLSwitch.

Create the VLANs on DLSwitch and place the switch in VTP Server mode. The default switch mode is Server:

```
DLSwitch#vlan database
DLSwitch(vlan)#vtp domain CORP
DLSwitch(vlan)#vlan 10 name Accounting
DLSwitch(vlan)#vlan 20 name Marketing
```

```
DLSwitch(vlan)#exit
```

Verify the VTP and VLAN configuration with the **show vlan** and **show vtp status commands**:

```
DLSwitch#show vlan
```

VLAN	Name	Status	Ports
1	default	active	Fa0/1, Fa0/2, Fa0/3, Fa0/4
			Fa0/5, Fa0/6, Fa0/7, Fa0/8
			Fa0/9, Fa0/10, Fa0/11, Fa0/12
			Fa0/13, Fa0/14, Fa0/15, Fa0/16
			Fa0/17, Fa0/18, Fa0/19, Fa0/20
			Fa0/21, Fa0/22, Fa0/23, Fa0/24
			Gi0/2
10	Accounting	active	
20	Marketing	active	
1002	fddi-default	active	
1003	token-ring-default	active	
1004	fddinet-default	active	
1005	trnet-default	active	

VLAN	Trans1	Trans2								
1	enet	100001	1500	-	-	-	-	-	0	0
10	enet	100010	1500	-	-	-	-	-	0	0
20	enet	100020	1500	-	-	-	-	-	0	0
1002	fddi	101002	1500	-	-	-	-	-	0	0

VLAN	Type	SAID	MTU	Parent	RingNo	BridgeNo	Stp	BrdgMode	Trans1	Trans2
1003	tr	101003	1500	-	-	-	-	srb	0	0
1004	fdnet	101004	1500	-	-	-	ieee	-	0	0
1005	trnet	101005	1500	-	-	-	ibm	-	0	0

```
Remote SPAN VLANs
------------------------------------------------------------------------
```

Primary	Secondary	Type	Ports

Type	SAID	MTU	Parent	RingNo	BridgeNo	Stp	BrdgMode

```
DLSwitch#show vtp status
VTP Version                     : 2
Configuration Revision          : 1
Maximum VLANs supported locally : 1005
Number of existing VLANs        : 7
VTP Operating Mode              : Server
VTP Domain Name                 : CORP
VTP Pruning Mode                : Disabled
VTP V2 Mode                     : Disabled
VTP Traps Generation            : Disabled
MD5 digest                      : 0x31 0x31 0xF4 0x65 0x66 0x67 0x37 0x63
Configuration last modified by 0.0.0.0 at 3-1-93 00:01:18
Local updater ID is 0.0.0.0 (no valid interface found)
```

Configure the DLSwitch ports for the proper VLAN. You can use the **interface range** command to configure several interfaces at the same time. By default, all ports are in VLAN 1. You need to move the ports that belong to VLANs 10 and 20:

```
DLSwitch(config)#interface range fastethernet 0/5 - 14
DLSwitch(config-if-range)#switchport mode access
DLSwitch(config-if-range)#switchport access vlan 10

DLSwitch(config)#interface range fastethernet 0/15 - 24
DLSwitch(config-if-range)#switchport mode access
```

```
DLSwitch(config-if-range)#switchport access vlan 20
```

Verify the port configuration with the **show vlan** command:

```
DLSwitch#show vlan
VLAN Name                             Status    Ports
---- --------------------------       --------- -------------------------------
1    default                          active    Fa0/1, Fa0/2, Fa0/3, Fa0/4
                                                Gi0/2
10   Accounting                       active    Fa0/5, Fa0/6, Fa0/7, Fa0/8
                                                Fa0/9, Fa0/10, Fa0/11, Fa0/12
                                                Fa0/13, Fa0/14
20   Marketing                        active    Fa0/15, Fa0/16, Fa0/17, Fa0/18
                                                Fa0/19, Fa0/20, Fa0/21, Fa0/22
                                                Fa0/23, Fa0/24
1002 fddi-default                     active
1003 token-ring-default               active
1004 fddinet-default                  active
1005 trnet-default                    active

VLAN Type  SAID     MTU   Parent RingNo BridgeNo Stp  BrdgMode Trans1 Trans2
---- ----- -------- ----- ------ ------ -------- ---- -------- ------ ------
1    enet  100001   1500  -      -      -        -    -        0      0
10   enet  100010   1500  -      -      -        -    -        0      0
20   enet  100020   1500  -      -      -        -    -        0      0
1002 fddi  101002   1500  -      -      -        -    -        0      0
1003 tr    101003   1500  -      -      -        -    srb      0      0

VLAN Type  SAID     MTU   Parent RingNo BridgeNo Stp  BrdgMode Trans1 Trans2
---- ----- -------- ----- ------ ------ -------- ---- -------- ------ ------
1004 fdnet 101004   1500  -      -      -        ieee -        0      0
1005 trnet 101005   1500  -      -      -        ibm  -        0      0

Remote SPAN VLANs
------------------------------------------------------------------------------


Primary Secondary Type              Ports
------- --------- ----------------- ------------------------------------------
```

Step 3

Configure the VLANs on the ALSwitch.

The ALSwitch is the client. It must join the domain in Client mode:

```
ALSwitch#vlan database
ALSwitch(vlan)#vtp client
ALSwitch(vlan)#vtp domain CORP
ALSwitch(vlan)#exit
```

Verify the VLAN configuration with the **show vlan** command. If the message "Domain name already set to CORP" is displayed, it is because the ports auto-negotiate a trunking protocol, in which case the domain and VLANs are learned through VTP.

```
DLSwitch#show vlan
```

1. Can you see VLANs 10 and VLAN 20?

2. Why or why not?

Step 4

Create a trunk link between DLSwitch and ALSwitch.

Set the port to trunking with 802.1Q encapsulation on DLSwitch.

Note: The encapsulation in some IOS versions might be set to auto, which does not allow the user to set the switchport mode to trunking. If this is the case, you must configure the encapsulation first.

```
DLSwitch(config)#interface gigabitethernet 0/1
DLSwitch(config-if)#switchport trunk encapsulation dot1q
DLSwitch(config-if)#switchport mode trunk
DLSwitch(config-if)#exit
```

The 2950 switches do not need the encapsulation to be configured. These switches default to 802.1Q. Some IOS versions do not include other options. Console into ALSwitch switch and configure trunking:

```
ALSwitch(config)#interface gigabitethernet 0/1
ALSwitch(config-if)#switchport mode trunk
ALSwitch(config-if)#exit
```

Verify the VLAN configuration with the **show vlan** command. Note that Gi0/1 is not in a VLAN because it is a trunk. Also note that both VLANs 10 and 20 are listed in the output for ALSwitch:

```
ALSwitch(config)#show vlan

VLAN Name                             Status    Ports
---- -------------------------------- --------- -------------------------------
1    default                          active    Fa0/1, Fa0/2, Fa0/3, Fa0/4
                                                Fa0/5, Fa0/6, Fa0/7, Fa0/8
                                                Fa0/9, Fa0/10, Fa0/11, Fa0/12
                                                Gi0/2
10   Accounting                       active
20   Marketing                        active
1002 fddi-default                     active
1003 token-ring-default               active
1004 fddinet-default                  active
1005 trnet-default                    active

VLAN Type  SAID   MTU  Parent RingNo BridgeNo Stp  BrdgMode Trans1 Trans2
---- ----- ------ ---- ------ ------ -------- ---- -------- ------ ------
1    enet  100001 1500 -      -      -        -    -        0      0
10   enet  100010 1500 -      -      -        -    -        0      0
20   enet  100020 1500 -      -      -        -    -        0      0
1002 fddi  101002 1500 -      -      -        -    -        0      0
1003 tr    101003 1500 -      -      -        -    srb      0      0
1004 fdnet 101004 1500 -      -      -        ieee -        0      0
1005 trnet 101005 1500 -      -      -        ibm  -        0      0
```

Move the ports into the appropriate VLANs:

```
ALSwitch(config)#interface range fastethernet 0/5 - 8
ALSwitch(config-if-range)#switchport access vlan 10
ALSwitch(config-if-range)#exit
```

```
ALSwitch(config)#interface range fastethernet 0/9 - 12
ALSwitch(config-if-range)#switchport access vlan 20
ALSwitch(config-if-range)#exit
```

Verify the port configuration with **show vlan** command:

```
ALSwitch#show vlan
VLAN Name                             Status    Ports
---- -------------------------------- --------- -------------------------------
1    default                          active    Fa0/1, Fa0/2, Fa0/3, Fa0/4
                                                Gi0/2
10   Accounting                       active    Fa0/5, Fa0/6, Fa0/7, Fa0/8
20   Marketing                        active    Fa0/9, Fa0/10, Fa0/11, Fa0/12
1002 fddi-default                     active
1003 token-ring-default               active
1004 fddinet-default                  active
1005 trnet-default                    active

VLAN Type  SAID   MTU  Parent RingNo BridgeNo Stp  BrdgMode Trans1 Trans2
---- ----- ------ ---- ------ ------ -------- ---- -------- ------ ------
1    enet  100001 1500 -      -      -        -    -        0      0
10   enet  100010 1500 -      -      -        -    -        0      0
20   enet  100020 1500 -      -      -        -    -        0      0
1002 fddi  101002 1500 -      -      -        -    -        0      0
1003 tr    101003 1500 -      -      -        -    srb      0      0
1004 fdnet 101004 1500 -      -      -        ieee -        0      0
1005 trnet 101005 1500 -      -      -        ibm  -        0      0

Remote SPAN VLANs
-------------------------------------------------------------------------


Primary Secondary Type          Ports
------- --------- ------------- -----------------------------------------------
```

You also can use the **show vtp status** and **show vtp counters** commands to verify and troubleshoot trunking issues:

```
ALSwitch#show vtp status
VTP Version                     : 2
Configuration Revision          : 1
Maximum VLANs supported locally : 250
Number of existing VLANs        : 7
VTP Operating Mode              : Client
VTP Domain Name                 : CORP
VTP Pruning Mode                : Disabled
VTP V2 Mode                     : Disabled
VTP Traps Generation            : Disabled
MD5 digest                      : 0xB4 0x57 0x1A 0x95 0x99 0x85 0x6D 0x49
Configuration last modified by 0.0.0.0 at 3-1-93 00:13:27
ALSwitch#show vtp counters
VTP statistics:
Summary advertisements received    : 4
Subset advertisements received     : 1
Request advertisements received    : 0
Summary advertisements transmitted : 5
Subset advertisements transmitted  : 1
Request advertisements transmitted : 2
Number of config revision errors   : 0
Number of config digest errors     : 0
Number of V1 summary errors        : 0


VTP pruning statistics:

Trunk          Join Transmitted Join Received   Summary advts received from
                                                non-pruning-capable device
```

```
------------  ----------------  -------------  -------------------------
Gi0/1            0                  0             0
```

Step 5

Verify the VLAN trunking at Layer 3.

Connect one workstation to VLAN 10 on ALSwitch. Connect a second workstation to VLAN 10 on ALSwitch. Test connectivity with the **ping** command.

Note: Change the workstation IP address when connecting to different VLANs.

---

1. Did the ping work?

Now move both workstations to VLAN 20 on ALSwitch. Use ping to test the connection.

2. Did the ping work?

Test the connections between VLANs. Connect one workstation to VLAN 10 and the other to VLAN 20. Use ping to test the connection.

3. Did the ping work?

Step 6

Create the Layer 3 VLAN interfaces to route between VLANs.

In the 3550, the IOS consists of a single image instead of a separate CatOS image for the switching engine and an IOS image for the route processor. Inter-VLAN routing is configured from a command-line interface. You do not need to configure internal trunks or internal EtherChannels. No internal Layer 2 ports and internal Layer 3 interfaces are connecting through the switch backplane.

Use the **interface vlan vlan-id** command to create the interface. Then use the **ip routing** command to enable routing between VLANs:

```
DLSwitch(config)#interface vlan 1
DLSwitch(config-if)#ip address 172.16.1.1 255.255.255.0
DLSwitch(config-if)#no shutdown

DLSwitch(config)#interface vlan 10
DLSwitch(config-if)#ip address 172.16.10.1 255.255.255.0

DLSwitch(config)#interface vlan 20
DLSwitch(config-if)#ip address 172.16.20.1 255.255.255.0
DLSwitch(config)#ip routing
```

Use the **show ip interface brief** command to verify the IP interface configuration:

```
DLSwitch#show ip interface brief

Interface         IP-Address       OK? Method Status      Protocol
Vlan1             172.16.1.1       YES manual up          up
Vlan10            172.16.10.1      YES manual up          up
Vlan20            172.16.20.1      YES manual up          up
```

```
FastEthernet0/1         unassigned      YES unset  administratively down down
FastEthernet0/2         unassigned      YES unset  administratively down down

--Output Omitted--
```

Step 7

Verify routing between VLANs.

Connect one workstation to VLAN 10 and one to VLAN 20. Use ping to test connectivity. Remember to change the workstation IP address and gateway to match the subnet.

1. Did the ping work?

_____

2. Why is a routing protocol unnecessary in this network?

_____

Save the configurations for use in the next lab.

Lab 4.3.3: Routing Between an External Router and an Internal Route Processor

Estimated Time: 90 Minutes

Objective

In this lab, you configure routing between an internal route processor and an external router. Figure 4-3 shows a topology for this lab.

Figure 4-3 Topology for Lab 4.3.3

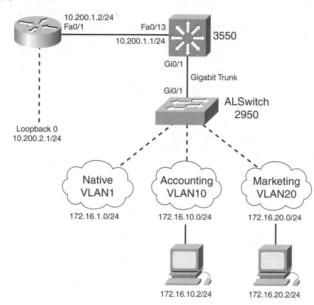

Scenario

The network switching equipment currently includes a 3550 distribution layer switch and a 2950 access layer switch. The network is segmented into three functional VLANs for better network management. The VLANs include Accounting and Marketing for the users. The default name is used for the native VLAN 1 network management. The 3550 is used for routing between the VLANs. A separate network with a 2600 router connects to a remote office. The company executive wants the accounting and marketing departments to be able to access the remote office when necessary. To facilitate the new requirement, you will connect the 2600 directly to the 3550.

The network design information is shown here.

Switch	VTP Domain	VTP Mode
DLSwitch	CORP	Server
ALSwitch	CORP	Client

The VLAN configuration information is shown here.

VLAN ID	VLAN Name	VLAN Subnet	DLSwitch	ALSwitch Ports
1	Default (Native)	172.16.1.0	Fa0/1-4 Gi0/2	Fa0/1-4 Fa0/13-24 Gi0/2
10	Accounting	172.16.10.0	Fa0/5-12	Fa0/5-8
20	Marketing	172.16.20.0	Fa0/14-24	FA0/9-12
Trunk			Gi0/1 802.1Q	Gi0/1 802.1Q
Layer 3 Network		10.200.1.0	Fa0/13	

The internal route processor interface configuration information is shown here.

Interface	IP Address	VLAN
VLAN 1	172.16.1.1	1 Native
VLAN 10	172.16.10.1	10
VLAN 20	172.16.20.1	20
Layer 3 Interface	10.200.1.1	

Step 1

Note: If you are continuing from Lab 4.3.2 or if you have already loaded the saved configurations from that lab, proceed to Step 6. Otherwise, start with these instructions.

Do not cable the lab until you have erased all switch configurations and vlan.dat files.

Delete the VLAN database if it exists on any switches, and clear the configuration:

```
switch#delete flash:vlan.dat
Delete filename [vlan.dat]?
Delete flash:vlan.dat? [confirm]
switch#
switch#erase startup-config
Erasing the nvram filesystem will remove all files! Continue? [confirm]
DLSwitchA#reload

System configuration has been modified. Save? [yes/no]:n
Proceed with reload? [confirm]
```

Cable the lab according to Figure 4-3.

Configure the host name, passwords, and Telnet access on the switches.

Step 2

Configure the VLANs on DLSwitch.

Create the VLANs on DLSwitch. The 3550 defaults to VTP Server mode. Therefore, you do not need to configure it. If the 3550 is in Client mode, use the **vtp server** command:

```
DLSwitch#vlan database
DLSwitch(vlan)#vtp domain CORP
DLSwitch(vlan)#vlan 10 name Accounting
DLSwitch(vlan)#vlan 20 name Marketing
DLSwitch(vlan)#exit
```

Verify the VTP and VLAN configuration with the **show vlan** and **show vtp status** commands:

```
DLSwitch#show vlan
```

VLAN	Name	Status	Ports
1	default	active	Fa0/1, Fa0/2, Fa0/3, Fa0/4
			Fa0/5, Fa0/6, Fa0/7, Fa0/8
			Fa0/9, Fa0/10, Fa0/11, Fa0/12
			Fa0/13, Fa0/14, Fa0/15, Fa0/16
			Fa0/17, Fa0/18, Fa0/19, Fa0/20
			Fa0/21, Fa0/22, Fa0/23, Fa0/24
			Gi0/1, Gi0/2
10	Accounting	active	
20	Marketing	active	
1002	fddi-default	active	
1003	token-ring-default	active	
1004	fddinet-default	active	
1005	trnet-default	active	

VLAN	Type	SAID	MTU	Parent	RingNo	BridgeNo	Stp	BrdgMode	Trans1	Trans2
1	enet	100001	1500	-	-	-	-	-	0	0
10	enet	100010	1500	-	-	-	-	-	0	0
20	enet	100020	1500	-	-	-	-	-	0	0
1002	fddi	101002	1500	-	-	-	-	-	0	0

VLAN	Type	SAID	MTU	Parent	RingNo	BridgeNo	Stp	BrdgMode	Trans1	Trans2
1003	tr	101003	1500	-	-	-	-	srb	0	0
1004	fdnet	101004	1500	-	-	-	ieee	-	0	0
1005	trnet	101005	1500	-	-	-	ibm	-	0	0

```
Remote SPAN VLANs
------------------------------------------------------------------------


Primary Secondary Type              Ports
------- --------- ----------------- ------------------------------------------
DLSwitch#show vtp status
VTP Version                     : 2
Configuration Revision          : 1
Maximum VLANs supported locally : 1005
Number of existing VLANs        : 7
VTP Operating Mode              : Server
VTP Domain Name                 : CORP
VTP Pruning Mode                : Disabled
VTP V2 Mode                     : Disabled
VTP Traps Generation            : Disabled
MD5 digest                      : 0x31 0x31 0xF4 0x65 0x66 0x67 0x37 0x63
Configuration last modified by 0.0.0.0 at 3-1-93 00:01:18
Local updater ID is 0.0.0.0 (no valid interface found)
```

Place the ports into the proper VLAN. You can use the **interface range** command to configure several interfaces at the same time. By default, all ports are in VLAN 1. For this lab, move the ports that belong to VLAN 10 and 20:

```
DLSwitch(config)#interface range fastethernet 0/5 - 12
DLSwitch(config-if-range)#switchport mode access
DLSwitch(config-if-range)#switchport access vlan 10
DLSwitch(config)#interface range fastethernet 0/14 - 24
DLSwitch(config-if-range)#switchport mode access
DLSwitch(config-if-range)#switchport access vlan 20
```

Verify the port configuration with the **show vlan** command:

```
DLSwitch#show vlan

VLAN Name                             Status    Ports
---- -------------------------------- --------- -------------------------------
1    default                          active    Fa0/1, Fa0/2, Fa0/3, Fa0/4, Fa0/13
                                                Gi0/1, Gi0/2
10   Accounting                       active    Fa0/5, Fa0/6, Fa0/7, Fa0/8
                                                Fa0/9, Fa0/10, Fa0/11, Fa0/12
20   Marketing                        active    Fa0/14, Fa0/15, Fa0/16, Fa0/17, Fa0/18
                                                Fa0/19, Fa0/20, Fa0/21, Fa0/22
                                                Fa0/23, Fa0/24
1002 fddi-default                     active
1003 token-ring-default               active
1004 fddinet-default                  active
1005 trnet-default                    active

VLAN Type  SAID    MTU   Parent RingNo BridgeNo Stp  BrdgMode Trans1 Trans2
---- ----- ------- ----- ------ ------ -------- ---- -------- ------ ------
1    enet  100001  1500  -      -      -        -    -        0      0
10   enet  100010  1500  -      -      -        -    -        0      0
20   enet  100020  1500  -      -      -        -    -        0      0
1002 fddi  101002  1500  -      -      -        -    -        0      0
1003 tr    101003  1500  -      -      -        -    srb      0      0

VLAN Type  SAID    MTU   Parent RingNo BridgeNo Stp  BrdgMode Trans1 Trans2
---- ----- ------- ----- ------ ------ -------- ---- -------- ------ ------
1004 fdnet 101004  1500  -      -      -        ieee -        0      0
1005 trnet 101005  1500  -      -      -        ibm  -        0      0

Remote SPAN  VLANs
------------ --------------------------------------------------------------


Primary Secondary Type          Ports
------- --------- ------------- -----------------------------------------------
```

Step 3

Configure the VLANs on the ALSwitch.

The ALSwitch is the VTP client. The ALSwitch must join the domain in Client mode:

```
ALSwitch(vlan)#vtp client
ALSwitch(vlan)#vtp domain CORP
ALSwitch(vlan)#exit
```

Verify the VLAN configuration with the **show vlan** command.

1. Are VLANs 10 and 20 displayed?

_____

2. Why or why not?

_____

Step 4

Create a trunk link between DLSwitch and ALSwitch.

Set the port to trunking with 802.1Q encapsulation on the DLSwitch.

Note: The encapsulation in some IOS versions might be set to auto, which does not allow the user to set the switchport mode to trunking. If this is the case, you need to configure the encapsulation first.

```
DLSwitch(config)#interface gigabitethernet 0/1
DLSwitch(config-if)#switchport mode trunk
DLSwitch(config-if)#switchport trunk encapsulation dot1q
DLSwitch(config-if)#exit
```

You do not need to configure the encapsulation on the 2950 switches. These switches default to 802.1Q. Some IOS versions have no other options. Console into ALSwitch and configure trunking:

```
ALSwitch(config)#interface gigabitethernet 0/1
ALSwitch(config-if)#switchport mode trunk
ALSwitch(config-if)#exit
```

Verify the VLAN configuration with the **show vlan** command:

```
ALSwitch(config)#show vlan
```

VLAN	Name	Status	Ports
1	default	active	Fa0/1, Fa0/2, Fa0/3, Fa0/4
			Fa0/5, Fa0/6, Fa0/7, Fa0/8
			Fa0/9, Fa0/10, Fa0/11, Fa0/12
			Gi0/2
10	Accounting	active	
20	Marketing	active	
1002	fddi-default	active	
1003	token-ring-default	active	
1004	fddinet-default	active	
1005	trnet-default	active	

VLAN	Type	SAID	MTU	Parent	RingNo	BridgeNo	Stp	BrdgMode	Trans1	Trans2
1	enet	100001	1500	-	-	-	-	-	0	0
10	enet	100010	1500	-	-	-	-	-	0	0
20	enet	100020	1500	-	-	-	-	-	0	0
1002	fddi	101002	1500	-	-	-	-	-	0	0
1003	tr	101003	1500	-	-	-	-	srb	0	0
1004	fdnet	101004	1500	-	-	-	ieee	-	0	0
1005	trnet	101005	1500	-	-	-	ibm	-	0	0

Move the ports into the appropriate VLANs:

```
ALSwitch(config)#interface range fastethernet 0/5-8
ALSwitch(config-if-range)#switchport access vlan 10
ALSwitch(config-if-range)#exit

ALSwitch(config)#interface range fastethernet 0/9-12
ALSwitch(config-if-range)#switchport access vlan 20
ALSwitch(config-if-range)#exit
```

Verify the port configuration with the **show vlan** command:

```
ALSwitch#show vlan

VLAN Name                             Status    Ports
---- -------------------------------- --------- -------------------------------
1    default                          active    Fa0/1, Fa0/2, Fa0/3, Fa0/4
                                                Gi0/2
10   Accounting                       active    Fa0/5, Fa0/6, Fa0/7, Fa0/8
20   Marketing                        active    Fa0/9, Fa0/10, Fa0/11, Fa0/12
1002 fddi-default                     active
1003 token-ring-default               active
1004 fddinet-default                  active
1005 trnet-default                    active

VLAN Type  SAID    MTU   Parent RingNo BridgeNo Stp  BrdgMode Trans1 Trans2
---- ----- ------- ----- ------ ------ -------- ---- -------- ------ ------
1    enet  100001  1500  -      -      -        -    -        0      0
10   enet  100010  1500  -      -      -        -    -        0      0
20   enet  100020  1500  -      -      -        -    -        0      0
1002 fddi  101002  1500  -      -      -        -    -        0      0
1003 tr    101003  1500  -      -      -        -    srb      0      0
1004 fdnet 101004  1500  -      -      -        ieee -        0      0
1005 trnet 101005  1500  -      -      -        ibm  -        0      0


Remote SPAN VLANs
------------------------------------------------------------------------------


Primary Secondary Type              Ports
------- --------- ----------------- ------------------------------------------
```

You also can use the **show vtp status** and **show vtp counters** commands to verify and troubleshoot trunking:

```
ALSwitch#show vtp status
VTP Version                     : 2
Configuration Revision          : 1
Maximum VLANs supported locally : 250
Number of existing VLANs        : 7
VTP Operating Mode              : Client
VTP Domain Name                 : CORP
VTP Pruning Mode                : Disabled
VTP V2 Mode                     : Disabled
VTP Traps Generation            : Disabled
MD5 digest                      : 0xB4 0x57 0x1A 0x95 0x99 0x85 0x6D 0x49
Configuration last modified by 0.0.0.0 at 3-1-93 00:13:27

ALSwitch#show vtp counters
VTP statistics:
Summary advertisements received  : 4
Subset advertisements received   : 1
Request advertisements received  : 0
Summary advertisements transmitted : 5
Subset advertisements transmitted  : 1
Request advertisements transmitted : 2
Number of config revision errors : 0
Number of config digest errors   : 0
Number of V1 summary errors      : 0


VTP pruning statistics:

Trunk          Join Transmitted Join Received   Summary advts received from
                                                non-pruning-capable device
-------------- ---------------- --------------- ----------------------------
Gi0/1          0                0               0
```

Verify the VLAN trunking at Layer 3.

Connect one workstation to VLAN 10 on ALSwitch. Connect a second workstation to VLAN 10 on ALSwitch. Test connectivity with the **ping** command.

Note: Remember to change the workstation IP address when connecting to different VLANs.

---

1. Did the ping work?

Now, move both workstations to VLAN 20 on ALSwitch. Use the **ping** command to test the connection.

2. Did the ping work?

The last step is to test the connections between VLANs. Connect one workstation to VLAN 10 and the other to VLAN 20. Use the **ping** command to test the connection.

3. Did the ping work?

Step 5

Create the Layer 3 VLAN interfaces and use the **interface vlan** *vlan-id* command to route between VLANs.

The 3550 IOS consists of a single image, instead of a CatOS image for the switching engine and an IOS image for the route processor. Inter-VLAN routing is configured from a single command-line interface (CLI). You do not need to configure internal trunks or internal EtherChannels because no internal Layer 2 ports or internal Layer 3 interfaces connect through the switch backplane:

```
DLSwitch(config)#interface vlan 1
DLSwitch(config-if)#ip address 172.16.1.1 255.255.255.0
DLSwitch(config-if)#no shutdown

DLSwitch(config-)#interface vlan 10
DLSwitch(config-if)#ip address 172.16.10.1 255.255.255.0

DLSwitch(config)#interface vlan 20
DLSwitch(config-if)#ip address 172.16.20.1 255.255.255.0
```

Verify the interfaces with the **show ip interface brief** command:

```
DLSwitch#show ip interface brief

Interface       IP-Address      OK? Method Status                Protocol
Vlan1           172.16.1.1      YES manual up                    up
Vlan10          172.16.10.1     YES manual up                    up
Vlan20          172.16.20.1     YES manual up                    up
FastEthernet0/1 unassigned      YES unset  administratively down down
FastEthernet0/2 unassigned      YES unset  administratively down down

--Output Omitted--
```

Step 6

Verify routing between the VLANs.

Connect a workstation to VLAN 10 and another to VLAN 20. Use the **ping** command to test connectivity. Remember to change the workstation IP address and gateway to match the subnet.

1. Did the ping work?

Step 7

Connect the 2600 Fast Ethernet 0/1 router port to the Catalyst 3500 Fast Ethernet 0/13 port. Configure Fast Ethernet 0/0 on the 2600:

```
Router(config)#hostname 2600
2600(config)#interface fastethernet 0/1
2600(config-if)#ip address 10.200.1.2 255.255.255.0
2600(config-if)#no shutdown
2600(config-if)#exit
```

Configure the loopback interface that will be used to test external connectivity:

```
2600(config)#interface loopback 0
2600(config-if)#ip address 10.200.2.1 255.255.255.0
2600(config-if)#exit
```

Configure EIGRP as the routing protocol. You must configure a routing protocol so that the routers can learn about external networks:

```
2600(config)#router eigrp 100
2600(config-router)#no auto-summary
2600(config-router)#network 10.200.1.0
2600(config-router)#network 10.200.2.0
2600(config-router)#exit
```

Step 8

Configure the Layer 3 interface on the 3550.

The 3550 supports Layer 2 interfaces and Layer 3 physical interfaces. If a port on the switch is connected to an independent network without VLANs, convert it to a Layer 3 interface. You can use the **no switchport** command for this purpose:

```
DLSwitch(config)#interface fastethernet 0/13
DLSwitch(Config-if)#no switchport
DLSwitch(Config-if)#ip address 10.200.1.1 255.255.255.0
DLSwitch(config-if)#exit
```

You need a routing protocol to pass network information between the 2600 router and Catalyst 3550. Configure EIGRP as the DLSwitch routing protocol. You must enable IP routing on the device:

```
DLSwitch(config)#ip routing
```

Configure EIGRP as the routing protocol:

```
DLSwitch(config)#router eigrp 100
DLSwitch(config-router)#no auto-summary
DLSwitch(config-router)#network 10.200.1.0
DLSwitch(config-router)#network 172.16.1.0
DLSwitch(config-router)#network 172.16.10.0
DLSwitch(config-router)#network 172.16.20.0
DLSwitch(config-router)#exit
```

Step 9

Verify proper routing between networks.

Use the **show ip route** command on the DLSwitch to verify routing.

1. Which network is learned through EIGRP on DLSwitch?

_____

Use **show ip route** on the remote router to check the routing table.

Use the **ping** command to test connectivity between the workstation and the loopback address.

Chapter 5

Multilayer Switching

Lab 5.4.1: Monitoring Cisco Express Forwarding

Estimated Time: 120 Minutes

Objective

In this lab, you monitor the default behavior of Cisco Express Forwarding (CEF). Figure 5-1 shows the topology for this lab.

Figure 5-1 Topology for Lab 5.4.1

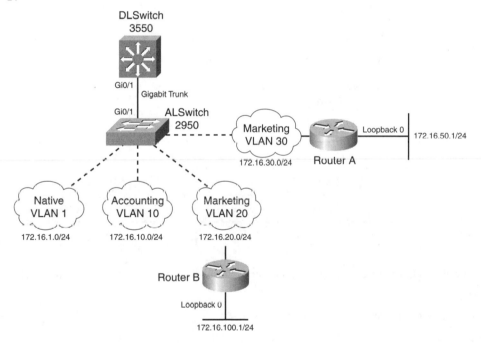

Scenario

In this lab, the network switching equipment currently includes a 3550 distribution layer switch and a 2950 access switch. The network is segmented into four functional VLANs for better network management. VLANs include Accounting, Engineering, and Marketing for the users. VLAN 1 is used for the native VLAN. Currently, the 3550 switch provides inter-VLAN routing. By default, the switch uses CEF. The network administrator wants to monitor CEF and verify proper operation of CEF.

The VTP configuration information is shown here.

Switch	VTP Domain	VTP Mode
DLSwitch	CORP	Server
ALSwitch	CORP	Client

The VLAN configuration information is shown here.

VLAN ID	VLAN Name	VLAN Subnet	DLSwitch	ALSwitch Ports
1	Default (Native)	172.16.1.0	Fa0/1-24 Gi0/2	Fa0/1-3 Fa0/13-24 Gi0/2
10	Accounting	172.16.10.0		Fa0/4-6
20	Marketing	172.16.20.0		FA0/7-9
30	Engineering	172.16.30.0		FA0/10-12
Trunk			Gi0/1 802.1Q	Gi0/1 802.1Q

The internal router processor interface configuration information is shown here.

Interface	IP Address	VLAN
VLAN1	172.16.1.1	1 Native
VLAN10	172.16.10.1	10
VLAN20	172.16.20.1	20
VLAN30	172.16.30.1	30

Step 1

Do not cable the lab until you have erased the router configurations, switch configurations, and switch vlan.dat file and reloaded the devices.

Build the network according to Figure 5-1:

```
DLSwitch#delete flash
Delete filename [flash]?
Enter vlan.dat at the Delete prompt.
DLSwitch#erase start
Switch#reload
```

Configure both switches with the proper host name and enable Telnet access on both switches.

Step 2

On the DLSwitch, configure the VTP domain name and create and name the VLANs as shown here. The DLSwitch will be the VTP server and should already be in the default Server mode:

```
DLSwitch#vlan database
DLSwitch(vlan)#vtp domain CORP
DLSwitch(vlan)#vlan 10 name Accounting
DLSwitch(vlan)#vlan 20 name Marketing
DLSwitch(vlan)#vlan 30 name Engineering
DLSwitch(vlan)#exit
```

Now verify the VLAN configuration with the **show vlan brief** command. Verify the VTP configuration with the **show vtp status** command. The DLSwitch should be in the Server mode, and the VTP domain name should be CORP:

```
DLSwitch#show vlan brief

VLAN Name                             Status    Ports
---- -------------------------------- --------- -------------------------------
1    default                          active    Fa0/2, Fa0/3, Fa0/4, Fa0/5
                                                Fa0/6, Fa0/7, Fa0/8, Fa0/9
                                                Fa0/10, Fa0/11, Fa0/12, Fa0/13
                                                Fa0/14, Fa0/15, Fa0/16, Fa0/17
                                                Fa0/18, Fa0/19, Fa0/20, Fa0/21
                                                Fa0/22, Fa0/23, Fa0/24, Gi0/1
                                                Gi0/2
10   Accounting                       active
20   marketing                        active
30   Engineering                      active
1002 fddi-default                     active
1003 token-ring-default               active
1004 fddinet-default                  active
1005 trnet-default                    active
```

Step 3

Configure the ALSwitch as a VTP client. The ALSwitch should pick up the VTP domain name from the server DLSwitch, but you can enter it again:

```
ALSwitch#vlan database
ALSwitch(vlan)#vtp client
ALSwitch(vlan)#vtp domain CORP
ALSwitch(vlan)#exit
```

If the message "Domain name already set to CORP" is displayed, it is because the ports auto-negotiate a trunking protocol. In that case, the domain and VLANs will be learned through VTP.

Verify the VTP and VLAN configurations with the **show vtp status** and **show vlan brief** commands.

1. Can you see VLAN 10, VLAN 20, and VLAN 30?

_____

2. Why or why not?

_____

Step 4

Create a trunk link between the DLSwitch and ALSwitch.

On the DLSwitch, set the port to trunking with the 802.1Q encapsulation.

Note: In some IOS versions, you can set the encapsulation to auto, which prohibits the user from setting the switchport mode to trunking. If this is the case, you need to configure the encapsulation first.

```
DLSwitch(config)# interface gigabiteternet 0/1
DLSwitch(config-if)#switchport mode trunk
DLSwitch(config-if)#switchport trunk encapsulation dot1q
DLSwitch(config-if)#exit
```

Follow the same procedure for the ALSwitch:

```
ALSwitch(config)# interface gigabiteternet 0/1
ALSwitch(config-if)#switchport mode trunk
ALSwitch(config-if)#exit
```

Note: The trunk encapsulation type is not specified on a 2950 switch because it supports only 802.1Q.

Now move the ports into the appropriate VLANs:

```
ALSwitch(config)#interface range fastethernet 0/4 - 6
ALSwitch(config-if-range)#switchport access vlan 10
ALSwitch(config-if-range)#exit

ALSwitch(config)#interface range fastethernet 0/7 - 9
ALSwitch(config-if-range)#switchport access vlan 20
ALSwitch(config-if-range)#exit

ALSwitch(config)#interface range fastethernet 0/10 - 12
ALSwitch(config-if-range)#switchport access vlan 30
ALSwitch(config-if-range)#exit
```

Verify the port trunking:

```
ALSwitch#show interfaces trunk
Port       Mode            Encapsulation  Status         Native vlan
Gi0/1      on              802.1q         trunking       1
Port       Vlans allowed on trunk
Gi0/1      1-4094
Port       Vlans allowed and active in management domain
Gi0/1      1,10,20,30
Port       Vlans in spanning tree forwarding state and not pruned
Gi0/1      1,10,20,30
```

Step 5

Verify the VLAN trunking at Layer 3.

Connect one workstation to VLAN 10 on the ALSwitch. Connect a second workstation to VLAN 10 on the ALSwitch. Use the **ping** command to test the connection.

Note: If the lab is rack mounted permanently, you must use the routers as the end devices.

Note: Remember to change the workstation IP address when connecting to different VLANs.

1. Does the ping work?

Now move both workstations to VLAN 20 on the ALSwitch. Use **ping** to test the connection.

2. Does the ping work?

Test the connections between VLANs. Connect one workstation to VLAN 10 and the other to VLAN 20. Can you use the ping between these workstations?

Step 6

In the 3550, the IOS consists of a single image, rather than a separate CatOS image for the switching engine. The 3550 also has an IOS image for the route processor. Inter-VLAN routing is configured from a single command-line interface (CLI). You do not need to configure internal trunks or internal EtherChannels. Internal Layer 2 ports and internal Layer 3 interfaces no longer connect through the switch backplane. To route between VLANs, create the Layer 3 VLAN interfaces. Use the command **interface vlan** *vlan-id* to create the interface:

```
DLSwitch(config)#interface vlan 1
DLSwitch(config-if)#ip address 172.16.1.1 255.255.255.0
DLSwitch(config-if)#no shutdown
DLSwitch(config)#interface vlan 10
DLSwitch(config-if)#ip address 172.16.10.1 255.255.255.0
DLSwitch(config)#interface vlan 20
DLSwitch(config-if)#ip address 172.16.20.1 255.255.255.0
DLSwitch(config)#interface vlan 30
DLSwitch(config-if)#ip address 172.16.30.1 255.255.255.0
DLSwitch(config-if)#^Z
```

Verify the interfaces with the **show ip interface brief** command:

```
DLSwitch#show ip interface brief

Interface          IP-Address      OK? Method Status               Protocol
Vlan1              172.16.1.1      YES manual up                    up
Vlan10             172.16.10.1     YES manual up                    up
Vlan20             172.16.20.1     YES manual up                    up
Vlan30             172.16.30.1     YES manual up                    up
FastEthernet0/1    unassigned  YES unset  administratively down down
FastEthernet0/2    unassigned  YES unset  administratively down down

--Output Omitted--
```

Use the **show ip route** command to see if the switch is routing:

```
DLSwitch#show ip route
Default gateway is not set

Host            Gateway         Last Use    Total Uses Interface
ICMP redirect cache is empty
```

Notice that the switch is still behaving as a Layer 2 device. After you create the VLANs, you still must enable routing.

Enable routing with the **ip routing** global configuration command:

```
DLSwitch(config)#ip routing
DLSwitch(config)#router rip
DLSwitch(config-router)#version 2
DLSwitch(config-router)#no auto-summary
DLSwitch(config-router)#network 172.16.0.0
DLSwitch(config-router)#exit
```

Now check the routing table again with the **show ip route** command:

```
DLSwitch#show ip route
Codes: C - connected, S - static, I - IGRP, R - RIP, M - mobile, B - BGP
       D - EIGRP, EX - EIGRP external, O - OSPF, IA - OSPF inter area
       N1 - OSPF NSSA external type 1, N2 - OSPF NSSA external type 2
       E1 - OSPF external type 1, E2 - OSPF external type 2, E - EGP
       i - IS-IS, L1 - IS-IS level-1, L2 - IS-IS level-2, ia - IS-IS inter area
       * - candidate default, U - per-user static route, o - ODR
       P - periodic downloaded static route

Gateway of last resort is not set

     172.16.0.0/24 is subnetted, 4 subnets
C       172.16.30.0 is directly connected, Vlan30
C       172.16.20.0 is directly connected, Vlan20
C       172.16.10.0 is directly connected, Vlan10
C       172.16.1.0 is directly connected, Vlan1
```

The DLSwitch now provides Layer 2 and Layer 3 functions.

Step 7

Configure RouterA and RouterB. Set the host name and the IP address of the interface. Run Routing Information Protocol (RIP) as the routing protocol:

```
Router(config)#hostname RouterA
RouterA(config)#interface loopback 0
RouterA(config-if)#ip address 172.16.50.1 255.255.255.0
RouterA(config)#interface fastethernet 0/0
RouterA(config-if)#ip address 172.16.30.5 255.255.255.0
RouterA(config-if)#no shutdown
RouterA(config)#router rip
RouterA(config-router)#version 2
RouterA(config-router)#no auto-summary
RouterA(config-router)#network 172.16.0.0
RouterA(config-router)#exit

Router(config)#hostname RouterB
RouterB(config)#interface loopback 0
RouterB(config-if)#ip address 172.16.100.1 255.255.255.0
RouterB(config)#interface fastethernet0/0
RouterB(config-if)#ip address 172.16.20.5 255.255.255.0
RouterB(config-if)#no shutdown
RouterB(config)#router rip
RouterB(config-router)#version 2
RouterB(config-router)#no auto-summary
RouterB(config-router)#network 172.16.0.0
RouterB(config-router)#exit
```

Verify the routing between RouterA and RouterB with the **show ip route** command:

```
DLSwitch#show ip route
Codes: C - connected, S - static, I - IGRP, R - RIP, M - mobile, B - BGP
       D - EIGRP, EX - EIGRP external, O - OSPF, IA - OSPF inter area
       N1 - OSPF NSSA external type 1, N2 - OSPF NSSA external type 2
       E1 - OSPF external type 1, E2 - OSPF external type 2, E - EGP
       i - IS-IS, L1 - IS-IS level-1, L2 - IS-IS level-2, ia - IS-IS inter area
       * - candidate default, U - per-user static route, o - ODR
       P - periodic downloaded static route

Gateway of last resort is not set
```

```
       172.16.0.0/24 is subnetted, 6 subnets
R        172.16.50.0 [120/1] via 172.16.30.5, 00:00:15, Vlan30
C        172.16.30.0 is directly connected, Vlan30
C        172.16.20.0 is directly connected, Vlan20
C        172.16.10.0 is directly connected, Vlan10
C        172.16.1.0 is directly connected, Vlan1
R        172.16.100.0 [120/1] via 172.16.20.5, 00:00:01, Vlan20
```

Check the routing table on RouterA and RouterB.

Now test the connectivity by using the **ping** command. Ping from RouterA to loopback 0 interface on RouterB.

1. Does the ping work?

Step 8

Cisco Express Forwarding (CEF) is a Layer 3 IP switching technology that optimizes network performance. CEF implements an advanced IP lookup and forwarding algorithm to deliver maximum Layer 3 switching performance. CEF is less CPU intensive than fast switching route caching. This allows more CPU processing power to be dedicated to packet forwarding. In the Catalyst 3550 switch, the hardware uses CEF to achieve Gigabit speed line rate IP traffic. In dynamic networks, fast switching cache entries frequently are invalidated because of routing changes. This can cause traffic to be process switched using the routing table, instead of fast switched using the route cache. CEF uses the Forwarding Information Base (FIB) lookup table to perform destination-based switching of IP packets.

CEF is enabled globally by default. If for some reason it is disabled, re-enable it by using the **ip cef** global configuration command.

To display the CEF status, use the **show ip cef** command:

```
DLSwitch#show ip cef
Prefix              Next Hop           Interface
0.0.0.0/32          receive
172.16.1.0/24       attached           Vlan1
172.16.1.0/32       receive
172.16.1.1/32       receive
172.16.1.2/32       172.16.1.2         Vlan1
172.16.1.255/32     receive
172.16.10.0/24      attached           Vlan10
172.16.10.0/32      receive
172.16.10.1/32      receive
172.16.10.255/32    receive
172.16.20.0/24      attached           Vlan20
172.16.20.0/32      receive
172.16.20.1/32      receive
172.16.20.5/32      172.16.20.5        Vlan20
172.16.20.255/32    receive
172.16.30.0/24      attached           Vlan30
172.16.30.0/32      receive
172.16.30.1/32      receive
172.16.30.5/32      172.16.30.5        Vlan30
172.16.30.255/32    receive
172.16.50.0/24      172.16.30.5        Vlan30
172.16.100.0/24     172.16.20.5        Vlan20
224.0.0.0/4         drop
224.0.0.0/24        receive
255.255.255.255/32  receive
```

To verify whether CEF is enabled on an interface, use the **show ip interface** command:

```
DLSwitch#show ip interface vlan10
Vlan10 is up, line protocol is up
  Internet address is 172.16.10.1/24
  Broadcast address is 255.255.255.255
  Address determined by setup command
  MTU is 1500 bytes
  Helper address is not set
  Directed broadcast forwarding is disabled
  Outgoing access list is not set
  Inbound  access list is not set
  Proxy ARP is enabled
  Local Proxy ARP is disabled
  Security level is default
  Split horizon is enabled
  ICMP redirects are always sent
  ICMP unreachables are always sent
  ICMP mask replies are never sent
  IP fast switching is enabled
  IP fast switching on the same interface is disabled
  IP Flow switching is disabled
  IP CEF switching is enabled
  IP CEF Fast switching turbo vector
  IP multicast fast switching is enabled
  IP multicast distributed fast switching is disabled
  TCP/IP header compression is disabled
  RTP/IP header compression is disabled
  Probe proxy name replies are disabled
  Policy routing is disabled
  Network address translation is enabled, interface in domain outside
  WCCP Redirect outbound is disabled
  WCCP Redirect inbound is disabled
  WCCP Redirect exclude is disabled
  BGP Policy Mapping is disabled
```

Now check whether any packets were dropped with the **show cef drop** command:

```
DLSwitch#show cef drop
CEF Drop Statistics
Slot  Encap_fail  Unresolved Unsupported   No_route   No_adj  ChkSum_Err
RP        36487            0           0          0        6            0
```

Use the **show ip cef summary** command to display the CEF table summary:

```
DLSwitch#show ip cef detail
IP CEF with switching (Table Version 25), flags=0x0
  25 routes, 0 reresolve, 0 unresolved (0 old, 0 new), peak 0
  25 leaves, 14 nodes, 17760 bytes, 73 inserts, 48 invalidations
  0 load sharing elements, 0 bytes, 0 references
  universal per-destination load sharing algorithm, id D19B2C80
  4(2) CEF resets, 0 revisions of existing leaves
  Resolution Timer: Exponential (currently 1s, peak 1s)
  0 in-place/0 aborted modifications
  refcounts:  1595 leaf, 1568 node

  Table epoch: 0 (25 entries at this epoch)
```

```
Adjacency Table has 3 adjacencies
0.0.0.0/32, version 0, epoch 0, receive
172.16.1.0/24, version 18, epoch 0, attached, connected
0 packets, 0 bytes
  via Vlan1, 0 dependencies
    valid glean adjacency
172.16.1.0/32, version 4, epoch 0, receive
172.16.1.1/32, version 3, epoch 0, receive
172.16.1.2/32, version 22, epoch 0, connected, cached adjacency 172.16.1.2
0 packets, 0 bytes
  via 172.16.1.2, Vlan1, 0 dependencies
    next hop 172.16.1.2, Vlan1
    valid cached adjacency
172.16.1.255/32, version 5, epoch 0, receive
172.16.10.0/24, version 17, epoch 0, attached, connected
0 packets, 0 bytes
  via Vlan10, 0 dependencies
    valid glean adjacency
172.16.10.0/32, version 7, epoch 0, receive
172.16.10.1/32, version 6, epoch 0, receive
172.16.10.255/32, version 8, epoch 0, receive
172.16.20.0/24, version 16, epoch 0, attached, connected
0 packets, 0 bytes
  via Vlan20, 0 dependencies
    valid glean adjacency
172.16.20.0/32, version 10, epoch 0, receive
172.16.20.1/32, version 9, epoch 0, receive
172.16.20.5/32, version 23, epoch 0, connected, cached adjacency 172.16.20.5
0 packets, 0 bytes
  via 172.16.20.5, Vlan20, 0 dependencies
    next hop 172.16.20.5, Vlan20
    valid cached adjacency
172.16.20.255/32, version 11, epoch 0, receive
172.16.30.0/24, version 15, epoch 0, attached, connected
0 packets, 0 bytes
  via Vlan30, 0 dependencies
    valid glean adjacency
172.16.30.0/32, version 13, epoch 0, receive
172.16.30.1/32, version 12, epoch 0, receive
172.16.30.5/32, version 20, epoch 0, connected, cached adjacency 172.16.30.5
0 packets, 0 bytes
  via 172.10.30.5, Vlan30, 0 dependencies
    next hop 172.16.30.5, Vlan30
    valid cached adjacency
172.16.30.255/32, version 14, epoch 0, receive
172.16.50.0/24, version 21, epoch 0, cached adjacency 172.16.30.5
0 packets, 0 bytes
  via 172.16.30.5, Vlan30, 0 dependencies
    next hop 172.16.30.5, Vlan30
    valid cached adjacency
172.16.100.0/24, version 24, epoch 0, cached adjacency 172.16.20.5
0 packets, 0 bytes
  via 172.16.20.5, Vlan20, 0 dependencies
    next hop 172.16.20.5, Vlan20
    valid cached adjacency
224.0.0.0/4, version 19, epoch 0
0 packets, 0 bytes, Precedence routine (0)
224.0.0.0/24, version 2, epoch 0, receive
255.255.255.255/32, version 1, epoch 0, receive
```

You can use several other commands to monitor and troubleshoot CEF. If time permits, use the help option to check the output of all the commands.

Chapter 6

Redundancy

Estimated Time: 120 Minutes

Objective

In this lab, you configure Hot Standby Router Protocol (HSRP) on a pair of routers to provide redundant router services to a network. Figure 6-1 shows the topology for this lab.

Figure 6-1 Topology for Lab 6.5.1

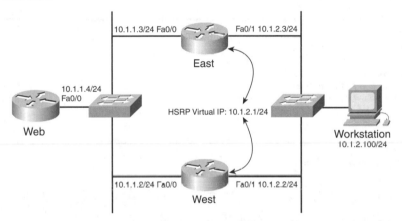

Scenario

Two routers are connected to the network, and the two default gateways do not provide a completely reliable path in the event of an outage. Configuring HSRP on the two routers provides a fast failover mechanism that is transparent to the users. This allows hosts on the LAN segment to maintain access to the Web router if a single point of failure occurs.

Step 1

Do not cable the lab until you have erased the router configurations, switch configurations, and switch vlan.dat file and reloaded the devices.

Cable the lab as shown in Figure 6-1.

If the routers are connected to Ethernet switches, it could take a few seconds for the switch to reach the Spanning Tree Protocol (STP) forwarding state. To maximize the benefits of HSRP, change the connected switch ports to spanning-tree PortFast. If the router is connected to a hub or switch with PortFast configured, the interface should come up almost immediately.

Step 2

Configure the Web router with a username, vty, and secret passwords; IP address; and enable HTTP management services:

```
Router(config)#hostname Web
Web(config)#interface fastethernet 0/0
Web(config-if)#ip address 10.1.1.4 255.255.255.0
Web(config-if)#no shutdown
Web(config-if)#line vty 0 4
Web(config-line)#password cisco
Web(config-line)#login
Web(config-line)#enable secret class
Web(config)#ip http server
```

Step 3

Configure the East and West routers for connectivity:

```
Router(config)#hostname West
West(config)#interface fastethernet 0/0
West(config-if)#ip address 10.1.1.2 255.255.255.0
West(config-if)#no shutdown
West(config-if)#interface fastethernet 0/1
West(config-if)#ip address 10.1.2.2 255.255.255.0
West(config-if)#no shutdown
West(config-if)#line vty 0 4
West(config-line)#password cisco
West(config-line)#login
West(config-line)#enable secret class
```

```
Router(config)#hostname East
East(config)#interface fastethernet0/0
East(config-if)#ip address 10.1.1.3 255.255.255.0
East(config-if)#no shutdown
East(config-if)#interface fastethernet 0/1
East(config-if)#ip address 10.1.2.3 255.255.255.0
East(config-if)#no shutdown
East(config-if)#line vty 0 4
East(config-line)#password cisco
East(config-line)#login
East(config-line)#enable secret class
```

Step 4

Configure Enhanced Interior Gateway Routing Protocol (EIGRP) on all routers:

```
Web(config)#router eigrp 10
Web(config-router)#network 10.0.0.0
```

```
West(config)#router eigrp 10
West(config-router)#network 10.0.0.0
```

```
East(config)#router eigrp 10
East(config-router)#network 10.0.0.0
```

Specify the default gateway for the workstation. Specify both routers as candidate default routers because two routers are present on each network.

Configure the workstation with the IP address 10.1.2.100/24 and the two default gateways 10.1.2.2 and 10.1.2.3.

Step 5

Ping the web server at address 10.1.1.4 from the workstation.

1. Is the **ping** command successful?

Step 6

If the ping to the web server or router is successful, unplug the cable connected to interface FastEthernet 0/1 on the West router.

1. Try to ping again. What happens?

---

2. Why is this happening?

Plug the cable back into the West router.

3. Try to ping again. Does it work?

Step 7

The HSRP will remove the single point of failure and provide a virtual gateway.

Currently, the routers use two IP addresses on each network, one for each router. HSRP allows the user to create a third virtual IP address that floats between the routers in case one of the routers fails. The 10.1.2.1 address will be used for the HSRP address on the 10.1.2.0 /24 network.

HSRP is enabled on an interface with the interface configuration **standby ip** command.

Turn on HSRP on the 10.1.2.0 network:

```
East(config)#interface fastethernet 0/1
East(config-if)#standby ip 10.1.2.1
East(config-if)#standby preempt
```

```
West(config)#interface fastethernet 0/1
West(config-if)#standby ip 10.1.2.1
West(config-if)#standby preempt
```

Step 8

Reconfigure the workstation. Remove the current default gateways and install just a single default gateway pointing to the HSRP virtual IP address of 10.1.2.1/24.

Step 9

Now try to ping the Web router at 10.1.1.4.

1. Does the ping work?

Step 10

Enter the **show standby** command on the East router before testing HSRP:

```
East#show standby
FastEthernet0/1 - Group 0
  Local state is Active, priority 100, may preempt
  Hellotime 3 sec, holdtime 10 sec
  Next hello sent in 1.552
  Virtual IP address is 10.1.2.1 configured
  Active router is local
  Standby router is 10.1.2.2 expires in 9.900
```

```
Virtual mac address is 0000.0c07.ac00
5 state changes, last state change 00:04:41
```

1. Which router becomes the active HSRP router?

___

2. How is the active HSRP router selected?

___

Remove the cable from interface FastEthernet 0/1 on the East router.

3. Try to ping again. Does it work?

___

Step 11

Enter the **show standby** command on the West router:

```
West#show standby
FastEthernet0/1 - Group 0
  Local state is Active, priority 100, may preempt
  Hellotime 3 sec, holdtime 10 sec
  Next hello sent in 1.306
  Virtual IP address is 10.1.2.1 configured
  Active router is local
  Standby router is unknown
  Virtual mac address is 0000.0c07.ac00
  2 state changes, last state change 00:01:40
```

1. Why does HSRP create a standby virtual MAC address?

___

Enter the **show standby** command on the East router:

```
East#show standby
FastEthernet0/1 - Group 0
  Local state is Init (interface down), priority 100, may preempt
  Hellotime 3 sec, holdtime 10 sec
  Virtual IP address is 10.1.2.1 configured
  Active router is unknown
  Standby router is unknown
  3 state changes, last state change 00:00:17
```

Plug the cable back into interface FastEthernet 0/1 on the East router. Try to ping again and enter the **show standby** command on both the East and West routers. Notice that the West router is still the active router, whereas the East router is now the standby router.

Step 12

Make the East router the active HSRP router by setting the standby priority to 150. The East router has the higher priority and wins the election because the default standby priority is 100.

The preempt keyword forces the router with the highest priority, which is the East router, to resume the role of the active HSRP router. The change occurs even if West is currently the active HSRP router. For example, when the East router standby interface FastEthernet 0/1 goes down and then comes back up, East resumes the role of the active router:

```
East(config-if)#interface fastethernet 0/1
East(config-if)#standby priority 150
East(config-if)#standby preempt

22:01:51: %STANDBY-6-STATECHANGE: FastEthernet0/7 Group 0 state Standby -> Active
```

Now issue the **show standby** command:

```
East#show standby
FastEthernet0/1 - Group 0
  Local state is Active, priority 150, may preempt
  Hellotime 3 sec, holdtime 10 sec
  Next hello sent in 0.164
  Virtual IP address is 10.1.2.1 configured
  Active router is local
  Standby router is 10.1.2.3 expires in 8.896
  Virtual mac address is 0000.0c07.ac00
  5 state changes, last state change 00:02:31
```

Notice that the East router has become the active HSRP router again.

Test the priority configuration by unplugging the cable from interface FastEthernet 0/1 on the East router and then issuing the **show standby** command on both routers. The East router shows that the interface is down, and the West router should assume the role of the active router.

Plug the cable back into interface FastEthernet 0/1 on the East router, and then issue the **show standby** command on both routers again. The East router should have resumed the active router role, and the West router should have become the standby router again.

Step 13

From the workstation, perform a **tracert** to the Web router. The **tracert** command traces the path of a packet, similar to the Cisco IOS **traceroute** command. The results should be similar to the following output:

```
C:\>tracert 10.1.1.4

Tracing route to 10.1.1.4 over a maximum of 30 hops

  1   <10 ms    10 ms   <10 ms  10.2.2.1
  2   <10 ms   <10 ms   <10 ms  10.1.1.4

Trace complete.
```

From the workstation, ping the Web router with a **–t** option. The **–t** option provides continuous pings. Disconnect the cable from interface FastEthernet 0/0 on the West router. Observe the output of the ping.

1. What was the result of removing the cable?

_____

From West, view the routing table:

```
West#show ip route
--output omitted--

Gateway of last resort is not set

     10.0.0.0/24 is subnetted, 2 subnets
C       10.1.2.0 is directly connected, fastethernet 0/1
D       10.1.1.0 [90/284160] via 10.1.2.3, 00:00:15, fastethernet 0/1
```

When the direct connection to the Web router is broken, the West router must use the FastEthernet 0/1 interface through the East router to pass packets to the web.

You can view the problem another way. Even if a ping is successful, connection could still be a problem. For example, the hops that the packet must traverse are hidden from the ping output. With the cable still disconnected from interface FastEthernet 0/0 on the West router, issue the **tracert** command to the Web router:

```
C:\>tracert 10.1.1.4

Tracing route to 10.1.1.4 over a maximum of 30 hops

  1   <10 ms   <10 ms    10 ms  10.2.2.1
  2   <10 ms   <10 ms   <10 ms  10.1.2.3
  3   <10 ms   <10 ms   <10 ms  10.1.1.4

Trace complete.
```

West could not pass the packet to the Web router on the FastEthernet 0/1 interface. Therefore, the packet had to be sent to East on 10.1.2.3. The packet was delivered successfully from East interface FastEthernet 0/0 to the Web router.

The solution to this problem is to use the **standby track** command, which ties the router standby priority to the availability of tracked interfaces. This command is important for providing redundancy for routers with interfaces that are not configured for HSRP. When a tracked interface fails, the hot standby priority on the device on which tracking has been configured is decreased by the specified value. If an interface is not tracked, state changes do not affect the hot standby priority on the configured interface.

Reconnect the cable between the Web router and the West router.

Then track the FastEthernet 0/0 interface on the West router. If the interface state changes, decrease the standby priority by at least 51:

```
West(config)#interface fastethernet 0/1
West(config-if)#standby track fastethernet 0/0 51
```

Verify standby track configuration:

```
West#show standby fastethernet 0/1
FastEthernet0/1 - Group 0
  Local state is Standby, priority 100, may preempt
  Hellotime 3 sec, holdtime 10 sec
  Next hello sent in 0.022
  Virtual IP address is 10.1.2.1 configured
  Active router is 10.1.2.3, priority 150 expires in 8.476
  Standby router is local
  7 state changes, last state change 00:39:34
  IP redundancy name is "hsrp-Fa0/1-0" (default)
  Priority tracking 1 interface, 1 up:
    Interface                Decrement  State
     FastEthernet0/0               51      Up
```

From the workstation, ping the Web router with the **–t** option. Disconnect the cable from interface FastEthernet 0/0 on the West router.

2. Did the network recover from the interface change?

From the workstation, perform a tracert to the Web router. The results should be similar to the following output:

```
C:\>tracert 10.1.1.4

Tracing route to 10.1.1.4 over a maximum of 30 hops

  1   <10 ms    10 ms   <10 ms  10.1.2.1
  2   <10 ms   <10 ms   <10 ms  10.1.1.4

Trace complete.
```

The output of the **tracert** command now shows that the optimal path from the workstation to the Web router was used.

This lab demonstrated the basic configuration of HSRP. HSRP provides fast failover for devices on a LAN segment containing two or more Cisco routers.

Lab 6.5.2: Multigroup Hot Standby Router Protocol

Estimated Time: 120 Minutes

Objective

In this lab, you configure Multigroup Hot Standby Router Protocol (MHSRP) on a pair of routers to provide redundant router services to a network. Figure 6-2 shows the topology for this lab.

Figure 6-2 Topology for Lab 6.5.2

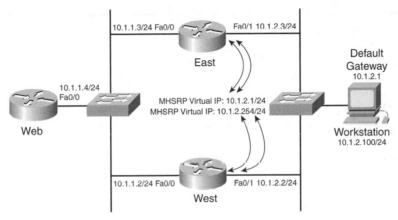

Scenario

Two routers are connected to the network. After installing HSRP, the user realizes that all the LAN traffic is forwarded through the active HSRP router. This is not the most efficient use of the bandwidth. Use MHSRP for load balancing between the East and the West routers.

Step 1

Do not cable the lab until you have erased the router configurations, switch configurations, and switch vlan.dat file and reloaded the devices.

Cable the lab as shown in Figure 6-2.

Step 2

Configure the Web router to act as a web server. Configure the router with a username, vty and secret passwords, IP address, and enable HTTP management services, as shown here:

```
Router(config)#hostname Web
Web(config)#interface fastethernet0/0
Web(config-if)#ip address 10.1.1.4 255.255.255.0
Web(config-if)#no shutdown
Web(config-if)#line vty 0 4
Web(config-line)# password cisco
Web(config-line)#login
Web(config-line)#enable secret class
Web(config)#ip http server
```

Step 3

Configure the East and West routers:

```
Router(config)#hostname West
West(config)#interface fastethernet 0/0
West(config-if)#ip address 10.1.1.2 255.255.255.0
West(config-if)#no shutdown
West(config-if)#interface fastethernet 0/1
West(config-if)#ip address 10.1.2.2 255.255.255.0
West(config-if)#no shutdown
West(config-if)#line vty 0 4
West(config-line)#password cisco
West(config-line)#login
West(config-line)#enable secret class
```

```
Router(config)#hostname East
East(config)#interface fastethernet 0/0
East(config-if)#ip address 10.1.1.3 255.255.255.0
East(config-if)#no shutdown
East(config-if)#interface fastethernet 0/1
East(config-if)#ip address 10.1.2.3 255.255.255.0
East(config-if)#no shutdown
East(config-if)#line vty 0 4
East(config-line)# password cisco
East(config-line)#login
East(config-line)#enable secret class
```

Step 4

Configure EIGRP on all routers:

```
Web(config)#router eigrp 10
Web(config-router)#network 10.0.0.0
```

```
West(config)#router eigrp 10
West(config-router)#network 10.0.0.0
```

```
East(config)#router eigrp 10
East(config-router)#network 10.0.0.0
```

Step 5

Turn on HSRP by using the **standby ip** command at the interface level.

Turn on HSRP on the 10.1.2.0 network:

```
West(config)#interface fastethernet 0/1
West(config-if)#standby ip 10.1.2.1
West(config-if)#standby preempt
```

```
East(config)#interface fastethernet 0/1
East(config-if)#standby ip 10.1.2.1
East(config-if)#standby preempt
```

Check the HSRP configuration with a **show standby** command on both routers.

Step 6

Ping the Web router at 10.1.1.4 from the workstation to test HSRP operation.

1. Was the ping successful?

If the ping did not work, go back and troubleshoot the configuration.

Change the IP address several times and ping 10.1.1.4 each time. Observe the lights on the routers and switch ports. Notice that the packets are forwarded over the same router each time. The HSRP standby router is sitting idle.

Step 7

To use both paths from the host network to the server network, configure MHSRP between the East and West routers. The East and West routers are configured with the same two HSRP groups. For group 1, East is the active router and West is the standby router. For group 2, West is the active router and East is the standby router. Configure half of the host default gateways using the HSRP group 1 virtual IP address. Configure the other half of the host default gateways using the HSRP group 2 virtual IP address.

Remove the original standby configuration before implementing MHSRP:

```
West(config)#interface fastethernet 0/1
West(config-if)#no standby ip 10.1.2.1
```

```
East(config)#interface fastethernet 0/1
East(config-if)#no standby ip 10.1.2.1
```

```
East(config)#interface fastethernet 0/1
East(config-if)#standby 1 ip 10.1.2.1
East(config-if)#standby 1 preempt
East(config-if)#standby 1 track fastethernet 0/0
East(config-if)#standby 2 ip 10.1.2.254
East(config-if)#standby 2 preempt
East(config-if)#standby 2 priority 95
East(config-if)#standby 2 track fastethernet 0/0
```

```
West(config)#interface fastethernet 0/1
West(config-if)#standby 1 ip 10.1.2.1
West(config-if)#standby 1 preempt
West(config-if)#standby 1 track fastethernet 0/0
West(config-if)#standby 1 priority 95
West(config-if)#standby 2 ip 10.1.2.254
West(config-if)#standby 2 preempt
West(config-if)#standby 2 track fastethernet 0/0
```

Check the HSRP configuration with a **show standby** command on both routers. The East router should be the active router for HSRP group 1 and the standby router for group 2. The West router should be the active router for group 2 and the standby router for group 1.

Step 8

You have created two default gateways for the LAN. You will configure half of the devices with one default gateway and the other half with the other gateway. Each router is the active HSRP for one of the virtual IP addresses.

Configure the workstation with the default gateway address of 10.1.2.1. Ping the Web router.

1. Was the ping successful?

_____

If the ping was unsuccessful, troubleshoot the network. Use the **show standby** command for assistance.

2. Which router forwarded the packets to the Web router?

_____

Now change the default gateway address on the workstation to 10.1.2.254. Ping the Web router.

3. Which router forwarded the packets to the Web router?

Now the network is load balancing between the two HSRP routers.

Test the redundancy of HSRP. Set the default gateway address to 10.1.2.1 on the workstation, and ping the Web router with the **-t** option. Disconnect the cable between the East router and the switch that is attached to the workstation while observing the ping output.

4. Did the network recover from the failure?

Reconnect the cable between the East router and the switch that is connected to the workstation. Then change the default gateway address of the workstation to 10.1.1.254. Again, use the **–t** option and ping the Web router. Disconnect the cable between the West router and the switch that is connected to the workstation.

5. Did the network recover from the failure?

Step 9

The track feature recovers the network when the far side links fail. Reconnect all the cables. Then disconnect the cable between the East router and the switch that is attached to the Web router. Set the default gateway address to 10.1.2.1, and ping the Web router with the **–t** option. Finally, reconnect the cable between the East router and the switch that is attached to the Web router.

1. Did the network recover from the failure?

Cisco AVVID

Currently, no lab activities are associated with this chapter. However, do review the objectives listed in Chapter 7 of the *CCNP 3: Network Troubleshooting Companion Guide*:

- Describe some of the major components of a Cisco AVVID network solution.
- Explain how Layer 2 multicast addresses map to Layer 3 multicast addresses.
- Explain the role of IGMP in multicasting.
- Understand the purpose of IGMP snooping and CGMP with switched traffic.
- Understand the operation of shared trees versus source trees in multicast routing.
- List the major multicast routing protocol solutions.
- Describe the role of the auxiliary VLAN with voice traffic.
- Explain the role of CoS, ToS, and DSCP in traffic classification.
- Understand the importance of QoS with IP telephony solutions.

A direct link to the Cisco AVVID site is http://www.cisco.com/en/US/netsol/ns340/ns19/ networking_solutions_market_segment_solutions_home.html.

Chapter 8

Quality of Service

Lab 8.9.1: Classifying Traffic Using Class of Service at the Access Layer

Estimated Time: 90 Minutes

Objective

For effective quality of service (QoS), you need to classify traffic as soon as possible. This allows routing and switching processes that can differentiate traffic and provide the required service levels. This lab introduces the use of the Layer 2 class of service (CoS) field as a means of classifying traffic entering the network at the access layer switch. The following key concepts are covered:

- Trust of an existing CoS, such as provided by an IP phone
- Manual configuration of CoS for devices that are incapable of setting it for themselves
- Manual configuration and overriding the CoS for devices that cannot be trusted

You can perform this lab using the Catalyst 2950T or 3550 switches. Figure 8-1 shows the topology for this lab.

Figure 8-1 Topology for Lab 8.9.1

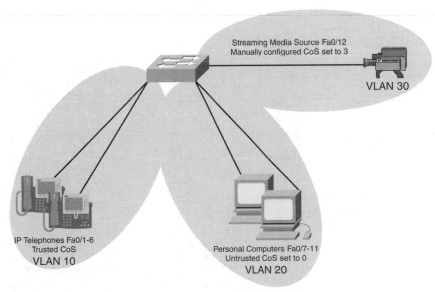

Scenario

A company's marketing department is expanding and has just obtained some additional floor space for five new staff members. Each staff member has a personal computer and an IP phone. In addition, the department has purchased a video web camera so that marketing presentations can be streamed to customers and employees. Configure the access layer switch for the new workgroup, and pay particular attention to the QoS requirements.

Step 1

Do not cable the lab until you have erased the switch configuration and vlan.dat files and reloaded the switch.

Cable the lab as shown in Figure 8-1.

If you are using a Catalyst 3550 for this lab, activate the QoS features of the switch from the global configuration mode:

```
Switch(config)#mls qos
```

If you are using a Catalyst 2950 for this lab, ignore this step because the QoS features of the 2950 are always available.

Step 2

Configure a VLAN Trunking Protocol (VTP) domain corp and assign VLANs to the interfaces, as shown in Figure 8-1:

```
Switch(config)#vtp domain corp
Switch(config)#vtp mode server
Switch(config)#interface range fastethernet 0/1 - 6
Switch(config-if-range)#switchport access vlan 10
Switch(config-if-range)#interface range fastethernet 0/7 - 11
Switch(config-if-range)#switchport access vlan 20
Switch(config-if-range)#interface fastethernet 0/12
Switch(config-if)#switchport access vlan 30
```

Step 3

The IP phones were purchased and the Ethernet CoS field was automatically set to 5. This is an appropriate value because it allows the access layer switch to pass these Ethernet frames, leaving the CoS intact. In other words, the CoS that is coming in on the IP phone interface's switch is trusted.

Configure interfaces 1 through 6 to trust the incoming CoS:

```
Switch(config)#interface range fastethernet 0/1 - 6
Switch(config-if-range)#mls qos trust cos
```

Step 4

The personal computers used in the marketing department do not have special QoS requirements. When you classify Ethernet frames originating from them with a CoS of 0, you represent a best-effort delivery priority.

Configure interfaces 7 through 11 with a default CoS of 0:

```
Switch(config)#interface range fastethernet 0/7 - 11
Switch(config-if-range)#mls qos cos 0
```

Step 5

The personal computers use a network interface card (NIC) that supports 802.1p. Therefore, the PCs can set the CoS. The marketing staff would never want to disrupt network services intentionally. However, if the CoS were set to a high value, data network traffic such as FTP could disrupt voice or video services seriously.

Configure interfaces 7 through 11 to override incoming CoS and set them to the default:

```
Switch(config-if-range)#mls qos cos override
```

Step 6

You need to give the video traffic priority treatment within the network. This is because video traffic has different requirements than voice traffic. Assign a separate CoS of 3, which ensures that other switches and routers within the network will identify the video traffic readily.

The camera is not capable of setting its own CoS. Configure a default CoS of 3 on interface 12:

```
Switch(config)#interface fastethernet 0/12
Switch(config-if)#mls qos cos 3
```

Step 7

It is possible that in the future, the marketing department will upgrade the camera to a more advanced model that supports setting of its own CoS. Configure the switch port so that if frames are received with the CoS already set, the switch will use that value instead of the default:

```
Switch(config-if-range)#mls qos trust cos
```

Step 8

Verify the QoS settings for each of the interfaces using the **show mls qos interface** command:

```
Switch#show mls qos interface fastethernet 0/1
FastEthernet0/1
trust state: trust cos
trust mode: trust cos
COS override: dis
default COS: 0
pass-through: none
trust device: none
```

1. What is the trust state for interface fa0/7?

_____

2. Which command brought about this trust state?

_____

3. Is it possible to use the commands **mls qos cos override** and **mls qos trust cos** on the same interface?

_____

Lab 8.9.2: Introduction to the Modular QoS Command-Line Interface

Estimated Time: 60 Minutes

Objective

Configuring QoS involves classifying, marking, and policing traffic flows. It is often necessary to apply the same rules to various classes of traffic or to apply the same policy to many interfaces on a switch. The IOS uses a modular QoS command-line interface (MQC) to avoid repetition and to make it easier to modify settings.

This lab introduces the MQC, which is an important part of the QoS configuration on an IOS-based switch or router.

This lab also introduces the concept of the Differentiated Services (or DiffServ) Code Point (DSCP), which you use to mark packets with a QoS identifier. Figure 8-2 shows the topology for this lab.

Figure 8-2 Topology for Lab 8.9.2

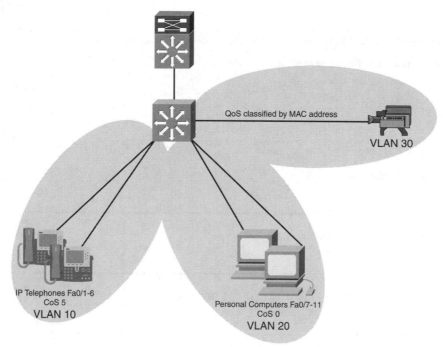

This lab is designed for use with the Catalyst 3550 switch and builds on Lab 8.9.1.

Scenario

The marketing department's access switch has been configured for Layer 2 class of service (CoS). However, this does not provide a QoS indicator that can be carried end-to-end through the network. To achieve this, you must mark the packets at Layer 3 using the DSCP field in the IP packet as the packets move into the distribution layer switch. In Lab 8.9.1, you marked traffic using the CoS as frames entered the access layer switch. In this lab, you will set a Layer 3 DSCP according to the existing Layer 2 CoS of the frames.

The marketing department personnel occasionally use an IP-based audio-conferencing phone. Because the department does not use this phone often, you do not need to reserve a switch port on every access layer switch. The workers would like to be able to unplug the nearest network device and plug the audio-conferencing phone into that port. Ensure that this device receives the same treatment as other voice traffic in the network.

Step 1

Do not cable the lab until you have erased the switch configuration file and vlan.dat file for the Dist1 switch and reloaded the switch. Cable the lab as shown in Figure 8-2.

Configure the host names for the Access1 and Dist1 switches. Then configure a gigabit trunk between the access and distribution layer switches:

```
Access1(config)#interface gigabitethernet 0/1
Access1(config-if-range)#switchport mode trunk

Dist1(config)#interface gigabitethernet 0/1
Dist1(config-if-range)#switchport trunk encapsulation dot1q
Dist1(config-if-range)#switchport mode trunk
```

Step 2

Before you use the Catalyst 3550, you must enable the QoS functionality by using the **mls qos** command:

```
Dist1(config)#mls qos
```

This step does not apply to the Catalyst 2950 because the QoS features of the 2950 are always available.

Step 3

You must identify traffic from the audio-conference device before you can classify it. In the previous lab, you used the incoming access port to identify frames and set the CoS. You cannot use an incoming port in this lab because the marketing people want to move the device from port to port. One mechanism that you could use to identify traffic from the audio-conference device is an IP access list. The problem with this solution is that the audio conference device requires different IP addresses if it is used on ports in different VLANs. This makes it more difficult to manage the Access Control List (ACL). The solution is to use a MAC-based ACL.

In this lab, you will use an example MAC address. Substitute the MAC address of an available PC to facilitate testing.

Configure a MAC ACL on the distribution layer switch to identify traffic originating from the audio conference device:

```
Dist1(config)#mac access-list extended audioconference
Dist1(config-ext-macl)#permit host 0000.0a00.0111 any
```

Step 4

Verify the configuration of the MAC ACL using the **show access-lists** command:

```
Dist1#show access-lists
Extended MAC access list audioconferencee
    permit host 0000.0a00.0111 any
```

Step 5

The first component of the modular QoS CLI is the class map. The class map defines the traffic types that will receive the same QoS treatment.

The **class-map** command uses various match statements to define the traffic. If the command uses **match-all**, the traffic must satisfy all the match statements. If the command uses **match-any**, traffic that matches any of the statements joins the traffic class.

You give each class map a name that references it.

Create a class map called voicetraffic that matches all the criteria specified:

```
Dist1(config)#class-map match-all voicetraffic
```

The **match** command identifies traffic that will become part of the class map. Use the following command to examine the possible criteria for a match:

```
Dist1(config-cmap)#match ?
```

Create a match using the named ACL that was defined previously:

```
Dist1(config-cmap)#match access-group name audioconference
```

Step 6

Verify the configuration using the **show class-map** command:

```
Dist1#show class-map
 Class Map match-all voicetraffic (id 2)
   Match access-group name audioconference

 Class Map match-any class-default (id 0)
```

The switch automatically creates a class map called class default. You also can assign match statements to this class map.

Step 7

After you define the traffic class with the class-map statement, define the actions that you should take on each class of traffic with the policy-map statement. Like the class map, you give the policy map a name:

```
Dist1(config)#policy-map from-access-layer
```

The format of the policy map is a reference to a traffic class and one or more actions that you must apply to the traffic. For the traffic class named voicetraffic, specify that the DSCP should be set to 40. When the **set** command is configured, use the question mark (?) to examine the extensive range of actions that you can take on a traffic class:

```
Dist1(config-pmap)#class voicetraffic
Dist1(config-pmap-c)#set ip dscp 40
```

After you specify an action for traffic originating from the audio-conference device, determine the QoS requirements of traffic originating from any other hosts that are attached to the access layer switch. Assume that the access layer switch has provided suitable CoS values and configure the class-default policy so that the CoS value of all other traffic is trusted:

```
Dist1(config-pmap)#class class-default
Dist1(config-pmap-c)#trust cos
```

Step 8

Use the **show policy-map** command to verify the policy map:

```
Dist1#show policy-map
Policy Map from-access-layer
  class  voicetraffic
   set ip dscp 40
  class  class-default
   trust cos
```

Step 9

The final configuration step for MQC is applying the policy to an interface. You accomplish this by using the **service-policy** command on the required interface:

```
Dist1(config)#interface gigabitethernet 0/1
Dist1(config-if)#service-policy input from-access-layer
```

Step 10

Use the **show mls qos interface gigabitethernet 0/1** command to verify that the service policy has been applied to the interface correctly:

```
Dist1#show mls qos interface gigabitethernet 0/1
gigabitethernet 0/1
Attached policy-map for Ingress: from-access-layer
trust state: not trusted
trust mode: not trusted
COS override: dis
default COS: 0
DSCP Mutation Map: Default DSCP Mutation Map
trust device: none
```

Lab 8.9.3: QoS Classification and Policing Using CAR

Estimated Time: 60 Minutes

Objective

In this lab, you use committed access rate (CAR) to classify and police traffic. Although you configure the classification and policing actions in this lab on one router, this is not a requirement for CAR. CAR commonly is used to classify traffic at a distribution router and then police the traffic on congested core routers. Figure 8-3 shows the topology for this lab.

Figure 8-3 Topology for Lab 8.9.3

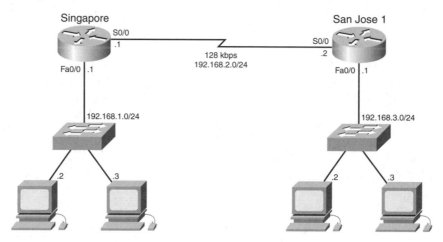

Scenario

Managing the bandwidth of the WAN link is difficult because the marketing departments in Singapore and San Jose frequently use peer-to-peer networking to exchange large graphics.

When you use CAR to classify traffic, you can lower the DSCP value of the traffic when excessive data rates occur. An analysis of current traffic patterns indicates that it is reasonable to allow up to 32 kbps of traffic between any two peers across the WAN link. All traffic up to the 32-kbps limit is permitted with a best-effort DSCP value of 8. If the peers attempt to exchange data across the WAN link at rates exceeding 32 kbps, traffic still is permitted to enter the network. However, the excessive traffic is given a DSCP value of 0, which ranks it lower than best-effort status.

On the WAN link, allow a maximum of 16 kbps of less than best-effort traffic with a DSCP value of 0. Drop any best-effort traffic that exceeds this bandwidth.

Step 1

Do not cable the lab until you have erased the switch and router configuration files and the switch vlan.dat files and reloaded the devices.

Build and configure the network according to Figure 8-3. Configure Enhanced Interior Gateway Routing Protocol (EIGRP) with an autonomous system of 100 as the routing protocol. The configuration of CAR will occur on the routers, so you can leave the access layer switches in their factory-default configuration.

Step 2

On each router, use an access list to define the peers that will be subject to CAR:

```
Singapore(config)#access-list 100 permit ip 192.168.1.0 0.0.0.255 192.168.3.0 0.0.0.255
```

```
SanJose1(config)#access-list 100 permit ip 192.168.3.0 0.0.0.255 192.168.1.0 0.0.0.255
```

Step 3

Use the **rate-limit** command to classify the traffic on each router at the Fa0/0 interface:

```
Router(config-if)#rate-limit {input ¦ output} [dscp dscp value][access-group [rate-limit] acl-index] bps burst-
normal burst-max conform-action action exceed-action action
```

Mark conforming traffic of up to 32 kbps with a DSCP value of 8 and nonconforming traffic in excess of 32 kbps with a DSCP value of 0. The traffic will then be forwarded.

Use question marks (?) extensively in the following commands to become familiar with the different QoS options that are available:

```
Singapore(config)#interface fastethernet 0/0
Singapore(config-if)#rate-limit input access-group 100 32000 3200 3200
conform-action set-dscp-transmit 8 exceed-action set-dscp-transmit 0
```

```
SanJose1(config)#interface fastethernet 0/0
SanJose1(config-if)#rate-limit input access-group 100 32000 3200 3200
conform-action set-dscp-transmit 8 exceed-action set-dscp-transmit 0
```

These commands mark only the traffic that uses the DSCP. Both conforming and nonconforming traffic will be transmitted.

Step 4

On the outbound WAN interfaces, police the traffic according to the requirements of keeping less than best-effort traffic with a DSCP value of 0 to a maximum of 16 kbps.

Police the traffic by dropping it if it is nonconformant:

```
SanJose1(config)#interface serial 0/0
SanJose1(config-if)#rate-limit output dscp 0 16000 1600 2000 conform-action
transmit exceed-action drop
```

```
Singapore(config)#interface serial 0/0
Singapore(config-if)#rate-limit output dscp 0 16000 1600 2000 conform-
action transmit exceed-action drop
```

Step 5

Ping between the peers across the WAN link to test the configuration. It might be helpful to experiment with Internet Control Message Protocol (ICMP) packets that are different sizes.

The following output was generated from a router used in place of the Singapore PC:

```
Singapore-host#ping
Protocol [ip]:
Target IP address: 192.168.3.2
Repeat count [5]: 1000
Datagram size [100]: 1500
Timeout in seconds [2]:
Extended commands [n]:
Sweep range of sizes [n]:
Type escape sequence to abort.
Sending 1000, 1500-byte ICMP Echos to 192.168.3.2, timeout is 2 seconds:
!!!!!!!!!!.!!!!!!!!!!!.!!!!!!!!!!!!.!!!!!!!!!!!!.!!!!!!!!!!!.!
```

Note that some of the 1500-byte packets exceeded the policed bandwidth on the WAN link and were dropped.

You should obtain similar results when using a PC. Use the command **ping 192.168.3.3 -n** *x* **-l** *y*, where *x* is the number of pings and *y* is the size of each packet in bytes. Continue increasing packet size until some packets are dropped:

```
C:\Documents and Settings\Singapore-PC>ping 192.168.3.3 -n 20 -l 6000
Pinging 192.168.3.3 with 6000 bytes of data:
Reply from 192.168.3.3: bytes=6000 time=773ms TTL=126
Reply from 192.168.3.3: bytes=6000 time=774ms TTL=126
Reply from 192.168.3.3: bytes=6000 time=773ms TTL=126
Request timed out.
Reply from 192.168.3.3: bytes=6000 time=774ms TTL=126
Reply from 192.168.3.3: bytes=6000 time=773ms TTL=126
Reply from 192.168.3.3: bytes=6000 time=773ms TTL=126
Request timed out.
Reply from 192.168.3.3: bytes=6000 time=773ms TTL=126
Reply from 192.168.3.3: bytes=6000 time=773ms TTL=126
Request timed out.
Reply from 192.168.3.3: bytes=6000 time=773ms TTL=126
Reply from 192.168.3.3: bytes=6000 time=773ms TTL=126
Reply from 192.168.3.3: bytes=6000 time=773ms TTL=126
Request timed out.
Reply from 192.168.3.3: bytes=6000 time=774ms TTL=126
Reply from 192.168.3.3: bytes=6000 time=773ms TTL=126
Reply from 192.168.3.3: bytes=6000 time=773ms TTL=126
Request timed out.

Ping statistics for 192.168.3.3:
Packets: Sent = 20, Received = 15, Lost = 5 (25% loss),
Approximate round trip times in milli-seconds:
Minimum = 773ms, Maximum = 774ms, Average = 773ms
```

Step 6

You can monitor the actions of CAR by using the **show interfaces rate-limit** command:

```
Singapore#show interfaces rate-limit
FastEthernet0/0
  Input
    matches: access-group 100
      params: 32000 bps, 3200 limit, 3200 extended limit
conformed 398 packets, 602572 bytes; action: set-dscp-transmit 8
exceeded 198 packets, 299772 bytes; action: set-dscp-transmit 0
      last packet: 44ms ago, current burst: 2140 bytes
      last cleared 00:12:15 ago, conformed 6000 bps, exceeded 3000 bps
Singapore#
Serial0/0
  Output
    matches: dscp 0
      params:  16000 bps, 1600 limit, 2000 extended limit
      conformed 244 packets, 324976 bytes; action: transmit
      exceeded 84 packets, 126336 bytes; action: drop
      last packet: 2876ms ago, current burst: 688 bytes
  last cleared 00:12:02 ago, conformed 3000 bps, exceeded 1000 bps
```

Note that packets are being classified according to their DSCP value on the FastEthernet interface. The packets are policed on the serial interface and dropped if necessary.

Congratulations! You have configured CAR to classify and police traffic.

Lab 8.9.4: Weighted Fair Queuing

Estimated Time: 60 Minutes

Objective

In this lab, you configure and optimize weighted fair queuing (WFQ). Figure 8-4 shows the topology for this lab.

Figure 8-4 Topology for Lab 8.9.4

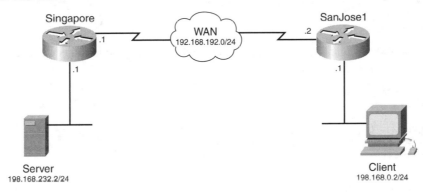

Scenario

As the network engineer for the International Travel Agency (ITA), you are responsible for WAN connectivity. As ITA has grown, traffic has increased on the WAN link. The network technicians recently have reported unreliable Telnet access between San Jose and regional sites. You discover that average WAN link utilization between Singapore and SanJose1 is near saturation. While investigating ways to increase bandwidth, you optimize WFQ as a temporary solution to meet the needs of all users.

Step 1

Do not cable the lab until you have erased the router configuration files and reloaded the routers.

Build the physical topology as shown in Figure 8-4.

Step 2

Configure the network as shown in Figure 8-4 and enable EIGRP with an autonomous system number of 100 as the routing protocol. Confirm connectivity by pinging between the hosts.

Step 3

View the default queuing strategy on the Singapore WAN link. The default queuing might be WFQ or first-in, first-out (FIFO), depending on the router IOS version and the bandwidth of the interface:

```
Singapore#show interfaces serial 0/0
Serial0/0 is up, line protocol is up
  Hardware is PowerQUICC Serial
  Internet address is 192.168.192.1/24
  MTU 1500 bytes, BW 128 Kbit, DLY 20000 usec,
     reliability 255/255, txload 1/255, rxload 1/255
  Encapsulation HDLC, loopback not set
  Keepalive set (10 sec)
  Last input 00:00:00, output 00:00:03, output hang never
  Last clearing of "show interface" counters never
  Input queue: 0/75/0/0 (size/max/drops/flushes); Total output drops: 0
```

```
Queueing strategy: weighted fair
Output queue: 0/1000/64/0 (size/max total/threshold/drops)
   Conversations  0/3/32 (active/max active/max total)
   Reserved Conversations 0/0 (allocated/max allocated)
   Available Bandwidth 96 kilobits/sec
5 minute input rate 0 bits/sec, 0 packets/sec
5 minute output rate 0 bits/sec, 0 packets/sec
   325 packets input, 21083 bytes, 0 no buffer
   Received 105 broadcasts, 0 runts, 0 giants, 0 throttles
   0 input errors, 0 CRC, 0 frame, 0 overrun, 0 ignored, 0 abort
   341 packets output, 23164 bytes, 0 underruns
   0 output errors, 0 collisions, 11 interface resets
   0 output buffer failures, 0 output buffers swapped out
   4 carrier transitions
   DCD=up  DSR=up  DTR=up  RTS=up  CTS=up
```

Issue the **show queue serial 0/0** command to view the queuing configuration on an interface. This command is not supported with FIFO queuing:

```
Singapore#show queue serial 0/0
  Input queue: 0/75/0/0 (size/max/drops/flushes); Total output drops: 0
  Queueing strategy: weighted fair
  Output queue: 0/1000/64/0 (size/max total/threshold/drops)
     Conversations  0/3/32 (active/max active/max total)
     Reserved Conversations 0/0 (allocated/max allocated)
     Available Bandwidth 96 kilobits/sec
```

If the serial interface of a router is using FIFO, you can configure WFQ by issuing the **fair-queue** command:

```
Singapore(config)#interface serial 0/0
Singapore(config-if)#fair-queue
```

On a congested FIFO interface, a low-volume, interactive session like Telnet is subject to intolerable delays, whereas high-bandwidth applications such as FTP monopolize available bandwidth. WFQ identifies and gives equal access to a variety of application protocols. You can think of WFQ as statistically multiplexing all applications. Low-volume sessions are given the necessary bandwidth, whereas high-volume sessions share the remainder. However, there is no guarantee of reserved bandwidth. Interfaces that are overwhelmed with traffic might be forced to drop packets.

Each communication session between hosts creates a flow. The router understands a flow as a record of attributes such as source and destination addresses, port numbers, and the inbound interface. Then the router can compare subsequent packets to existing flows. After the router identifies packets as belonging to a certain session, it buffers them accordingly.

To give each session equal router resources, a router can buffer a default maximum of 64 messages or packets in any one session. You must increase the congestion threshold to 128 packets for the ITA network. This allows the router to buffer more packets per session, but it decreases the number of sessions serviced at a time.

Queuing does not solve this problem because additional bandwidth is required. Queuing might increase performance problems because it demands additional router CPU cycles and forces the router to apply queuing logic to each packet. Therefore, queuing is either a temporary fix or a solution for times when interactive sessions fail because of latency or dropped packets.

Note: Queuing is only active when congestion is present. Congestion exists when any interface has one or more packets buffered in its queue. If all interfaces are clear of buffered packets, queuing is idle.

Step 4

Use the following command syntax to increase the congestion threshold value to 128 packets on both router WAN links:

```
Singapore(config)#interface serial 0/0
Singapore(config-if)#fair-queue 128
```

```
SanJose1(config)#interface serial 0/0
SanJose1(config-if)#fair-queue 128
```

Review the WFQ parameters on Serial 0/0:

```
SanJose1#show interface serial 0/0
Serial0/0 is up, line protocol is up
  Hardware is PowerQUICC Serial
  Internet address is 192.168.192.1/24
  MTU 1500 bytes, BW 128 Kbit, DLY 20000 usec,
     reliability 255/255, txload 1/255, rxload 1/255
  Encapsulation HDLC, loopback not set
  Keepalive set (10 sec)
  Last input 00:00:00, output 00:00:00, output hang never
  Last clearing of "show interface" counters never
  Input queue: 0/75/0/0 (size/max/drops/flushes); Total output drops: 0
  Queueing strategy: weighted fair
  Output queue: 0/1000/128/0 (size/max total/threshold/drops)
     Conversations  0/1/32 (active/max active/max total)
     Reserved Conversations 0/0 (allocated/max allocated)
     Available Bandwidth 96 kilobits/sec
  5 minute input rate 0 bits/sec, 0 packets/sec
  5 minute output rate 0 bits/sec, 0 packets/sec
     481 packets input, 30955 bytes, 0 no buffer
     Received 160 broadcasts, 0 runts, 0 giants, 0 throttles
     0 input errors, 0 CRC, 0 frame, 0 overrun, 0 ignored, 0 abort
     498 packets output, 33108 bytes, 0 underruns
     0 output errors, 0 collisions, 12 interface resets
     0 output buffer failures, 0 output buffers swapped out
     6 carrier transitions
     DCD=up  DSR=up  DTR=up  RTS=up  CTS=up
```

```
Singapore#show queue serial 0/0
  Input queue: 0/75/0/0 (size/max/drops/flushes); Total output drops: 0
  Queueing strategy: weighted fair
  Output queue: 0/1000/128/0 (size/max total/threshold/drops)
     Conversations  0/1/32 (active/max active/max total)
     Reserved Conversations 0/0 (allocated/max allocated)
     Available Bandwidth 96 kilobits/sec
```

When the WAN link is saturated and queuing is activated, each session can buffer up to 128 packets before dropping incoming packets. After the 128-packet discard threshold limit is reached for a particular flow, no packets are buffered until the queue for the flow drops to 25 percent of the discard threshold. In this case, the queue must reach 32 packets, which is 25 percent of 128. If packets are dropped, upper-layer protocols such as TCP can compensate and retransmit undelivered packets. This successfully changes the behavior of WFQ.

Step 5

Configure Windows file sharing on the Singapore host to see the effect of WFQ. Copy a large file from the Singapore host to the SanJose1 host. The file should be large enough to take 5 to 10 minutes to copy over the 128-kbps WAN link.

Step 6

Initiate a Telnet session between Singapore and SanJose1. The keystrokes should be echoed back in a timely fashion when WFQ is being used.

Step 7

Use the **no fair-queue** command to turn off WFQ on each serial interface. This results in FIFO queuing on the WAN link.

Step 8

Initiate another Telnet session between Singapore and SanJose1. The keystrokes should be echoed back after some latency and might be erratic. This makes it difficult to correct typing mistakes by using the **Backspace** key.

Lab 8.9.5: Configuring WRED on an Interface

Estimated Time: 60 Minutes

Objective

The Cisco implementation of random early detection (RED) is called weighted random early detection (WRED). WRED differs from other congestion-avoidance techniques because it attempts to anticipate and avoid congestion instead of controlling congestion after it occurs. WRED uses TCP congestion control and tries to control the average queue size by notifying end hosts when they should stop sending packets temporarily. WRED randomly drops packets before periods of high congestion to instruct the packet source to decrease its transmission rate. If the packet source is using TCP, WRED instructs it to decrease its transmission rate until all the packets reach their destination and the congestion is cleared.

WRED drops more packets from large users than small users. Therefore, sources that generate a lot of traffic are more likely to be slowed down than sources that generate limited amounts of traffic.

In this lab, you configure WRED in its simplest form. You use the default IP Precedence bits in a packet to determine the weighting. Figure 8-5 shows the topology for this lab.

Figure 8-5 Topology for Lab 8.9.5

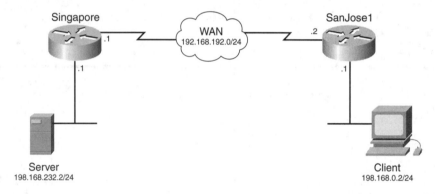

Scenario

The performance of the WAN link between Singapore and SanJose1 is not optimal. During a quiet period, large files are copied across the link to test the link throughput. This reveals that the throughput is considerably less than the 128-kbps bandwidth suggests. Network analysis indicates that the 128-kbps bottleneck causes the egress queue on the Singapore router to overflow when SanJose1 requests a large file. This causes TCP/IP to reduce its transmission speed drastically and increases the unnecessary retransmission of data. You can solve this problem by using WRED.

Step 1

Do not cable the lab until you have erased the router configuration files and reloaded the routers.

Build the physical topology as shown in Figure 8-5.

Step 2

Configure the network as shown in Figure 8-5 and enable EIGRP with an autonomous system number of 100 as the routing protocol. Confirm connectivity by pinging between the hosts.

Step 3

Use the interface **random-detect** command to enable WRED on the Serial 0/0 exit queues of each router:

```
Singapore(config-if)#random-detect
```

```
SanJose1(config-if)#random-detect
```

You do not need to specify other commands or parameters to configure WRED on the interface with the default parameter values.

Step 4

Use the **show interface** command to verify the configuration and operation of WRED.

```
Singapore#show interface serial 0/0
Serial0/0 is up, line protocol is up
  Hardware is PowerQUICC Serial
  Internet address is 192.168.192.1/24
  MTU 1500 bytes, BW 128 Kbit, DLY 20000 usec,
     reliability 255/255, txload 1/255, rxload 1/255
  Encapsulation HDLC, loopback not set
  Keepalive set (10 sec)
  Last input 00:00:00, output 00:00:03, output hang never
  Last clearing of "show interface" counters never
  Input queue: 0/75/0/0 (size/max/drops/flushes); Total output drops: 707
  Queueing strategy: random early detection(RED)
  5 minute input rate 0 bits/sec, 0 packets/sec
  5 minute output rate 0 bits/sec, 0 packets/sec
     72 packets input, 5041 bytes, 0 no buffer
     Received 56 broadcasts, 0 runts, 0 giants, 0 throttles
     3 input errors, 0 CRC, 3 frame, 0 overrun, 0 ignored, 0 abort
     151 packets output, 7317 bytes, 0 underruns
     0 output errors, 0 collisions, 3 interface resets
     0 output buffer failures, 0 output buffers swapped out
     11 carrier transitions
     DCD=up  DSR=up  DTR=up  RTS=up  CTS=up
```

You can view the thresholds that WRED is using to determine packet drop by implementing the **show queueing random-detect** command:

```
Singapore#show queueing random-detect
Current random-detect configuration:
  Serial0/0
    Queueing strategy: random early detection (WRED)
    Exp-weight-constant: 9 (1/512)
    Mean queue depth: 0
```

class	Random drop pkts/bytes	Tail drop pkts/bytes	Minimum thresh	Maximum thresh	Mark prob
0	0/0	0/0	20	40	1/10
1	0/0	0/0	22	40	1/10
2	0/0	0/0	24	40	1/10
3	0/0	0/0	26	40	1/10
4	0/0	0/0	28	40	1/10
5	0/0	0/0	31	40	1/10
6	0/0	0/0	33	40	1/10
7	0/0	0/0	35	40	1/10
rsvp	0/0	0/0	37	40	1/10

Step 5

Use the **random-detect** command to modify the default thresholds that WRED uses to determine packet drop. This command configures the weight factor that calculates the average queue length:

```
Singapore(config-if)#random-detect exponential-weighting-constant exponent
```

The following command configures parameters for packets with a specific IP Precedence:

```
Singapore(config-if)#random-detect precedence precedence min-threshold max-threshold
```

Experiment with these commands and observe any changes with the **show queueing random-detect** command.

The minimum threshold for IP Precedence 0 corresponds to half the maximum threshold for the interface. Repeat this command for each precedence. To configure RED instead of WRED, use the same parameters for each precedence.

Note: Do not change the default WRED parameter values unless the applications will benefit from the changed values.

Lab 8.9.6: Configuring WRED with CBWFQ

Estimated Time: 60 Minutes

Objective

Class-based weighted fair queuing (CBWFQ) extends the standard WFQ functionality to provide support for user-defined traffic classes. You define traffic classes for CBWFQ by using match criteria, such as protocols, Access Control Lists (ACLs), and input interfaces. Packets that satisfy the match criteria for a class constitute the traffic for the class. A FIFO queue is reserved for each class, and traffic that belongs to a class is directed to the queue for the class.

After you define a class according to its match criteria, you can assign characteristics to each class. To characterize a class, assign a bandwidth, weight, and maximum packet limit. The bandwidth that you assign to a class is the guaranteed bandwidth that is delivered to the class during congestion.

In this lab, you configure CBWFQ in conjunction with WRED. CBWFQ provides a guaranteed percentage of the output bandwidth, and WRED ensures that the TCP traffic is not sent faster than CBWFQ can forward it. Figure 8-6 shows the topology for this lab.

Figure 8-6 Topology for Lab 8.9.6

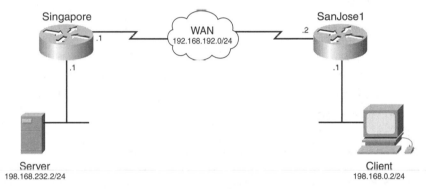

Scenario

Management would like to reduce costs by routing IP voice packets across the WAN. Access layer switches in the network are marking voice packets with a DSCP of 40. Ensure that these voice packets are guaranteed 40 percent of the available WAN bandwidth.

Step 1

Do not cable the lab until you have erased the router configuration files and reloaded the routers.

Build and configure the physical topology as shown in Figure 8-6. Use EIGRP with an autonomous system of 100 as the routing protocol.

Step 2

Use a class map to classify the traffic as the first step in providing QoS. The packets that should receive preferential treatment have already been marked with a DSCP of 40:

```
SanJose1(config)#class-map voice-class
SanJose1(config-cmap)#match ip dscp 40
```

```
Singapore(config)#class-map voice-class
Singapore(config-cmap)#match ip dscp 40
```

Step 3

Create a policy for the treatment of the traffic within the network through a policy map.

Begin by determining a policy for all traffic that is not voice. An efficient scheme for queuing general traffic is WFQ. This traffic class will be the **class-default**, and it will be a catchall for traffic that has not been classified specifically:

```
SanJose1(config)#policy-map wan-policy
SanJose1(config-pmap)#class class-default
SanJose1(config-pmap-c)#fair-queue
```

```
Singapore(config)#policy-map wan-policy
Singapore(config-pmap)#class class-default
Singapore(config-pmap-c)#fair-queue
```

Step 4

Create a policy for the treatment of the voice traffic by allowing 40 percent of the WAN link bandwidth:

```
SanJose1(config)#policy-map wan-policy
SanJose1(config-pmap)#class voice-class
SanJose1(config-pmap-c)#bandwidth percent 40
```

```
Singapore(config)#policy-map wan-policy
Singapore(config-pmap)#class voice-class
Singapore(config-pmap-c)#bandwidth percent 40
```

Step 5

Use the WRED method of congestion avoidance by adding the **random-detect** command to the policy map of both routers. If the 40 percent of bandwidth that is configured for voice-class traffic is exceeded, the default behavior is to drop any packets that cannot be accommodated immediately in the queue:

```
SanJose1(config)#policy-map wan-policy
SanJose1(config-pmap)#class voice-class
SanJose1(config-pmap-c)#random-detect
```

```
Singapore(config)#policy-map wan-policy
Singapore(config-pmap)#class voice-class
Singapore(config-pmap-c)#random-detect
```

Note: This step is included as a demonstration of how to provide WRED functionality by using the modular QoS CLI. WRED is designed to work with TCP streams that respond to dropped packets by reducing their transmission rate. Voice uses User Datagram Protocol (UDP) and is incapable of adjusting its rate. Voice networks should be designed to avoid packet loss.

Step 6

Use the **show run** and **show policy-map** commands to see the full structure of the policy map.

Step 7

Complete the configuration of QoS by using the MQC to apply the policy to an interface. Apply the policy to the outgoing serial interface on each router with the **service-policy** command:

```
SanJose1(config)#interface serial 0/0
SanJose1(config-if)#service-policy output wan-policy
```

```
Singapore(config)#interface serial 0/0
Singapore(config)#no fair-queue
Singapore(config-if)#service-policy output wan-policy
```

Step 8

Which **show** commands are used to verify the following?

Configuration of the class map

1.

Policy is applied correctly to the interface

2.

Lab 8.9.7: Configuring Low Latency Queuing (LLQ)

Objective

Low latency queuing (LLQ) enables the use of a single, strict priority queue within CBWFQ at the class level. You can make any class a priority queue by adding the **priority** keyword. Within a policy map, you can give one or more classes priority status. When you configure multiple classes within a single policy map as priority classes, all traffic from these classes is sent to the same, single, strict priority queue. Figure 8-7 shows the topology for this lab.

Figure 8-7 Topology for Lab 8.9.7

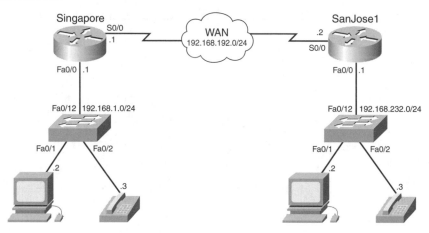

Scenario

Management informs you that it wants to reduce its costs by routing IP voice packets across your WAN. The IP phones in your network are not capable of setting QoS values themselves. Consequently, you must configure your access layer switch (2950T) to assign an IP DSCP of 48 to packets that originate from MAC addresses that are associated with your IP phones. You also must ensure that your WAN router guarantees these voice packets 80 kbps of WAN bandwidth. Finally, to achieve the lowest latency, you must create a priority queue for the voice traffic that is traversing the WAN link.

Step 1

Build and configure the physical topology as shown in Figure 8-7. The WAN link should use a clock rate of 1,000,000 bps, because this makes the difference between the voice bandwidth and the bandwidth that is available for other traffic more obvious.

Achieve basic IP connectivity among all devices by configuring EIGRP with an AS of 100 as your routing protocol. Initially, you can leave the switches with their default configuration.

Designate one PC at each location to simulate an IP phone connected to interface 0/2 of the local switch.

Step 2

Configure the access layer switch to mark traffic originating from the IP phones (PC, in this case) with a DSCP of 48:

```
SingaporeSwitch(config)#ip access-list standard phone
SingaporeSwitch(config-std-nacl)#permit 192.168.0.3
SingaporeSwitch(config)#class-map match-all voice-class
SingaporeSwitch(config-cmap)#match access-group name phone
SingaporeSwitch(config)#policy-map voice-policy
SingaporeSwitch(config-pmap)#class voice-class
SingaporeSwitch(config-pmap)#set ip dscp 48
```

```
SingaporeSwitch(config)#interface fastethernet 0/2
SingaporeSwitch(config-if)#service-policy input voice-policy
```

```
SanJose1Switch(config)#ip access-list standard phone
SanJose1Switch(config-std-nacl)#permit 192.168.232.3
SanJose1Switch(config)#class-map match-all voice-class
SanJose1Switch(config-cmap)#match access-group name phone
SanJose1Switch(config)#policy-map voice-policy
SanJose1Switch(config-pmap)#class voice-class
SanJose1Switch(config-pmap)#set ip dscp 48
SanJose1Switch(config)#interface fastethernet 0/2
SanJose1Switch(config-if)#service-policy input voice-policy
```

Notice that traffic is identified as originating from the IP phone on the basis of the IP phone's IP address. Any traffic that has this source address is classified as voice-class traffic, and a policy for this class of traffic sets the DSCP bits to a value of 48.

Step 3

After you have marked the traffic at the access layer, the next step is to create a policy for the treatment of the traffic within your WAN. Configure a class map on each router to classify frames with a DSCP of 48 as voice:

```
Singapore(config)#class-map voice-class
Singapore(config-cmap)#match ip dscp 48
```

```
SanJose1(config)#class-map voice-class
SanJose1(config-cmap)# match ip dscp 48
```

Step 4

Now that you have classified the router traffic, you apply the appropriate commands to a policy map to enable LLQ.

To begin, determine a policy for all traffic that is not voice. An efficient scheme for queuing general traffic is WFQ. This traffic class will be the **class-default** class, and it will be a catchall for traffic that you have not classified as voice:

```
SanJose1(config)#policy-map wan-policy
SanJose1(config-pmap)#class class-default
SanJose1(config-pmap-c)#fair-queue
```

```
Singapore(config)#policy-map wan-policy
Singapore(config-pmap)#class class-default
Singapore(config-pmap-c)#fair-queue
```

Step 5

Create a policy for the treatment of your voice traffic. Specifically, you need to allow 80 kbps of the WAN's bandwidth and specify that priority queuing be used for this class of traffic.

The command that provides this functionality is the **priority** *bandwidth* option of the policy map:

```
SanJose1(config)#policy-map wan-policy
SanJose1(config-pmap)#class voice-class
SanJose1(config-pmap-c)#priority 80
```

```
Singapore(config)#policy-map wan-policy
Singapore(config-pmap)#class voice-class
Singapore(config-pmap-c)#priority 80
```

Voice traffic that is queued to the priority queue is UDP-based; therefore, it is not adaptive to the early packet drop that is characteristic of WRED. Because WRED is ineffective, you cannot use the WRED **random-detect** command with the **priority** command. In addition, because you use policing to drop packets and a queue limit is not imposed, you cannot use the **queue-limit** command with the **priority** command.

Step 6

The final step in configuring QoS using the MQC is to apply the policy to an interface. Apply the policy to the outgoing serial interface on each router by using the **service-policy** command:

```
SanJose1(config)#interface s0/0
SanJose1(config-if)#service-policy output wan-policy
```

```
Singapore(config)#interface s0/0
Singapore(config-if)#service-policy output wan-policy
```

Step 7

When you specify the **priority** command for a class, it takes a *bandwidth* argument that specifies the maximum bandwidth in kbps. This parameter specifies the maximum amount of bandwidth that is allocated for packets belonging to the configured class. The bandwidth parameter both guarantees bandwidth to the priority class and restrains the flow of packets from the priority class. If congestion occurs, you can use policing to drop packets when the bandwidth is exceeded.

You can use the **debug priority** command to monitor LLQ and determine if the priority queue is overloaded and dropping packets.

Turn on priority debugging on the Singapore router:

```
Singapore# debug priority
```

At this stage, no traffic is flowing, so you should not see drops from the priority queue.

Step 8

Verify the configuration of LLQ using the following commands:

```
Router#show queue interface-type interface-number
```

```
Router#show policy-map interface interface-name
```

The **show policy-map interface** command displays the configuration of all classes that are configured for all traffic policies on the specified interface. It also displays if packets and bytes were discarded or dropped for the priority class in the traffic policy that is attached to the interface.

Step 9

Configure the workstations to allow file sharing. Copy a large file from the PC at Singapore to the PC at SanJose1. Simultaneously copy a file from the telephone (PC) at Singapore to the telephone at SanJose1.

What do you notice about the bandwidth utilization of the PC versus the telephone?

_____

Are packets being dropped?

_____

_____

Note: Do not expect the simulated voice traffic to achieve 80 kbps of throughput.

_____

Real voice traffic is UDP. Any packets that are dropped before crossing the WAN will not affect the data rate that the IP phone supplies. (The voice quality would suffer, though.) In this case, the throughput could be up to 80 kbps.

In this simulation, you are using TCP for the file copy. As packets are dropped, TCP retransmits from the point at which the packet was lost and reduces its window size in response to the congestion. These two factors drastically reduce the throughput across the link.

Lab 8.9.8: Configuring Generic Traffic Shaping (GTS)

Estimated Time: 60 Minutes

Objective

Generic traffic shaping (GTS) shapes traffic by reducing outbound traffic flow to avoid congestion. It does this by constraining traffic to a particular bit rate using the token bucket mechanism. GTS applies to a per-interface basis and can use access lists to select the traffic to shape.

In this lab, you configure GTS on an interface. Figure 8-8 shows the topology for this lab.

Figure 8-8 Topology for Lab 8.9.8

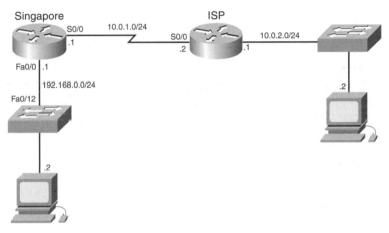

Scenario

Assume that the ISP has a policy of installing T1 links to all its customers and traffic shaping the data to match the bandwidth that the customer has paid for. Configure the customer router and the ISP router to shape traffic to a maximum rate of 128 kbps using GTS.

Step 1

Do not cable the lab until you have erased the switch and router configuration files and the switch vlan.dat files and reloaded the devices.

Build and configure the physical topology as shown in Figure 8-8. The WAN link should use a clock rate of approximately T1 speed, or 1,544,000 bps. This means that the routers must use the WIC2T serial modules. Use EIGRP with an autonomous system of 100 as the routing protocol. You can leave the switches in their default configuration.

Step 2

On each router serial interface, configure GTS using the **traffic-shape rate** command:

```
Router(config-if)#traffic-shape [group access-list-number | rate] bit-rate [burst-size [excess-burst-size]]
```

Note: The **traffic-shape** command uses either **group** or **rate**, depending on the presence or absence of an ACL.

The bit rate determines the average data rate that is permitted out of the specified interface. The burst size is the number of bits that you can send as a single burst within a time period. The instantaneous bit rate can be much higher than the average bit rate. You should configure the burst size so that no peaks overwhelm the input queue of the destination interface. The time period (T_c) over which the bit rate is measured is given by the following formula:

T_c = burst size/bit rate

The ISP requests that the burst size is limited to 12,800 bits. The ISP polices this rate and drops any packets that exceed this burst rate. Configure an excess burst size that is no higher than 12,800 bits:

```
Singapore(config)#interface serial 0/0
Singapore(config-if)#traffic-shape rate 128000 12800 12800
```

```
ISP(config)#interface serial 0/0
ISP(config-if)#traffic-shape rate 128000 12800 12800
```

Step 3

Verify the configuration of the **traffic-shape** command using the **show traffic-shape** command:

```
Singapore#show traffic-shape
Interface   Se0/0
       Access Target  Byte   Sustain   Excess    Interval  Increment Adapt
VC     List   Rate    Limit  bits/int  bits/int  (ms)      (bytes)   Active
-             128000  3200   12800     12800     100       1600      -
```

Verify the operation of GTS using the **show traffic-shape statistics** command:

```
Singapore #show traffic-shape statistics
               Access Queue   Packets   Bytes    Packets   Bytes    Shaping
I/F            List   Depth                      Delayed   Delayed  Active
Se0/0                 0       0         0        0         0        no
```

At this stage, no traffic is flowing, so no shaping is active.

Step 4

Enable file sharing on the PCs and copy a large file over the WAN link.

1. What is the maximum transfer speed achieved over the T1 WAN link?

_____

2. How else can you confirm that GTS is active?

_____

Lab 8.9.9: QoS Manually Configured Frame Relay Traffic Shaping

Estimated Time: 90 Minutes

Objective

Failing to perform traffic shaping before injecting traffic into a Frame Relay permanent virtual circuit (PVC) is likely to lead to dropped frames, because the traffic rate will exceed the guarantees of the service provider. In this lab, you use Frame Relay traffic shaping (FRTS) to shape traffic exiting a Frame Relay interface. You do this so that the traffic matches the committed information rate (CIR), committed burst (Bc), and excess burst (Be) that the service provider provides. Figure 8-9 shows the topology for this lab.

Figure 8-9 Topology for Lab 8.9.9

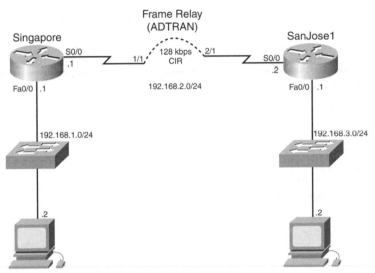

Scenario

You recently added a Frame Relay link between the Singapore and SanJose1 offices. The Frame Relay service provider guarantees a CIR of 128 kbps and a Bc of 256 kbps. Configure the routers so that these rates are not exceeded.

Step 1

Do not cable the lab until you have erased the switch and router configuration files and the switch vlan.dat files and reloaded the devices.

Build and configure the network according to Figure 8-9. Configure EIGRP with an autonomous system of 100 as the routing protocol. The configuration of FRTS occurs on the routers, which means that you can leave the access layer switches in the factory-default configuration.

Configure Frame Relay using subinterfaces as follows:

```
Singapore(config)#interface serial 0/0
Singapore(config-if)#encapsulation frame-relay
Singapore(config-if)#interface serial 0/0.103 point-to-point
Singapore(config-subif)#frame-relay interface-dlci 103
Singapore(config-fr-dlci)#ip address 192.168.2.1 255.255.255.0
```

```
SanJose1(config)#interface serial 0/0
SanJose1(config-if)#encapsulation frame-relay
SanJose1(config-if)#interface serial 0/0.301 point-to-point
SanJose1(config-subif)#frame-relay interface-dlci 301
SanJose1(config-fr-dlci)#ip address 192.168.2.2 255.255.255.0
```

Verify the configuration by pinging between the hosts and troubleshoot as necessary.

Step 2

On each router, configure a map class to define the shape of the traffic. The CIR should be 128 kbps. You can use any Bc as long as it is not greater than the Bc that the service provider specifies. A smaller Bc produces a smoother traffic flow because jitter is reduced. For voice traffic, keep Bc to 1 percent of the CIR. In this example, some jitter is acceptable in return for the higher performance that a larger Bc allows. Set the Bc at 12,800 bps. The application requires that traffic loss be minimized, so Be over the CIR is not allowed. This should prevent the service provider from marking any frames as discard eligible (DE) and prevent the frames from potentially being dropped.

Use the command **map-class frame-relay** *map-name* to create a map-class. Then use the question mark to examine the available options:

```
Singapore(config)#map-class frame-relay myclass
```

```
SanJose1(config)#map-class frame-relay myclass
```

Configure the Frame-Relay parameters as follows:

```
Singapore(config-map-class)#frame-relay cir 128000
Singapore(config-map-class)#frame-relay bc 12800
Singapore(config-map-class)#frame-relay be 0
Singapore(config-map-class)#frame-relay fair-queue
```

```
SanJose1(config-map-class)#frame-relay cir 128000
SanJose1(config-map-class)#frame-relay bc 12800
SanJose1(config-map-class)#frame-relay be 0
SanJose1(config-map-class)#frame-relay fair-queue
```

Step 3

To activate FRTS, apply the **frame-relay traffic-shaping** commands to the Frame Relay (S0/0) interface:

```
Singapore(config)#interface serial 0/0
Singapore(config-if)#frame-relay traffic-shaping
```

```
SanJose1(config)#interface serial 0/0
SanJose1(config-if)#frame-relay traffic-shaping
```

After FRTS is activated on the interface, you must specify the traffic shape or map class for each PVC using the **frame-relay class** statement on the subinterface:

```
Singapore(config-if)#interface serial 0/0.103
Singapore(config-subif)#frame-relay class myclass
```

```
SanJose1(config-if)#interface serial 0/0.301 point-to-point
SanJose1(config-subif)#frame-relay class myclass
```

Step 4

To test the traffic shaping, set up file sharing on the Singapore host and copy a large file to the SanJose1 host. After a couple of minutes of copying, use the **show interface serial 0/0** command to determine the average traffic rate:

```
Singapore#show interface serial 0/0
Serial0/0 is up, line protocol is up
  Hardware is PowerQUICC Serial
  MTU 1500 bytes, BW 1544 Kbit, DLY 20000 usec,
      reliability 255/255, txload 15/255, rxload 1/255
  Encapsulation FRAME-RELAY, loopback not set
  Keepalive set (10 sec)
  LMI enq sent  612, LMI stat recvd 612, LMI upd recvd 0, DTE LMI up
  LMI enq recvd 0, LMI stat sent  0, LMI upd sent  0
  LMI DLCI 0   LMI type is ANSI Annex D  frame relay DTE
  Broadcast queue 0/64, broadcasts sent/dropped 1438/0, interface broadcasts 1336  Last input 00:00:04, output
00:00:00, output hang never
  Last clearing of "show interface" counters 01:41:58
  Input queue: 0/75/0/0 (size/max/drops/flushes); Total output drops: 0
  Queueing strategy: fifo
  Output queue :0/40 (size/max)
  5 minute input rate 2000 bits/sec, 6 packets/sec
  5 minute output rate 91000 bits/sec, 12 packets/sec
     5185 packets input, 308420 bytes, 0 no buffer
     Received 0 broadcasts, 0 runts, 0 giants, 0 throttles
     0 input errors, 0 CRC, 0 frame, 0 overrun, 0 ignored, 0 abort
     6353 packets output, 5078253 bytes, 0 underruns
     0 output errors, 0 collisions, 0 interface resets
     0 output buffer failures, 0 output buffers swapped out
     0 carrier transitions
     DCD=up  DSR=up  DTR=up  RTS=up  CTS=up
```

Step 5

Try making the CIR much smaller, 10 kbps, and confirm that FRTS is in fact shaping the traffic.

Lab 8.9.10: Quality of Service Dynamic Frame Relay Traffic Shaping

Estimated Time: 60 Minutes

Objective

Failing to perform traffic shaping before injecting traffic into a Frame Relay PVC is likely to lead to dropped frames. These dropped frames occur as the traffic rate exceeds the guarantees of the service provider.

In this lab, you use dynamic FRTS to shape traffic that is exiting a Frame Relay interface. You do this so that the traffic flow responds to backward explicit congestion notification (BECN) that it receives from the Frame Relay switch. Figure 8-10 shows the topology for this lab.

Figure 8-10 Topology for Lab 8.9.10

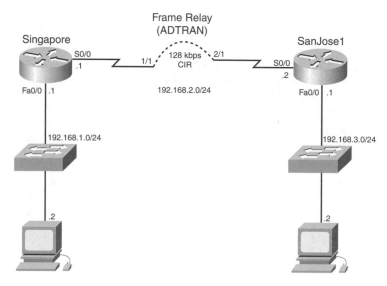

Scenario

You have added a Frame Relay link between the offices in Singapore and San Jose. The Frame Relay service provider guarantees a CIR of 128 Kbps and a Bc of 256 kbps. As a user, it is important to take advantage of the ability of the Frame Relay to burst above the CIR. Use dynamic traffic shaping to minimize any traffic loss during periods when the Frame Relay provider network might become congested.

Step 1

Do not cable the lab until you have erased the switch and router configuration files and the switch vlan.dat files and reloaded the devices.

Build and configure the network according to Figure 8-10. Configure EIGRP with an autonomous system of 100 as the routing protocol. The configuration of FRTS occurs on the routers, so you can leave the access layer switches in their factory-default configuration.

You should configure the Frame Relay using the subinterfaces as follows:

```
Singapore(config)#interface serial 0/0
Singapore(config-if)#encapsulation frame-relay
Singapore(config-if)#interface serial 0/0.103 point-to-point
```

```
Singapore(config-subif)#frame-relay interface-dlci 103
Singapore(config-subif)#ip address 192.168.2.1 255.255.255.0
```

```
SanJose1(config)#interface serial 0/0
SanJose1(config-if)#encapsulation frame-relay
SanJose1(config-if)#interface serial 0/0.301 point-to-point
SanJose1(config-subif)#frame-relay interface-dlci 301
SanJose1(config-subif)#ip address 192.168.2.2 255.255.255.0
```

Verify the configuration by pinging between the hosts, and troubleshoot as necessary.

Step 2

On each router, specify the maximum rate that should be used over the Frame Relay link with the **traffic-shape rate** command. In this example, set the maximum rate to the Bc speed of 256 kbps. Use the interface **traffic-shape adaptive** command to allow the interface to recognize BECNs and adjust its output rate accordingly:

```
Singapore(config-if)#interface serial 0/0.103 point-to-point
Singapore(config-subif)#traffic-shape rate 256000
Singapore(config-subif)#traffic-shape adaptive 128000
```

```
SanJose1(config-if)#interface serial 0/0.301 point-to-point
SanJose1(config-subif)#traffic-shape rate 256000
SanJose1(config-subif)#traffic-shape adaptive 128000
```

Note that the **traffic-shape adaptive** command takes a parameter that defines the traffic rate to be used when BECNs are received. Normally, you set this value to the CIR of the virtual circuit. The actual data rate falls between these two values.

Step 3

You can verify adaptive traffic shaping configuration by using the **show traffic-shape** command:

```
Singapore#show traffic-shape serial 0/0.103
```

```
Interface   Se0/0.17
          Access Target Byte  Sustain  Excess   Interval Increment Adapt
VC        List   Rate   Limit bits/int bits/int (ms)     (bytes)   Active
-                256000 1984  7936     7936     31       992       BECN
```

Congratulations! You have configured Frame Relay to automatically adapt its transmission rate to the congestion in the Frame Relay switch.

Lab 8.9.11: Configuring Link Fragmentation and Interleaving

Estimated Time: 120 Minutes

Objective

In this lab, you configure Link Fragmentation and Interleaving (LFI) to control latency over a low-speed WAN link. Figure 8-11 shows the topology for this lab.

Figure 8-11 Topology for Lab 8.9.11

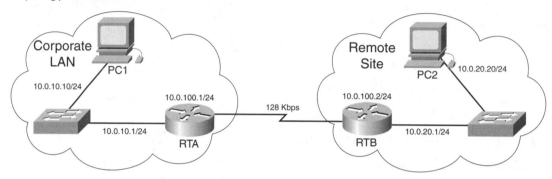

Scenario

The International Travel Agency has a low-speed, 128-kbps WAN link to a remote office. To save costs, the agency wants to send its long-distance voice traffic over this link. The system works correctly when voice traffic travels across the WAN link on its own. However, even a small simultaneous transfer of data packets results in a severely degraded or unusable voice call. Configure LFI to ensure that small delay-sensitive voice packets do not get stuck behind large data packets traveling across the WAN link.

Step 1

Do not cable the lab until you have erased the switch and router configuration files and the switch vlan.dat files and reloaded the devices.

Build and configure the network according to Figure 8-11. Use EIGRP as the routing protocol, and set the clock rate to 128 kbps.

Use the **ping** and **show ip route** commands to test the connectivity among all interfaces. The two PCs should be able to ping each other.

Step 2

Configure file sharing on PC 1 and verify files that can be transferred from PC 1 to PC 2. You will use the transfer of files from PC 1 to PC 2 to create data traffic to compete with the simulated voice traffic.

Step 3

To simulate voice traffic traveling across the WAN link, ping PC 2 from the command prompt on PC 1. Use the following ping parameters to generate a continuous stream of small packets:

```
Ping -t -l 60 -w 5000 10.0.20.20
```

The **-t** option pings the specified host until it is stopped. Use Ctrl-Break to suspend and Ctrl-C to stop. The **-l** option specifies a packet length of 60 bytes, and **-w 5000** instructs ping to wait up to 5 seconds before declaring that a timeout has occurred. By default, ping waits only 2 seconds. Type **ping** and press **Enter** at the PC command prompt to see the various options available.

1. What is the average time for a packet to cross the WAN link? _____ ms

2. What is the acceptable latency for voice traffic?

_____ ms

Step 4

Use PC 2 to copy a large file from PC 1. Then examine the continuous ping that is running on PC 1.

1. What is the average time for a packet to cross the WAN link? _____ ms

2. Would this be acceptable for voice traffic?

_____

_____

Note: The **ping** command measures the round-trip time, whereas the latency requirements for voice are stated in terms of a one-way trip. However, because the link is heavily congested in one direction only, most of the latency is experienced in the PC 1 to PC 2 direction.

Step 5

The amount of latency experienced is the result of voice packets waiting in the router queue for the data packets to cross the WAN link. You could attempt problem resolution by implementing some kind of priority queuing scheme. However, a voice packet will arrive just as a data packet has started its journey across the WAN link. The voice packet will have to wait for the data packet to be sent before it can be forwarded across the WAN link. If the data packet is 1500 bytes in length, the wait could be up to 93 ms:

$$1500 \text{ (bytes)} * 8 \text{ (bits)} / 128{,}000 \text{ (bandwidth)} = 93 \text{ ms}$$

Clearly, even giving priority to voice packets cannot guarantee low latency when the link is shared with large packets.

To guarantee a low latency, you need to fragment any large packets into smaller pieces. The IOS feature that allows this to occur is LFI.

LFI makes use of the PPP multilink ability to break up and reassemble traffic across multiple physical links. LFI also can break up and reassemble fragments across a single physical link. To achieve this, you must create a PPP multilink virtual interface and link this to the physical interface.

Begin by removing the IP address from the physical interface and configuring PPP multilink:

```
RTA(config)#interface serial 0/0
RTA(config-if)#no ip address
RTA(config-if)#encapsulation ppp
RTA(config-if)#ppp multilink
RTA(config-if)#shutdown
```

```
RTB(config)#interface serial 0/0
RTB(config-if)#no ip address
RTB(config-if)#encapsulation ppp
RTB(config-if)#ppp multilink
RTB(config-if)#shutdown
```

Step 6

Configure a PPP multilink virtual interface called multilink 1 and set the IP address:

```
RTA(config)#interface multilink 1
RTA(config-if)#ip address 10.0.100.1 255.255.255.0
```

```
RTB(config)#interface multilink 1
RTB(config-if)#ip address 10.0.100.2 255.255.255.0
```

Step 7

Use the **ppp multilink fragment-delay** command to instruct the routers to break up any large packets into fragments that will not take longer than 10 ms to cross the WAN link:

```
RTA(config)#interface multilink 1
RTA(config-if)#ppp multilink fragment-delay 10
RTA(config-if)#bandwidth 128
```

```
RTB(config)#interface multilink 1
RTB(config-if)#ppp multilink fragment-delay 10
RTB(config-if)#bandwidth 128
```

The **bandwidth** command is an essential element because the router uses this value in conjunction with the **ppp multilink fragment-delay** command to determine the size of the fragments.

Step 8

The **ppp multilink fragment-delay** command used in Step 7 breaks up larger packets. PPP still delivers all the fragments belonging to one packet before forwarding any new packets. You can change this behavior by using the **ppp multilink interleave** command:

```
RTA(config)#interface multilink 1
RTA(config-if)#ppp multilink interleave
```

```
RTB(config)#interface multilink 1
RTB(config-if)#ppp multilink interleave
```

Step 9

At this point, large packets have been broken into smaller fragments, and PPP will interleave new packets subject to whatever queuing strategy is in place. However, if the queuing strategy is FIFO, the voice packets likely will get caught behind a stream of fragmented data packets. By turning on WFQ, intermittent traffic gets a better chance of accessing the media:

```
RTA(config)#interface multilink 1
RTA(config-if)#fair-queue
```

```
RTB(config)#interface multilink 1
RTB(config-if)#fair-queue
```

Step 10

It is now necessary to tell the router that the virtual interface, multilink 1, will use physical interface S0/0:

```
RTA(config)#interface serial 0/0
RTA(config-if)#ppp multilink group 1
RTA(config-if)#no shutdown
```

```
RTB(config)#interface serial 0/0
RTB(config-if)#ppp multilink group 1
RTB(config-if)#no shutdown
```

Step 11

Verify the operation of the PPP multilink bundle by using the **show ppp multilink** command:

```
RTA#show ppp multilink

Multilink1, bundle name is RTA
  Bundle up for 00:42:54
  0 lost fragments, 0 reordered, 0 unassigned
  0 discarded, 0 lost received, 1/255 load
  0x244F received sequence, 0x3477 sent sequence
  Member links: 1 active, 0 inactive (max not set, min not set)
    Serial0/0, since 00:42:54, last rcvd seq 00244E 160 weight RTA#
```

Step 12

Verify the operation of the LFI feature by using the **debug ppp multilink fragments** command.

CAUTION: This **debug** command generates a large volume of console information. It might be difficult to turn off the debug if a file is being copied across the WAN link. Use this command with caution in a live network environment.

```
RTA#debug ppp multilink fragments
Multilink fragments debugging is on
RTA#
*Mar 1 00:55:58.063: Se0/0 MLP: O frag 00004FD1 size 160
*Mar 1 00:55:58.067: Se0/0 MLP: I frag C00031FA size 50 direct
*Mar 1 00:55:58.083: Se0/0 MLP: O frag 00004FD2 size 160
*Mar 1 00:55:58.083: Se0/0 MLP: O frag 00004FD3 size 160
*Mar 1 00:55:58.103: Se0/0 MLP: O frag 00004FD4 size 160
*Mar 1 00:55:58.103: Se0/0 MLP: O frag 00004FD5 size 160
*Mar 1 00:55:58.123: Se0/0 MLP: O frag 00004FD6 size 160
*Mar 1 00:55:58.123: Se0/0 MLP: O frag 00004FD7 size 160
*Mar 1 00:55:58.143: Se0/0 MLP: O frag 40004FD8 size 94
*Mar 1 00:55:58.143: Se0/0 MLP: O frag 80004FD9 size 160
*Mar 1 00:55:58.151: Se0/0 MLP: O frag 00004FDA size 160
*Mar 1 00:55:58.171: Se0/0 MLP: O frag 00004FDB size 160
*Mar 1 00:55:58.171: Se0/0 MLP: O frag 00004FDC size 160
*Mar 1 00:55:58.191: Se0/0 MLP: O frag 00004FDD size 160
```

Note that the large packets are broken down into 160-byte fragments.

1. How many milliseconds does it take to transmit 160 bytes at 128 kbps?

Step 13

Repeat the file and copy and ping test of Steps 2 and 3. Notice that the reduced ping times are well within the latency requirements of voice traffic. If everything is configured correctly, the ping times should be reduced to approximately 30 ms.

Step 14

Although the configuration performed so far is capable of providing the low latency that is required for voice traffic, the limitations of WFQ will become apparent. As you add more streams of traffic, WFQ will provide fair access to each of the streams. This eventually will result in insufficient bandwidth to support a voice call. What is really required is guaranteed bandwidth for the voice traffic.

To provide guaranteed bandwidth, begin by identifying the voice traffic with access lists:

```
RTA(config)#access-list 102 permit udp any any range 16384 32767
RTA(config)#access-list 103 permit tcp any eq 1720 any
RTA(config)#access-list 103 permit tcp any any eq 1720
```

```
RTB(config)#access-list 102 permit udp any any range 16384 32767
RTB(config)#access-list 103 permit tcp any eq 1720 any
RTB(config)#access-list 103 permit tcp any any eq 1720
```

UDP represents voice, and TCP represents call management. They are defined using separate access lists because the QoS requirements differ.

Step 15

Create class maps that define the classes of traffic using the ACLs:

```
RTA(config)#class-map match-all voice-signaling
RTA(config-cmap)#match access-group 103
RTA(config)#class-map match-all voice-traffic
RTA(config-cmap)#match access-group 102
```

```
RTB(config)#class-map match-all voice-signaling
RTB(config-cmap)#match access-group 103
RTB(config)#class-map match-all voice-traffic
RTB(config-cmap)#match access-group 102
```

Step 16

Create a policy map that defines the QoS requirements for the classes of traffic. Ensure that 8 kbps of bandwidth is available to support voice signaling. Voice traffic is priority queued, and all other traffic is subject to a weighted fair queue:

```
RTA(config)#policy-map voice-policy
RTA(config-pmap)#class voice-signaling
RTA(config-pmap-c)#bandwidth 8
RTA(config-pmap-c)#class voice-traffic
RTA(config-pmap-c)#priority 48
RTA(config-pmap-c)#class class-default
RTA(config-pmap-c)#fair-queue
```

```
RTB(config)#policy-map voice-policy
RTB(config-pmap)#class voice-signaling
RTB(config-pmap-c)#bandwidth 8
RTB(config-pmap-c)#class voice-traffic
RTB(config-pmap-c)#priority 48
RTB(config-pmap-c)#class class-default
RTB(config-pmap-c)#fair-queue
```

Step 17

Finally, apply the QoS policy to the outbound WAN interfaces:

```
RTA(config)#interface multilink 1
RTA(config-if)#no fair-queue
RTA(config-if)#service-policy output voice-policy
```

```
RTB(config)#interface multilink 1
RTB(config-if)#no fair-queue
RTB(config-if)#service-policy output voice-policy
```

Lab 8.9.12: QoS Compressed Real Time Protocol

Estimated Time: 60 Minutes

Objective

Compressed Real Time Protocol (cRTP) allows the significant overhead that is associated with voice packet headers to be compressed substantially over point-to-point links. Configure cRTP if the network has slow links and you need to save the bandwidth. Figure 8-12 shows the topology for this lab.

Figure 8-12 Topology for Lab 8.9.12

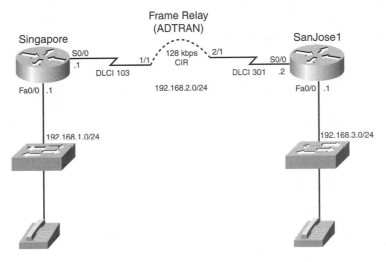

Scenario

The number of voice calls made over the Frame Relay link has increased dramatically over the past few months. Occasionally, voice quality has suffered because congestion is being experienced on the low-bandwidth WAN link. Management insists that this problem be addressed immediately.

Given that the majority of traffic is voice, you can use cRTP to improve the situation.

Note: Unless you have access to voice traffic, this lab is an exercise in configuration only.

Step 1

Do not cable the lab until you have erased the switch and router configuration files and the switch vlan.dat files and reloaded the devices.

Build and configure the network according to Figure 8-12. Configure EIGRP with an autonomous system of 100 as the routing protocol. The configuration of cRTP will occur on the routers, so you can leave the access layer switches in their factory-default (erase startup-configuration) configuration.

Configure the Frame Relay using subinterfaces:

```
Singapore(config)#interface serial 0/0
Singapore(config-if)#encapsulation frame-relay
```

```
Singapore(config-if)#interface serial 0/0.103 point-to-point
Singapore(config-subif)#frame-relay interface-dlci 103
Singapore(config-subif)#ip address 192.168.2.1 255.255.255.0
```

```
SanJose1(config)#interface serial 0/0
SanJose1(config-if)#encapsulation frame-relay
SanJose1(config-if)#interface serial 0/0.301 point-to-point
SanJose1(config-subif)#frame-relay interface-dlci 301
SanJose1(config-subif)#ip address 192.168.2.2 255.255.255.0
```

Verify the configuration by pinging between the hosts, and troubleshoot as necessary.

Step 2

You can configure an interface with cRTP, in which case any Frame Relay map inherits the configuration. Use the following command:

```
Router(config-if)#frame-relay ip rtp header-compression [passive]
```

Note: In a non-Frame Relay environment, such as a point-to-point serial link, you can use the same command without the **frame-relay** prefix.

You also can configure an individual Frame Relay map with cRTP with the following command:

```
Router(config-if)#frame-relay map ip ip-address dlci [broadcast] rtp header-compression [active ¦ passive]
```

If you include the **passive** keyword, the Cisco IOS Software compresses outgoing Real-Time Transport Protocol (RTP) packets. This compression takes place only if incoming RTP packets on the same interface are compressed. When you use the command without the **passive** keyword, the software compresses all RTP traffic.

Configure cRTP on both ends of the WAN link:

```
Singapore(config-subif)#frame-relay ip rtp header-compression
Singapore(config-subif)#frame-relay ip rtp compression-connections 20
```

```
SanJose1(config-subif)#frame-relay ip rtp header-compression
SanJose1(config-subif)#frame-relay ip rtp compression-connections 20
```

By default, the IOS only allows for the compression for 16 simultaneous voice traffic flows. The **frame-relay ip rtp compression-connections** command allows you to vary this number.

Step 3

You can monitor the operation of cRTP with the **show frame-relay ip rtp header-compression** command. Notice that the output can indicate the amount of bandwidth being saved:

```
SanJose1#show ip rtp header-compression serial 0/0
RTP/UDP/IP header compression statistics:
DLCI 301          Link/Destination info: point-to-point dlci
Interface Serial0/0:
    Rcvd:    0 total, 0 compressed, 0 errors
             0 dropped, 0 buffer copies, 0 buffer failures
    Sent:    0 total, 0 compressed,
             0 bytes saved, 0 bytes sent
    Connect: 20 rx slots, 20 tx slots,
             0 long searches, 0 misses 0 collisions, 0 negative cache hits
```

Congratulations! You have configured cRTP to manage the congested voice link successfully.

Chapter 9

Monitoring and Security

Lab 9.9.1: Creating a Switched Port Analyzer (SPAN) Session

Estimated Time: 90 Minutes

Objective

In this lab, you create a Switched Port Analyzer (SPAN) session to monitor network traffic remotely. Figure 9-1 shows the topology for this lab.

Figure 9-1 Topology for Lab 9.9.1

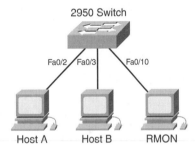

Scenario

The effective monitoring of network traffic in a fully switched network can be challenging. SPAN is included in the 2950, 3550, and 6500 switches. Therefore, you can copy and forward the LAN traffic that single or multiple switch ports receive or transmit to a monitoring port. Then you can capture and analyze this mirrored traffic.

A company recently upgraded to fully switched network architecture. To optimize network performance, you will monitor network traffic for analysis purposes. You will use the SPAN features of Cisco switches to enable this process. You will implement a SPAN session on an access layer 2950 switch to test the potential of port-centric traffic monitoring.

You will load and run protocol analysis software, such as Protocol Inspector or Optiview Protocol Expert, on a host that will act as the Remote Monitor (RMON). You must configure two hosts with IP addresses in the same subnet so that they can share network traffic.

Step 1

Do not cable the lab until you have erased the switch configuration and vlan.dat file and reloaded the switch.

Cable the lab as shown in Figure 9-1.

Enter global configuration mode in the switch IOS. Create a monitor session on the switch by defining the source interface of a monitor session called session 1:

```
Switch(config)#monitor session 1 source interface fastethernet 0/2
```

Step 2

Create a destination port, FastEthernet 0/10, to receive the mirrored traffic being sent to and transmitted from FastEthernet 0/2, which is the source port:

```
Switch(config)#monitor session 1 destination interface fastethernet 0/10
```

1. What does the switch advertise when switch port FastEthernet 0/10 becomes a destination port?

_____

_____

Step 3

Use the **show monitor** command to verify that the session has been configured correctly:

```
Switch#show monitor session 1
```

The following output should be displayed:

```
Switch#show monitor session 1
Session 1
---------
   Type:           Local Session
Source Ports:
RX Only:        None
TX Only:        None
Both:           Fa0/2
Source VLANs:
RX Only:        None
TX Only:        None
Both:           None
      Source RSPAN VLAN:    None
Destination Ports:    Fa0/10
      Encapsulation:  Native
Reflector Port:       None
Filter VLANs:         None
Dest RSPAN VLAN:      None

Switch#_
```

Configure Host A with address 192.168.1.1 and Host B with address 192.168.1.2. Use the subnet mask 255.255.255.0 for both hosts. The monitoring host that is attached to the SPAN destination port can be in any network. Ping continuously from Host A to Host B. The RMON should pick up the ICMP traffic received by FastEthernet port 0/2 and forwarded by FastEthernet port 0/2 to FastEthernet port 0/3.

1. Are other packets being forwarded to the destination port? If so, what are they?

_____

Step 4

Add an additional port to the session for mirroring onto the destination port:

```
Switch(config)#monitor session 1 source interface fastethernet 0/2 ,
             fastethernet 0/3
```

An additional port called FastEthernet 0/3 is added to monitoring session 1. You can add multiple ports by adding a space after the interface number, a comma, another space, and an additional port/port number. You can add a continuous series of ports by using a dash (—) instead of a comma to separate the initial port and the final port in a sequence.

1. Send another ping from Host A to Host B. Why should the amount of ICMP traffic increase that the RMON collects?

_____

_____

TFTP a file from Host A to Host B and observe the different packet types that are being monitored.

Step 5

Remove port FastEthernet 0/3 from the monitored port list:

```
Switch(config)#no monitor session 1 source interface fastethernet 0/3
```

Step 6

Use the **show monitor** command to verify that this has occurred:

```
Switch#show monitor session 1
```

1. Send an additional ping from Host A to Host B. How has removing port FastEthernet 0/3 from the monitor session affected the amount of data captured?

_____

_____

_____

Step 7

Remove SPAN monitoring from the switch.

Enter global configuration mode:

```
Switch(config)#no monitor session 1
```

A **show monitor session 1** reveals that the SPAN session has been deleted from the switch.

Lab 9.9.2: Creating a VSPAN Session

Estimated Time: 90 Minutes

Objective

In this lab, you create a VLAN Switched Port Analyzer (VSPAN) session to monitor network traffic remotely. Figure 9-2 shows the topology for this lab.

Figure 9-2 Topology for Lab 9.9.2

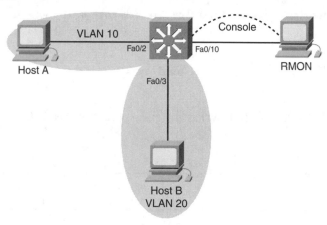

Scenario

Effective monitoring of network traffic in fully switched networks can be challenging. However, you can make it easier by including VSPAN in 3550 and 6500 switches. When you use VSPAN, you can copy and forward to a monitoring port the LAN traffic that single or multiple VLANs receive or transmit. You then can capture and analyze this mirrored traffic.

A company recently upgraded to a fully switched network architecture. To optimize network performance, the company decided to monitor network traffic for analysis purposes. You will use the VSPAN features of Cisco switches to enable this process. You will implement a VSPAN session on a distribution layer 3550 switch to explore the potential of VLAN-based traffic monitoring.

You will load and run protocol analysis software, such as Protocol Inspector or Optiview Protocol Expert, on a host that will act as the RMON for this session. You need to configure two hosts, Host A and Host B, with IP addresses in different subnets to represent hosts in different VLANs.

Step 1

Do not cable the lab until you have erased the switch configuration and vlan.dat file and reloaded the switch.

Cable the lab as shown in Figure 9-2.

Enter global configuration mode in the switch IOS. Create a VLAN that contains FastEthernet port 0/2 called VLAN 10:

```
Switch(config)#interface fastethernet 0/2
Switch(config-if)#switchport access VLAN 10
```

Next, create a VLAN that contains FastEthernet port 0/3 called VLAN 20:

```
Switch(config)#interface fastethernet 0/3
Switch(config-if)#switchport access VLAN 20
Switch(config)#exit
```

Step 2

Ensure that previous SPAN-based sessions are cleared from the switch.

In global configuration mode, enter the following command:

```
Switch(config)#no monitor session all
```

Step 3

Configure routing between VLAN 10 and VLAN 20. You can do this by creating switch virtual interfaces (SVIs) for VLAN 10 and VLAN 20. Assign IP addresses within VLAN 10 and VLAN 20 to the respective interfaces and enable **ip routing** in global configuration mode. Remember to configure the Host A and Host B default gateway with the SVI IP addresses of their respective VLAN interfaces:

```
Switch(config)#interface vlan 10
Switch(config-if)#ip address 192.168.10.1 255.255.255.0
Switch(config-if)#interface vlan 20
Switch(config-if)#ip address 192.168.20.1 255.255.255.0
Switch(config-if)#exit
Switch(config)#ip routing
```

Test connectivity by pinging between the VLANs and troubleshoot where necessary.

1. What does this do to the amount of traffic that the VSPAN destination port receives?

_____

_____

_____

Step 4

Create a monitor session on the switch by defining the source VLAN of a monitor session called session 1:

```
Switch(config)#monitor session 1 source VLAN 10 rx
```

The **rx** is specified because VSPAN sessions can occur only based on traffic that the VLAN switch ports receive.

Step 5

Create a destination port, which receives the mirrored traffic that is being sent to source ports within VLAN 10:

```
Switch(config)#monitor session 1 destination interface fastethernet 0/10
```

1. What does the switch advertise when FastEthernet port 0/10 becomes a destination port?

_____

_____

_____

You can take encapsulation into account when trunking has been configured on a switch. The full command, which is not used in this lab, is as follows:

```
Switch(config)#monitor session session_number destination interface module/interface
  encapsulation [isl¦dot1q]
```

Lab 9.9.3: Creating an RSPAN Session

Estimated Time: 120 Minutes

Objective

In this lab, you create a Remote Switched Port Analyzer (RSPAN) session on two switches to monitor network traffic remotely. Figure 9-3 shows the topology for this lab.

Figure 9-3 Topology for Lab 9.9.3

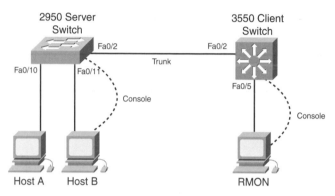

Scenario

Effective monitoring of network traffic in fully switched networks can be challenging. However, you can make the process easier by including RSPAN in 2950, 3550, and 6500 series switches. Using RSPAN, you can copy and forward LAN traffic that's received or transmitted by switch ports or VLANs to a monitoring port on a remote switch. Then you can capture and analyze this mirrored traffic.

A company recently upgraded to fully switched network architecture. To optimize network performance, the company decided to monitor network traffic for analysis purposes. After the company tried SPAN sessions and VSPAN sessions on a single switch, it decided to progress to RSPAN session trials. It will monitor traffic generated on one switch and use a remote switch port as the destination for the monitored traffic.

Load and run protocol analysis software, such as Protocol Inspector or Optiview Protocol Expert, on a host that will act as the RMON. You also need to configure two hosts that have IP addresses in the same subnet so that they can share network traffic.

Step 1

Do not cable the lab until you have erased the switch configuration and vlan.dat file and reloaded the switch.

Cable the network devices according to Figure 9-3 and configure the host names "Server" and "Client3550" in the 2950 and 3550 switches respectively.

Step 2

Enter global configuration mode in the Server switch IOS. Clear any previous monitor sessions:

```
Server(config)#no monitor session 1
```

Step 3

From privileged mode, enter the VLAN database and create a VLAN Trunking Protocol (VTP) server and domain name so that you can propagate VLAN information from the Server switch to the attached Client switch:

```
Server#vlan database
Server(vlan)#vtp server
Server(vlan)#vtp domain schnauzer
```

On the Client 3550, enter the VLAN database and create a VTP client in the same domain:

```
Client3550#vlan database
Client3550(vlan)#vtp client
Client3550(vlan)#vtp domain schnauzer
```

Step 4

Create a unique VLAN for the RSPAN session. You will forward this VLAN through a VLAN trunk to its destination port in the same way as normal traffic. The RSPAN VLAN must be a unique VLAN. It cannot be a native VLAN of any of the active switch ports:

```
Server(config)#vlan 901
Server(config-vlan)#remote-span
Server(config-vlan)#exit
```

Step 5

Create the trunk between the Server switch and the Client switch. Perform the same procedure on both switches:

```
Server(config)#interface fastethernet 0/2
Server(config-if)#switchport trunk native vlan 99
Server(config-if)#switchport mode trunk
```

```
Client3350(config)#interface fastethernet 0/2
Client3350(config-if)#switchport trunk native vlan 99
Client3350(config-if)#switchport trunk encapsulation dot1q
Client3350(config-if)#switchport mode trunk
```

Step 6

Verify that the trunks are set correctly at both ends using the **show interface fastethernet 0/2 trunk** command. Output for both switches should indicate that the RSPAN VLAN is present as an allowed VLAN in the schnauzer management domain.

Step 7

The Server switch will be the source for the RSPAN session. Configure two ports as source ports for mirrored traffic:

- FastEthernet port 0/10 will be monitored for bidirectional traffic.

- FastEthernet port 0/11 will be monitored only for received traffic.

```
Server(config)#monitor session 1 source interface fastethernet 0/10 both
Server(config)#monitor session 1 source interface fastethernet 0/11 rx
```

Step 8

Now configure a reflector port on the RSPAN source switch. This is an actual physical port set to loopback mode. To redirect copies of the monitored traffic onto the RSPAN VLAN for transport to the destination switch, enter the following:

```
Server(config)#monitor session 1 destination remote vlan 901 reflector-port fastethernet 0/12
Server(config)#end
```

1. What happened when you entered this command? Why?

_____

_____

_____

Step 9

Confirm that you have configured the RSPAN session correctly by using the **show monitor session** command:

```
Server#show monitor session 1
```

You should see the following output:

```
Server#show monitor session 1
Session 1
---------
  Type          : remote Source Session
Source Ports  :
RX Only:              Ra0/11
TX Only:              None
Both:                 Ra0/10
Source VLANs:
RX Only:              None
TX Only:              None
Both:                 None
      Source RSPAN VLAN:           None
Destination Ports:         None
Reflector Port:            Fa0/12
Filter VLANs:              None
Dest RSPAN VLAN:           901
```

Step 10

The client switch acts as the RSPAN session destination. You need to configure it to transfer the RSPAN VLAN traffic from the trunk toward the nominated destination port. The first command identifies the RSPAN source VLAN. The second command defines the port that you should forward the RSPAN VLAN traffic to:

```
Client3550(config)#monitor session 1 source remote vlan 901
Client3550(config)#monitor session 1 destination interface fastethernet 0/5
Client3550(config)#end
```

Step 11

Confirm that you have configured the RSPAN session correctly. Use the **show monitor session** command:

```
Client3550#show monitor session 1
```

You should see the following output:

```
Client3550#show monitor session 1
Session 1
---------
  Type                    : Remote Destination Session
Source Ports      :
RX Only:              None
TX Only:              None
Both:                 None
Source VLANs :
RX Only:              None
TX Only:              None
Both:                 None
```

```
Source RSPAN VLAN:        901
Destination Ports:        Fa0/5
Reflector Port:           None
Filter VLANs:             None
Dest RSPAN VLAN:          None
```

Generate some pings between Host A and Host B. Forward the Layer 3 traffic that Host A generates to Host C, the remote monitor.

Step 12

Now alter the characteristics of one of the source ports, FastEthernet 0/10, from monitoring bidirectional traffic to monitoring only received traffic:

```
Server(config)#no monitor session 1 source interface fastethernet 0/10 both
Server(config)#monitor session 1 source interface fastethernet 0/10 rx
```

In privileged mode, confirm that the monitor session characteristics have changed with the **show monitor session** command. Generate a ping from Host A to Host B.

1. What happened to the volume and types of traffic that Host C logged?

Step 13

Remove one of the source ports from the RSPAN session:

```
Server(config)#no monitor session 1 source interface fastethernet 0/10
Server(config)#end
```

Again, in privileged mode, use the **show monitor session** command to confirm that the monitor session characteristics have changed. Generate additional pings from Host A to Host B.

1. What happened to the volume and types of traffic that Host C logged?

Lab 9.9.4: Setting Encrypted Passwords

Estimated Time: 60 Minutes

Objective

In this lab, you configure passwords on switch console ports and virtual terminal lines. Figure 9-4 shows the topology for this lab.

Figure 9-4 Topology for Lab 9.9.4

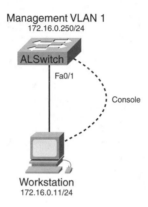

Scenario

Corporate headquarters has recently become concerned about network security. Headquarters issued a directive for regional staff members to secure local Ethernet switches with passwords on the console port and virtual terminal lines to prevent unauthorized access to the network. For added security, you must encrypt all passwords that are saved in the switch configuration.

Step 1

Do not cable the lab until you have erased the switch configuration and vlan.dat file and reloaded the switch.

Build and configure the network according to Figure 9-4. Use the **ping** command to verify the Ethernet connection to the switch.

Step 2

Enter global configuration mode and configure the console port to use the password letmein to authenticate users:

```
ALSwitch(config)#line console 0
ALSwitch(config-line)#password letmein
```

Enable password checking on the console port:

```
ALSwitch(config-line)#login
ALSwitch(config-line)#exit
```

Step 3

Configure the virtual terminal lines to use the password telnetin to authenticate users:

```
ALSwitch(config)#line vty 0 15
ALSwitch(config-line)#password telnetin
```

Enable password checking on the vty lines:

```
ALSwitch(config-line)#login
ALSwitch(config-line)#exit
```

Step 4

Check the running configuration on the switch to confirm that you have entered the passwords correctly:

```
--output omitted--
ALSwitch(config)#end
ALSwitch#show running-config

!
line con 0
 password letmein
 login
line vty 0 4
 password telnetin
 login
line vty 5 15
 password telnetin
 login
!
--output omitted--
```

Step 5

Re-enter global configuration mode and enable password encryption on the switch:

```
ALSwitch(config)#service password-encryption
```

Check the running configuration again:

```
--output omitted--
ALSwitch(config)#end
ALSwitch#show running-config

!
line con 0
 password 7 00081612095E0208
 login
line vty 0 4
 password 7 06120A2D424B1D100B
 login
line vty 5
 password 7 06120A2D424B1D100B
 login
line vty 6 15
 password 7 120D001B1C0E180D24
 login
!
--output omitted--
```

Notice that the clear-text passwords have been encrypted. The numbers that were used to represent the encrypted password might not be the same as the numbers shown.

1. What does the 7 mean in the output password 7 120D001B1C0E180D24?

_____

Step 6

Log out of the switch and reconnect to the console to test the password.

Note: Passwords are case-sensitive.

```
ALSwitch#exit
ALSwitch con0 is now available
Press RETURN to get started.
User Access Verification
Password:
ALSwitch>
```

Step 7

Connect to the switch using Telnet to test the vty line password.

Step 8

Connect to the switch using either the console port or a Telnet session, and remove the line passwords:

```
--output omitted--
ALSwitch(config)#line console 0
ALSwitch(config-line)#no login
ALSwitch(config-line)#no password
ALSwitch(config-line)#line vty 0 15
ALSwitch(config-line)#no login
ALSwitch(config-line)#no password
ALSwitch(config-line)#end
ALSwitch#
1w3d: %SYS-5-CONFIG_I: Configured from console by console
ALSwitch#show running-config

!
line con 0
line vty 0 4
 no login
line vty 5 15
 no login
--output omitted--
```

Lab 9.9.5: Using Local Usernames and Passwords

Estimated Time: 60 Minutes

Objective

In this lab, you configure multiple local usernames with passwords. You will use these for login authentication on the console port and virtual terminal lines. Figure 9-5 shows the topology for this lab.

Figure 9-5 Topology for Lab 9.9.5

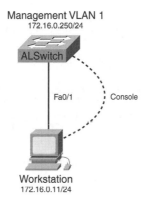

Management VLAN 1
172.16.0.250/24

ALSwitch

Fa0/1   Console

Workstation
172.16.0.11/24

Scenario

Corporate headquarters wants to increase network security by implementing individual user accounts on the switches for the network administrators, Alice, Bob, and Carol. Regional staff members are to secure local Ethernet switches with local usernames and passwords on the switches. This will prevent unauthorized access to the network and provide better logging information about access to the network switches. For added security, all passwords that are saved in the switch configuration also must be encrypted.

Step 1

Do not cable the lab until you have erased the switch configuration and vlan.dat file and reloaded the switch.

Build and configure the network according to Figure 9-5. Use the **ping** command to verify the Ethernet connection to the switch.

Step 2

Enter global configuration mode to create a user account for Alice, Bob, and Carol. The password for Alice is fantastic. The password for Bob is switching. The password for Carol is equipment:

```
ALSwitch(config)#username Alice password fantastic
ALSwitch(config)#username Bob password switching
ALSwitch(config)#username Carol password equipment
ALSwitch(config)#enable secret class
```

Step 3

Enter line configuration mode for line console 0.

Then enable login authentication using local accounts on the console port:

```
ALSwitch(config)#line console 0
ALSwitch(config-line)#login local
```

Finally, enable login authentication using local accounts on the virtual terminal lines:

```
ALSwitch(config)#line vty 0 15
ALSwitch(config-line)#login local
```

Step 4

Check the running configuration on the switch to confirm that you have entered the passwords correctly:

```
--output omitted--
ALSwitch(config)#end
ALSwitch#
00:14:52: %SYS-5-CONFIG_I: Configured from console by console
ALSwitch#show running-config
Building configuration...

Current configuration : 1069 bytes
!
version 12.1
no service pad
service timestamps debug uptime
service timestamps log uptime
no service password-encryption
!
hostname ALSwitch
!
!
username Alice password 0 fantastic
username Bob password 0 switching
username Carol password 0 equipment
--output omitted--
!
line con 0
 login local
line vty 0 4
 login local
line vty 5 15
 login local
!
--output omitted--
```

1. What does the 0 mean in the output username Carol password 0 equipment?

Step 5

Re-enter global configuration mode and enable password encryption on the switch:

```
ALSwitch(config)#service password-encryption
```

Check the running configuration again:

```
ALSwitch#show running-config
Building configuration...

Current configuration : 1111 bytes
!
version 12.1
```

```
no service pad
service timestamps debug uptime
service timestamps log uptime
service password-encryption
!
hostname ALSwitch
!
!
username Alice password 7 104808171116011F0507
username Bob password 7 071C36455A0A110C1915
username Carol password 7 06031E34455E041C0B03
--output omitted--
```

Notice that the clear-text passwords have been encrypted. The numbers that were used to represent the encrypted password might not be the same as the numbers shown.

1. What does the 7 mean in the output username Carol password 7 06031E34455E041C0B03?

Step 6

Log out of the switch and reconnect to the console to test the user accounts and passwords:

Note: Passwords are case-sensitive.

```
ALSwitch con0 is now available
Press RETURN to get started.
User Access Verification
Username: Bob
Password:
ALSwitch>
```

Log in at least once with each user account and password. Test what happens when you enter incorrect passwords and usernames.

Step 7

Enter global configuration mode. Return to privileged mode without making changes to the switch configuration:

```
ALSwitch#conf t
Enter configuration commands, one per line.  End with CNTL/Z.
ALSwitch(config)#end
ALSwitch#
00:29:47: %SYS-5-CONFIG_I: Configured from console by Bob on console
```

1. What changes in the log message after you exit global configuration mode?

Step 8

Connect to the switch using either the console port or a Telnet session and remove the user account settings:

```
ALSwitch(config)#no username Bob
ALSwitch(config)#no username Alice
ALSwitch(config)#no username Carol
ALSwitch(config)#line console 0
ALSwitch(config-line)#no login
ALSwitch(config-line)#line vty 0 15
ALSwitch(config-line)#no login
```

```
ALSwitch(config-line)#end
ALSwitch#
00:36:31: %SYS-5-CONFIG_I: Configured from console by Bob on console
ALSwitch#show running-config
Building configuration...

Current configuration : 953 bytes
!
version 12.1
no service pad
service timestamps debug uptime
service timestamps log uptime
service password-encryption
!
hostname ALSwitch
--output omitted--
!
!
ip subnet-zero

!
line con 0
line vty 0 4
 no login
line vty 5 15
 no login
!
```

Lab 9.9.6: Using Advanced Username Options

Estimated Time: 60 Minutes

Objective

In this lab, you configure multiple user accounts with advanced options to limit privilege levels and use strong encryption to secure passwords. Figure 9-6 shows the topology for this lab.

Figure 9-6 Topology for Lab 9.9.6

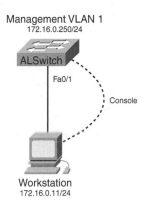

Scenario

Corporate headquarters wants to give first-level help desk staff low-level access to network switches for monitoring purposes. The network administrators, Alice, Bob, and Carol, want to have their own accounts on the switch. The help desk staff must be able to log in to the switch without a password. The three network administrators must enter privileged mode automatically after authenticating with the switch.

A strong encryption algorithm must protect the passwords for the network administrator accounts because the help desk staff will have access to the switch.

Step 1

Do not cable the lab until you have erased the switch configuration and vlan.dat file and reloaded the switch.

Build and configure the network according to Figure 9-6. Use the **ping** command to verify the Ethernet connection to the switch.

Step 2

Enter global configuration mode and create a new account for the help desk. The help desk account does not have a password.

Create the account for the help desk and set the account privilege to Level 3:

```
ALSwitch(config)#username Helpdesk nopassword
ALSwitch(config)#username Helpdesk privilege 3
```

Step 3

Enable login authentication for local accounts on the console port and virtual terminal lines:

```
ALSwitch(config)#line console 0
ALSwitch(config-line)#login local
ALSwitch(config-line)#line vty 0 15
ALSwitch(config-line)#login local
```

Step 4

Exit the global configuration mode and check the running configuration of the switch:

```
ALSwitch(config)#end
ALSwitch#
00:05:35: %SYS-5-CONFIG_I: Configured from console by console
ALSwitch#show running-config
Building configuration...

Current configuration : 1093 bytes
!
version 12.1
no service pad
service timestamps debug uptime
service timestamps log uptime
no service password-encryption
!
hostname ALSwitch
!
!
username Helpdesk privilege 3 nopassword
--output omitted--

!
line con 0
 login local
line vty 0 4
 login local
line vty 5 15
 login local
!
--output omitted--
```

Step 5

Re-enter global configuration mode and create user accounts for Alice, Bob, and Carol. You must use strong encryption to store the passwords for these accounts. The password for Alice is fantastic. The password for Bob is switching. The password for Carol is equipment:

```
ALSwitch(config)#username Alice secret fantastic
ALSwitch(config)#username Bob secret switching
ALSwitch(config)#username Carol secret equipment
```

Check the running configuration again:

```
ALSwitch(config)#end
ALSwitch#
00:09:52: %SYS-5-CONFIG_I: Configured from console by console
ALSwitch#show running-config
Building configuration...

Current configuration : 1256 bytes
!
version 12.1
no service pad
service timestamps debug uptime
service timestamps log uptime
no service password-encryption
!
hostname ALSwitch
!
!
username Helpdesk privilege 3 nopassword
username Alice secret 5 $1$vBnC$kw40PgOX0yQQyM1KzOmv71
username Bob secret 5 $1$f3mK$C5PUyHwjT0T0fvNgPDwT60
username Carol secret 5 $1$808J$XeiJBlrFTCLUaZhBcE/y..
--output omitted--
```

1. You have not used the **service password-encryption** command. Why are the passwords for Alice, Bob, and Carol not stored in clear text?

2. What does the 5 mean in the output username Carol secret 5 $808J$XeiJBlrFTCLUaZhBcE/y..?

Step 6

Enter global configuration mode. Configure the accounts for the network administrators so that they enter privileged mode automatically after authenticating with the switch:

```
ALSwitch(config)#username Alice privilege 15
ALSwitch(config)#username Bob privilege 15
ALSwitch(config)#username Carol privilege 15
```

Step 7

Check the running configuration of the switch:

```
ALSwitch(config)#end
ALSwitch#
00:21:34: %SYS-5-CONFIG_I: Configured from console by console
ALSwitch#show running-config
Building configuration...

Current configuration : 1295 bytes
!
version 12.1
no service pad
service timestamps debug uptime
service timestamps log uptime
no service password-encryption
!
hostname ALSwitch
!
!
username Helpdesk privilege 3 nopassword
username Alice privilege 15 secret 5 $1$vBnC$kw40PgOX0yQQyM1KzOmv71
username Bob privilege 15 secret 5 $1$f3mK$C5PUyHwjT0T0fvNgPDwT60
username Carol privilege 15 secret 5 $1$808J$XeiJBlrFTCLUaZhBcE/y..
--output omitted--
```

Step 8

Log out of the switch and reconnect as help desk.

Note: Passwords are case-sensitive.

```
itch con0 is now available
Press RETURN to get started.
User Access Verification
Username: Helpdesk
ALSwitch#
```

1. The help desk account appears to have been entered into privileged mode automatically. Check the list of available commands using **?**. Does the Helpdesk username have full privileged mode?

_____

_____

2. What are some of the core commands that help desk users cannot use? Try to examine or change the switch configuration.

_____

_____

_____

Step 9

Log out of the switch. Log on again as one of the network administrator accounts:

```
ALSwitch con0 is now available
Press RETURN to get started.
User Access Verification
Username: Carol
Password:
ALSwitch#
```

1. Do the network administrators get complete privileged mode access automatically after authenticating?

_____

Lab 9.9.7: Configuring the Management VLAN on a Single Switch

Estimated Time: 60 Minutes

Objective

In this lab, you configure and use a nondefault management VLAN. This lab uses the **config-vlan** and **vlan database** modes to configure VLANs. Figure 9-7 shows the topology for this lab.

Figure 9-7 Topology for Lab 9.9.7

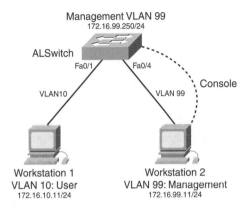

Scenario

Corporate headquarters decided to improve network management security by implementing VLANs to separate user and management traffic.

Step 1

Do not cable the lab until you have erased the switch configuration and vlan.dat file and reloaded the switch.

Build the network according to Figure 9-7. Assign IP addresses to the workstations. Configure the switch name, but do not configure VLANs and do not assign an IP address to the switch.

Step 2

From privileged mode, enter VLAN database mode:

```
ALSwitch#vlan database
ALSwitch(vlan)#
```

Create VLAN 10 and name it Users:

```
ALSwitch(vlan)#vlan 10 name Users
VLAN 10 modified:
Name: Users
```

Verify that you have created the VLAN:

```
ALSwitch(vlan)#show
```

1. Which VLAN numbers and names are displayed?

Step 3

Exit VLAN database mode:

```
ALSwitch(vlan)#exit
APPLY completed.
Exiting....
ALSwitch#
```

Display summary VLAN information from privileged mode:

```
ALSwitch#show vlan
```

VLAN	Name	Status	Ports
1	default	active	Fa0/1, Fa0/2, Fa0/3, Fa0/4
			Fa0/5, Fa0/6, Fa0/7, Fa0/8
			Fa0/9, Fa0/10, Fa0/11, Fa0/12
			Gi0/1, Gi0/2
10	Users	active	
1002	fddi-default	active	
1003	token-ring-default	active	
1004	fddinet-default	active	
1005	trnet-default	active	

VLAN	Type	SAID	MTU	Parent	RingNo	BridgeNo	Stp	BrdgMode	Trans1	Trans2
1	enet	100001	1500	-	-	-	-	-	0	0
10	enet	100010	1500	-	-	-	-	-	0	0
1002	fddi	101002	1500	-	-	-	-	-	0	0
1003	tr	101003	1500	-	-	-	-	srb	0	0
1004	fdnet	101004	1500	-	-	-	ieee	-	0	0
1005	trnet	101005	1500	-	-	-	ibm	-	0	0

```
Remote SPAN VLANs
------------------------------------------------------------------------
```

Primary	Secondary	Type	Ports
-------	---------	-----------------	--

Step 4

Enter global configuration mode.

Use the config-vlan configuration mode to create VLAN 99 and name it Mgt:

```
ALSwitch(config)#vlan 99
ALSwitch(config-vlan)#name Mgt
```

Return to privileged mode and verify the VLAN configuration:

```
ALSwitch(config-vlan)#end
ALSwitch#show vlan
00:44:11: %SYS-5-CONFIG_I: Configured from console by console
```

VLAN	Name	Status	Ports
1	default	active	Fa0/1, Fa0/2, Fa0/3, Fa0/4
			Fa0/5, Fa0/6, Fa0/7, Fa0/8
			Fa0/9, Fa0/10, Fa0/11, Fa0/12
			Gi0/1, Gi0/2
10	Users	active	
99	Mgt	active	
1002	fddi-default	active	
1003	token-ring-default	active	
1004	fddinet-default	active	
1005	trnet-default	active	

VLAN	Type	SAID	MTU	Parent	RingNo	BridgeNo	Stp	BrdgMode	Trans1	Trans2
1	enet	100001	1500	-	-	-	-	-	0	0
10	enet	100010	1500	-	-	-	-	-	0	0
99	enet	100099	1500	-	-	-	-	-	0	0
1002	fddi	101002	1500	-	-	-	-	-	0	0
1003	tr	101003	1500	-	-	-	-	srb	0	0
1004	fdnet	101004	1500	-	-	-	ieee	-	0	0
1005	trnet	101005	1500	-	-	-	ibm	-	0	0

```
Remote SPAN VLANs
------------------------------------------------------------------


Primary Secondary Type            Ports
------- --------- ---------------- ----------------------------------------
```

1. Can you establish a Telnet connection from either PC to the switch? Explain why or why not.

_____

_____

_____

Step 5

Enter global configuration mode.

Assign an IP address to VLAN 99 on the switch:

```
ALSwitch(config)#interface vlan 99
ALSwitch(config-if)#ip address 172.16.99.250 255.255.255.0
ALSwitch(config-if)#no shutdown
```

1. Can you establish a Telnet connection from either workstation to the switch? Explain why or why not.

_____

_____

_____

Step 6

Make port FastEthernet0/1 a member of VLAN 10:

```
ALSwitch(config)#interface fastethernet 0/1
ALSwitch(config-if)#switchport mode access
ALSwitch(config-if)#switchport access vlan 10
```

Make port FastEthernet0/4 a member of VLAN 99:

```
ALSwitch(config)#int fastethernet0/4
ALSwitch(config-if)#switchport mode access
ALSwitch(config-if)#switchport access vlan 99
```

1. Now is it possible to establish a Telnet connection from either workstation to the switch? Explain why or why not.

_____

_____

_____

Return to privileged mode and verify the VLAN configuration:

```
ALSwitch(config-if)#end
ALSwitch#
00:54:52: %SYS-5-CONFIG_I: Configured from console by console
ALSwitch#show vlan

VLAN Name                             Status    Ports
---- -------------------------------- --------- -------------------------------
1    default                          active    Fa0/2, Fa0/3, Fa0/5, Fa0/6
                                                Fa0/7, Fa0/8, Fa0/9, Fa0/10
                                                Fa0/11, Fa0/12, Gi0/1, Gi0/2
10   Users                            active    Fa0/1
99   Mgt                              active    Fa0/4
1002 fddi-default                     active
1003 token-ring-default               active
1004 fddinet-default                  active
1005 trnet-default                    active

VLAN Type  SAID       MTU   Parent RingNo BridgeNo Stp  BrdgMode Trans1 Trans2
---- ----- ---------- ----- ------ ------ -------- ---- -------- ------ ------
1    enet  100001     1500  -      -      -        -    -        0      0
10   enet  100010     1500  -      -      -        -    -        0      0
99   enet  100099     1500  -      -      -        -    -        0      0
1002 fddi  101002     1500  -      -      -        -    -        0      0
1003 tr    101003     1500  -      -      -        -    srb      0      0
1004 fdnet 101004     1500  -      -      -        ieee -        0      0
1005 trnet 101005     1500  -      -      -        ibm  -        0      0

Remote SPAN VLANs
------------------------------------------------------------------------------


Primary Secondary Type              Ports
------- --------- ----------------- -------------------------------------------
```

Note: VLANs 10 and 99 now have associated interfaces.

Step 7

Try to ping the switch IP address 172.16.99.250 from workstation 1.

1. Did it work? Why or why not?

Try to ping the switch IP address 172.16.99.250 from workstation 2.

2. Did it work? Why or why not?

Try to open a Telnet session to the switch from workstation 1.

3. Did it work? Why or why not?

_____

_____

_____

Try to open a Telnet session to the switch from workstation 2.

4. Did it work? Why or why not?

_____

_____

_____

Configure the vty lines for Telnet access into the switch:

```
ALSwitch(config)#line vty 0 15
ALSwitch(config-line)#password cisco
ALSwitch(config-line)#login
ALSwitch(config-line)#end
```

A Telnet session from workstation 2 should be successful now.

Lab 9.9.8: Restricting Virtual Terminal Sessions with Access Lists

Estimated Time: 60 Minutes

Objective

In this lab, you define and apply access lists to restrict access to virtual terminal sessions on the switch. Figure 9-8 shows the topology for this lab.

Figure 9-8 Topology for Lab 9.9.8

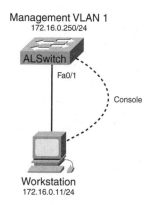

Scenario

Corporate headquarters decided to implement a specific switch-management terminal in the IT department. Configure the switch to allow Telnet sessions from a single host, but not from other hosts in the same subnet.

Step 1

Do not cable the lab until you have erased the switch configuration and vlan.dat file and reloaded the switch.

Build and configure the network according to Figure 9-8. Use the **ping** command to verify the Ethernet connectivity to the switch.

Step 2

Use the global configuration mode to create a standard access list to permit traffic from the workstation at 172.16.0.11. Prohibit all other traffic:

```
ALSwitch(config)#access-list 99 permit 172.16.0.11
ALSwitch(config)#access-list 99 deny any
```

Step 3

Enter line configuration mode and apply this access list to all vty lines:

```
ALSwitch(config)#line vty 0 15
ALSwitch(config-line)#access-class 99 in
```

Configure a password on the vty lines to enable Telnet sessions:

```
ALSwitch(config)#line vty 0 15
ALSwitch(config)#password cisco
ALSwitch(config)#login
```

Step 4

Return to privileged mode and verify the switch configuration:

```
ALSwitch(config-line)#end
ALSwitch#
00:03:45: %SYS-5-CONFIG_I: Configured from console by console
ALSwitch#show running-config
Building configuration...

Current configuration : 1050 bytes
!
version 12.1
no service pad
service timestamps debug uptime
service timestamps log uptime
no service password-encryption
!
hostname ALSwitch
--output omitted--
!


!
access-list 99 permit 172.16.0.11
access-list 99 deny    any
!
line con 0
line vty 0 4
 access-class 99 in
'password cisco
 login
line vty 5 15
 access-class 99 in
'password cisco
 login
!
end
```

Step 5

Try to open a Telnet session from the workstation to the switch.

1. Did it work? Why or why not?

Step 6

Change the IP address of the workstation to 172.16.0.12 / 24.

Try to open a Telnet session from the workstation to the switch.

1. Did it work? Why or why not?

Note: You can use the same setup and configurations for Lab 9.9.9.

Lab 9.9.9: Restricting Web Interface Sessions with Access Lists

Estimated Time: 60 Minutes

Objective

In this lab, you define and apply access lists to restrict access to the web interface on the switch. Figure 9-9 shows the topology for this lab.

Figure 9-9 Topology for Lab 9.9.9

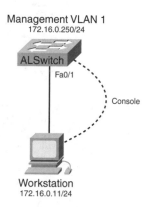

Management VLAN 1
172.16.0.250/24

ALSwitch

Fa0/1

Console

Workstation
172.16.0.11/24

Scenario

Corporate headquarters has decided to implement a specific switch management terminal in the IT department. Configure the switch to allow Internet browser sessions from a single host but not from other hosts in the same subnet.

Step 1

Do not cable the lab until you have erased the switch configuration and vlan.dat file and reloaded the switch.

Build and configure the network according to Figure 9-9. Use the **ping** command to verify the Ethernet connectivity to the switch.

Step 2

Use the global configuration mode to create a standard access list to permit traffic from the workstation at 172.16.0.11. Prohibit all other traffic:

```
ALSwitch(config)#access-list 99 permit 172.16.0.11
ALSwitch(config)#access-list 99 deny any
```

Step 3

Enable the HTTP server on the switch and apply the access list to the HTTP server process:

```
ALSwitch(config)#ip http server
ALSwitch(config)#ip http access-class 99
```

Note: The **ip http server** command should be enabled on the switch by factory default.

Step 4

Return to privileged mode and verify the switch configuration:

```
ALSwitch(config-line)#end
ALSwitch#
00:14:04: %SYS-5-CONFIG_I: Configured from console by console
ALSwitch#show running-config
Building configuration...

Current configuration : 1050 bytes
!
version 12.1
no service pad
service timestamps debug uptime
service timestamps log uptime
no service password-encryption
!
hostname ALSwitch
!


!
ip http server
ip http access-class 99
--output omitted--
!
access-list 99 permit 172.16.0.11
access-list 99 deny   any
!
--output omitted--
```

Step 5

Try to open an Internet browser session from the workstation to the switch.

1. Did it work? Why or why not?

_____

_____

Step 6

Change the IP address of the workstation to 172.16.0.12 / 24.

Try to open an Internet browser session from the workstation to the switch.

1. Did it work? Why or why not?

_____

_____

Lab 9.9.10: Configuring Protected Ports

Estimated Time: 60 Minutes

Objective

In this lab, you configure private VLAN edge-protected ports. Figure 9-10 shows the topology for this lab.

Figure 9-10 Topology for Lab 9.9.10

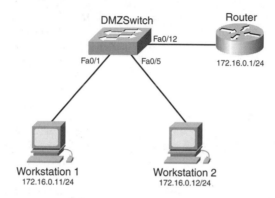

Scenario

Configure the DMZ switch so that the servers on ports 1 through 8 cannot interact directly with each other. All servers need to be able to communicate with the firewall that is connected to port 12.

Step 1

Do not cable the lab until you have erased the router and switch configuration files and the switch vlan.dat file and reloaded the devices.

Configure the network as shown in Figure 9-10, including IP addresses on both workstations and the router. Use the **ping** command to confirm connectivity among all the devices.

Step 2

Select ports 1 through 8.

Note: Be sure to include a space on either side of the hyphen.

```
DMZSwitch(config)#interface range fa0/1 - 8
```

Step 3

Enable port protection on these interfaces and then return to privileged EXEC mode:

```
DMZSwitch(config-if-range)#switchport protected
DMZSwitch(config-if-range)#end
DMZSwitch#
```

Step 4

Attempt to ping between the workstations.

1. Was the ping successful? Why or why not?

_____

_____

Attempt to ping the router from either workstation.

2. Was the ping successful? Why or why not?

_____

_____

Step 5

Disable port protection for Workstation 2, which is port FastEthernet 0/5, and return to privileged EXEC mode:

```
DMZSwitch#configure terminal
DMZSwitch#interface fastethernet 0/5
DMZSwitch(config-if)#no switchport protected
DMZSwitch(config-if)#end
DMZSwitch#
```

Step 6

Attempt to ping among the workstations.

1. Was the ping successful? Why or why not?

_____

_____

Attempt to ping the router from Workstation 1.

2. Was the ping successful? Why or why not?

_____

_____

Attempt to ping the router from Workstation 2.

3. Was the ping successful? Why or why not?

_____

_____

Lab 9.9.11: Configuring VLAN Maps

Estimated Time: 90 Minutes

Objective

In this lab, you configure VLAN Access Control Lists (ACLs) for IP addresses in a common VLAN. Figure 9-11 shows the topology for this lab.

Figure 9-11 Topology for Lab 9.9.11

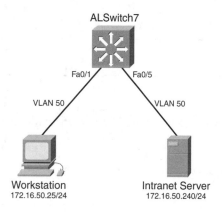

Scenario

The Human Resources (HR) director has decided to improve security by implementing VLAN ACLs. This will make it possible to control user traffic within the HR department VLAN. You must configure the switch that is handling all the HTTP traffic for the HR department to control access to the HR intranet server, limiting it to a small range of IP addresses.

Dynamic Host Configuration Protocol (DHCP) allocates an address from the pool 172.16.50.1 to 172.16.50.127/24 to all the client machines in the HR subnet. Only hosts in the range 172.16.50.16 to 172.16.50.31 are allowed to access the web server.

Step 1

Do not cable the lab until you have erased the switch configuration file and the switch vlan.dat file and reloaded the device.

Build and configure the network according to Figure 9-11. Create VLAN 50 with the name HR and assign interfaces FastEthernet 0/1 through 0/5 to VLAN 50.

The HR client at 172.16.50.25/24 should be able to access the web server running on the HR intranet server at 172.16.50.240/24.

Step 2

Using the information provided in Figure 9-11, create a named extended access list that matches the profile of the authorized traffic. Be as specific as possible with the ACL so that other traffic flows are unaffected:

```
ALSwitch7(config)#ip access-list extended HRServerAllowed
ALSwitch7(config-ext-nacl)#permit tcp 172.16.50.16 0.0.0.15 host 172.16.50.240 eq www
ALSwitch7(config-ext-nacl)#end
```

Verify the ACL configuration:

```
ALSwitch7#show ip access-list
Extended IP access list HRServerAllowed
    permit tcp 172.16.50.16 0.0.0.15 host 172.16.50.240 eq www
```

Then create another access list that matches the profile of the traffic that must be blocked. Again, be as specific as possible with the ACL so that other traffic flows are unaffected:

```
ALSwitch7(config)#ip access-list extended HRServerBlocked
ALSwitch7(config-ext-nacl)#permit tcp 172.16.50.0 0.0.0.127 host 172.16.50.240 eq www
ALSwitch7(config-ext-nacl)#end
```

Verify the ACL configuration:

```
ALSwitch7#show ip access-list
Extended IP access list HRServerAllowed
    permit tcp 172.16.50.16 0.0.0.15 host 172.16.50.240 eq www
Extended IP access list HRServerBlocked
    permit tcp 172.16.50.0 0.0.0.127 host 172.16.50.240 eq www
```

1. Why is the ACL HRServerBlocked using a permit statement?

_____

_____

Now create a third access list to allow all other IP traffic through the VLAN map:

```
ALSwitch7(config)#ip access-list extended HRServerDefaults
ALSwitch7(config-ext-nacl)#permit ip any any
ALSwitch7(config-ext-nacl)#end
```

Verify the ACL configuration:

```
ALSwitch7#show ip access-list
Extended IP access list HRServerAllowed
      permit tcp 172.16.50.16 0.0.0.15 host 172.16.50.240 eq www
Extended IP access list HRServerBlocked
      deny tcp 172.16.50.0 0.0.0.127 host 172.16.50.240 eq www
Extended IP access list HRServerDefaults
      permit ip any any
```

Step 3

Create a VLAN access map named HRServerMap with a sequence number of 10:

```
ALSwitch7(config)#vlan access-map HRServerMap 10
```

Bind the access list HRServerAllowed to the VLAN access map HRServerMap 10. Set the action to forward packets matching the ACL, and then return to global configuration mode:

```
ALSwitch7(config-access-map)#match ip address HRServerAllowed
ALSwitch7(config-access-map)#action forward
ALSwitch7(config-access-map)#exit
ALSwitch7(config)#
```

Add to the VLAN access map with a sequence number of 20, binding the access list HRServerBlocked to the VLAN access map HRServerMap. Set the action to drop packets matching the ACL, and then return to global configuration mode:

```
ALSwitch7(config)#vlan access-map HRServerMap 20
ALSwitch7(config-access-map)#match ip address HRServerBlocked
ALSwitch7(config-access-map)#action drop
ALSwitch7(config-access-map)#exit
ALSwitch7(config)#
```

Bind the access list HRServerDefault to the VLAN access map HRServerMap by using a sequence number of 30. Set the action to forward packets matching the ACL, and then return to privileged mode:

```
ALSwitch7(config)#vlan access-map HRServerMap 30
ALSwitch7(config-access-map)#match ip address HRServerDefault
ALSwitch7(config-access-map)#action forward
ALSwitch7(config-access-map)#end
ALSwitch7#
```

Verify the VLAN access map configuration so far:

```
ALSwitch7#show vlan access-map
Vlan access-map "HRServer" 10
  Match clauses:
    ip address: HRServerAllowed
  Action:
    forward
Vlan access-map "HRServerMap" 20
  Match clauses:
    ip address: HRServerBlocked
  Action:
    drop
Vlan access-map "HRServerMap" 30
  Match clauses:
    ip address: HRServerDefault
  Action:
    forward
ALSwitch7#
```

Step 4

Enable VLAN filtering on VLAN 50 in global config mode using the newly created VLAN access map. Use **?** if you forget the syntax used to apply the VLAN access map.

1. What is the command to apply the VLAN access map HRServerMap to the HR VLAN?

Return to privileged mode, and verify the VLAN filter configuration:

```
ALSwitch7#show vlan filter
VLAN Map HRServerMap is filtering VLANs:
  50
ALSwitch7#
```

Step 5

Verify connectivity between the workstation and the HR intranet server using the **ping** command. Troubleshoot if necessary.

1. Can the workstation connect to the web server that is running on the HR intranet server? Explain.

Step 6

Change the IP address on the client workstation to 172.16.50.125/24.

Verify connectivity between the workstation and the HR intranet server using the **ping** command. Troubleshoot if necessary.

1. Can the workstation connect to the web server that is running on the HR Intranet server? Explain.

Transparent LAN Services

Currently, no lab activities are associated with this chapter. However, do review the objectives listed in Chapter 10 of the *CCNP 3: Network Troubleshooting Companion Guide*:

- Identify the characteristics of an Ethernet service.

- Describe the transparent LAN services architectures.

- Compare benefits of transparent LAN service over legacy services.

- Describe Cisco transparent LAN service solutions.

- Describe transparent LAN service implementations.

A useful link for Metro Ethernet access services, including transparent LAN services, is http://www.cisco.com/en/US/netsol/ns341/ns396/ns223/networking_solutions_audience_business_benefit09186a00801b977b.html.

You can find Cisco Metro Ethernet switching products at http://www.cisco.com/en/US/netsol/ns341/ns396/ns223/networking_solutions_audience_promotion0900aecd800d9d67.html.